Lecture Notes in Computer Science 12669

More information about this subseries at http://www.springer.com/series/7407

Markus Roggenbach (Ed.)

Recent Trends in Algebraic Development Techniques

25th International Workshop, WADT 2020
Virtual Event, April 29, 2020
Revised Selected Papers

Springer

Editor
Markus Roggenbach
Swansea University
Swansea, UK

ISSN 0302-9743 ISSN 1611-3349 (electronic)
Lecture Notes in Computer Science
ISBN 978-3-030-73784-9 ISBN 978-3-030-73785-6 (eBook)
https://doi.org/10.1007/978-3-030-73785-6

LNCS Sublibrary: SL1 – Theoretical Computer Science and General Issues

This Springer imprint is published by the registered company Springer Nature Switzerland AG
The registered company address is: Gewerbestrasse 11, 6330 Cham, Switzerland

Preface

The 25th International Workshop on Algebraic Development Techniques 2020 (WADT) took place under the auspices of the IFIP Working Group 1.3 on "Foundations of System Specification". It was originally scheduled to take place during April 25–26, 2020, as a physical workshop co-located with the European Joint Conferences on Theory and Practice of Software (ETAPS) in Dublin, Ireland. However, due to the COVID-19 pandemic, the physical event had to be canceled and WADT 2020 took place as a virtual event on April 29, 2020.

For the *physical workshop*, there was a line-up of two invited talks as well as 14 contributed presentations addressing questions around axiomatisation, verification of distributed systems, deductive verification, semantics of programming languages, parallel graph transformations, tool support, string diagrams, and hybrid and modal logics, by authors from China, Denmark, France, Germany, Italy, the Netherlands, Portugal, and the UK.

At the *virtual workshop* only a subset of nine out of the 14 contributed talks could be presented. Authors were hindered from participating in the virtual workshop due to reasons such as slow Internet connections, lack of access to university facilities and therefore being unable to prepare their talks, and increased workload due to the necessary change of university teaching from physical to virtual delivery. WADT 2020, the first virtual WADT ever, was held free of charge and open for anyone interested. The workshop was able to attract an audience of about 45–50 participants worldwide. It provided an opportunity to present recent and ongoing work, to virtually meet and catch up with colleagues, and to discuss new ideas and future trends.

As with previous WADT events, all authors were invited after the workshop to submit full papers, which underwent a thorough peer review process. Each paper was reviewed by three referees. This volume contains those papers that were accepted by the Program Committee. I wish to thank all authors, the members of the Program Committee, the special stream chairs Andrea Corradini, Alexander Knapp, and Marieke Huismann for their diligent work in the selection process, and the external reviewers for their support in evaluating the papers. A further special thanks goes to Andrea Corradini who kindly supported me in the process of compiling these proceedings.

The algebraic approach to system specification encompasses many aspects of the formal design of software systems. Originally born as formal method for reasoning about abstract data types, it now covers new specification frameworks and programming paradigms (such as object-oriented, aspect-oriented, agent-oriented, logic, and higher-order functional programming) as well as a wide range of application areas (including concurrent, distributed, and mobile systems).

WADT 2020 invited contributions in four different streams:

– *Graph Transformation* (chair: Andrea Corradini, Italy), which addressed theoretical, application-oriented or tool-related aspects of graph transformation, or any combination of them.

- *System Modelling* (chair: Alexander Knapp, Germany), which sought contributions in the (co-)algebraic and model-based tradition of system specification and verification.
- *Deductive Software Verification* (chair: Marieke Huisman, the Netherlands), which addressed theoretical or tool-related contributions in the area of deductive software verification. Also experience reports were welcome.
- *General Stream* (chair: Markus Roggenbach, UK), which covered topics such as foundations of algebraic specification; other approaches to formal specification, including process calculi and models of concurrent, distributed, and cyber-physical systems; specification languages, methods, and environments; semantics of conceptual modelling methods and techniques; integration of formal specification techniques; formal testing and quality assurance, validation, and verification; and algebraic approaches to cognitive sciences, including computational creativity.

WADT can look back on a proud history of workshops. The first workshop took place in 1982 in Sorpesee, followed by Passau (1983), Bremen (1984), Braunschweig (1986), Gullane (1987), Berlin (1988), Wusterhausen (1990), Dourdan (1991), Caldes de Malavella (1992), S. Margherita (1994), Oslo (1995), Tarquinia (1997), Lisbon (1998), Chateau de Bonas (1999), Genoa (2001), Frauenchiemsee (2002), Barcelona (2004), La Roche en Ardenne (2006), Pisa (2008), Etelsen (2010), Salamanca (2012), Sinaia (2014), Gregynog (2016), and Egham (2018).

I hope that reading the contributions in this volume will bring as much joy as the WADT community had at our virtual workshop in April 2020.

February 2021 Markus Roggenbach

Organization

General Chair

Markus Roggenbach	Swansea University, UK

Program Committee Chairs

Andrea Corradini	Universitàdi Pisa, Italy
Marieke Huisman	University of Twente, the Netherlands
Alexander Knapp	Universität Augsburg, Germany
Markus Roggenbach	Swansea University, UK

Steering Committee

Andrea Corradini, Italy
José Fiadeiro, UK
Rolf Hennicker, Germany
Alexander Knapp, Germany
Hans-Jörg Kreowski, Germany
Till Mossakowski, Germany
Fernando Orejas, Spain
Leila Ribeiro, Brazil
Markus Roggenbach (Chair), UK
Grigore Roşu, USA

Program Committee

Wolfgang Ahrendt	Chalmers University of Technology, Sweden
Claire Dross	AdaCore, France
Francisco Durán	Universidad de Málaga, Spain
Rachid Echahed	CNRS and University of Grenoble, France
José Luiz Fiadeiro	University of Dundee, UK
Reiko Heckel	University of Leicester, UK
Leen Lambers	Universität Potsdam, Germany
Stephan Merz	Inria Nancy, France
Rosemary Monahan	Maynooth University, Ireland
Till Mossakowski	University of Magdeburg, Germany
Iulian Ober	University of Toulouse, France
Peter Ölveczky	University of Oslo, Norway
Wytse Oortwijn	ETH Zurich, Switzerland
Fernando Orejas	Universitat Politècnica de Catalunya, Spain

Carlos Gustavo Lopez Pombo	Universidad de Buenos Aires and CONICET, Argentina
Pierre-Yves Schobbens	University of Namur, Belgium
Leila Ribeiro	Universidade Federal do Rio Grande do Sul, Brazil
Ionut Tutu	Romanian Academy, Romania
Mattias Ulbrich	Karlsruhe Institute of Technology, Germany
Antonio Vallecillo	Universidad de Málaga, Spain

Additional Reviewers

Xiaohong Chen
Mihai Codescu

Contents

Invited Paper

On Completeness of Liveness Synthesis for Parametric Timed Automata (Extended Abstract)

Jaco van de Pol[1,2(✉)] and Laure Petrucci[3]

[1] Department of Computer Science, University of Aarhus, Aarhus, Denmark
jaco@cs.au.dk
[2] FMT, University of Twente, Enschede, The Netherlands
[3] LIPN, CNRS UMR 7030, Université Sorbonne Paris Nord, Villetaneuse, France

Abstract. We discuss what kind of completeness guarantees can be provided by semi-algorithms for the synthesis of the set of parameters under which a parametric timed automata meets some liveness property.

1 Introduction

After the initial successes of model checking for the verification of discrete systems, several quantitative extensions have been introduced. The two main directions are probabilistic systems and timed systems. These extensions allow for a more precise design and analysis of systems, by reasoning for instance about probabilities of errors, failure rates, performance, worst case response times and proper settings of timeout values.

A common problem in quantitative reasoning is how to obtain realistic numeric values. In particular during the early design phase, the proper quantitative values are not yet known. However, the analysis results could be sensitive to these values. This naturally leads to *parametric models*, in which concrete values are replaced by symbolic parameters, as in "the message is lost with probability p", or "the message will arrive within t seconds".

The introduction of parameters raises new verification problems [5]. On the one hand, *parametric model checking* asks whether the model is correct for all values of the parameters (satisfying some condition). Here correctness refers to some requirement specified as a temporal logic property. More interestingly, the *parameter synthesis* problem asks for the set of parameters for which the required property holds. Ideally, this set of solutions is represented in a finite manner, for instance by a set of constraints. In a sense, synthesis is more constructive than analysis, since it helps the designer to obtain the proper quantitative values.

In this contribution,[1] we focus on the particular case of parameter synthesis for parametric timed automata (PTA) [1,2]. Like timed automata (TA), they extend finite automata with real-valued clocks that are constrained by location

[1] The full version of this paper will be presented at TACAS [3].

M. Roggenbach (Ed.): WADT 2020, LNCS 12669, pp. 3–10, 2021.
https://doi.org/10.1007/978-3-030-73785-6_1

invariants and transition guards. But in *parametric* TA, a clock constraint compares a clock value with a symbolic parameter. Here, we assume that the property is already encoded in the accepting locations of the automaton. We distinguish reachability (some accepting location is reachable) and liveness (some accepting location can be visited infinitely often).

Unfortunately, model checking is undecidable for parametric timed automata, both for reachability and liveness. As a consequence, the set of parameter solutions cannot be synthesized either. One line of research studies decidability of reachablity [13] and liveness [6,10] for syntactic subclasses.

Another strategy is to resort to semi-algorithms, which are not guaranteed to terminate, but yield sound results if they terminate. This contribution studies the kind of completeness guarantees that can be provided by semi-algorithms for the parameter synthesis for liveness properties of parametric timed automata.

2 Parametric Timed Automata and Parametric Zones

We recall Parametric Timed Automata (PTA) and an important vehicle to study them, Parametric Zone Graphs (PZG); see [2,15] for full definitions. A PTA has a finite set of locations (ℓ); we write ℓ_0 for the initial location and Acc for the set of accepting locations. A PTA also has a finite set of real-valued clocks, which are constrained by location invariants. Transitions between locations are guarded by clock constraints and may reset some clocks. Each constraint is a conjunction of linear inequalities over clocks and parameters in a set P, and can be represented as a convex polyhedron (zone). A PTA T can be instantiated with a rational parameter valuation $p : P \to \mathbb{Q}_{\geq 0}$, to obtain a plain TA $T[p]$.

The *abstract* semantics of a PTA is described by a single PZG, which captures the behaviour for all parameter instances and clock values, symbolically. Abstract states are pairs $\mathbf{s} = (\ell, Z)$, for a location ℓ and a non-empty convex polyhedron (zone) Z. Here a single zone describes an uncountably infinite set of parameter

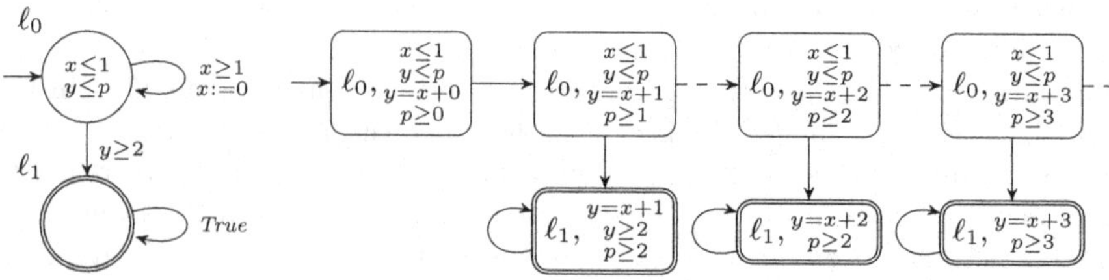

(a) PTA (b) Parametric Zone Graph

Fig. 1. This PTA has locations $\{\ell_0, \ell_1\}$, clocks $\{x, y\}$ and parameter p. The initial location ℓ_0 has an invariant consisting of two inequalities, one parametric. Its self loop is enabled if $x \geq 1$ and it resets clock x. Clocks x and y increase at the same rate, so after i transitions in ℓ_0, $y = x + i$ (note that clock y is never reset). If $y \geq 2$ a transition can happen to accepting location ℓ_1, which admits an unconditional infinite loop. The corresponding PZG is infinite. This example has an accepting run if and only if $p \geq 2$.

and clock values by a set of linear constraints. The transition relation $(\ell_1, Z_1) \Rightarrow (\ell_2, Z_2)$ reflects a step $\ell_1 \rightarrow \ell_2$ in the PTA from any point in Z_1 to some point in Z_2, reached after some valid time delay.

Since we are interested in liveness properties, the accepting states are interpreted as a Büchi condition: an infinite path from the initial state is accepting if it passes through an accepting state infinitely often. An *accepting lasso* is a special case, consisting of a path from the initial state to some accepting state, and then a non-empty cycle from that accepting state to itself. In a finite graph, there is an accepting path if and only if there is an accepting lasso. In infinite graphs we have to be more careful, as the following examples show Fig. 2 and Fig. 3.

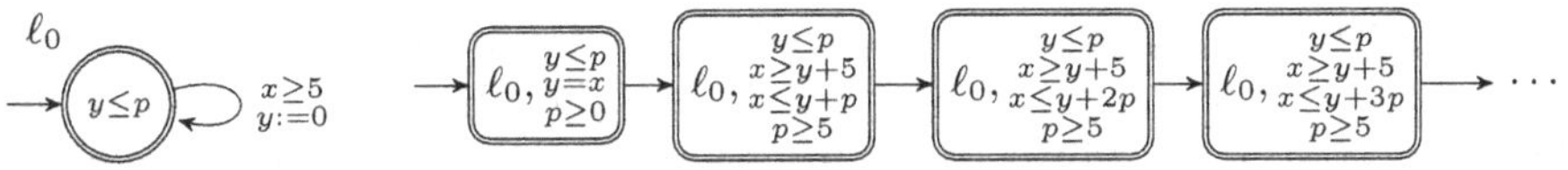

(a) PTA (b) PZG with infinite accepting run, but no loop

Fig. 2. In this example, the PZG has an infinite accepting run but no accepting cycle. Note that the transition can only become enabled when $p \geq 5$. After $i > 0$ transitions, $y + 5 \leq x \leq y + ip$. There is an infinite accepting run if and only if $p \geq 5$.

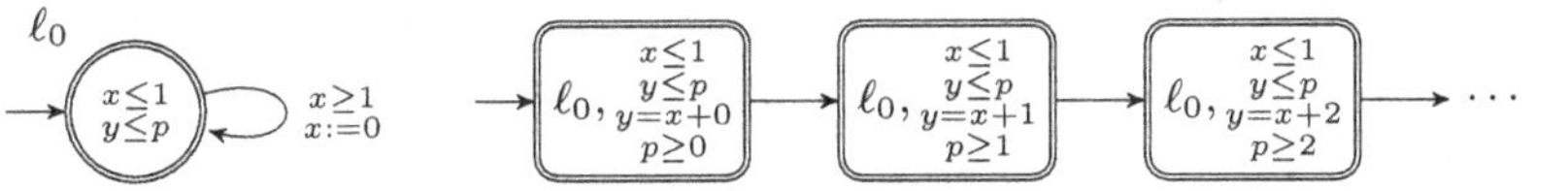

(a) PTA (b) PZG with spurious accepting run

Fig. 3. In this example, the PZG seems to have an infinite accepting run, but this is a spurious run, since the intersection of all zones along the path is empty. Indeed, no concrete TA-instance would admit an infinite (accepting) run.

The *parameter synthesis problem* takes a PTA T as input. Its solution $Sol(T)$ is the set of rational parameter valuations p, for which the TA $T[p]$ has an infinite accepting run. The set of solutions doesn't need to be convex, so the result is typically presented as a collection (union) of convex polyhedra. Figure 4 shows a PTA where the set of solutions is $p \in \{1, 2, 3, \ldots\}$, showing that the set of solutions cannot always be presented as a finite disjunction of convex sets.

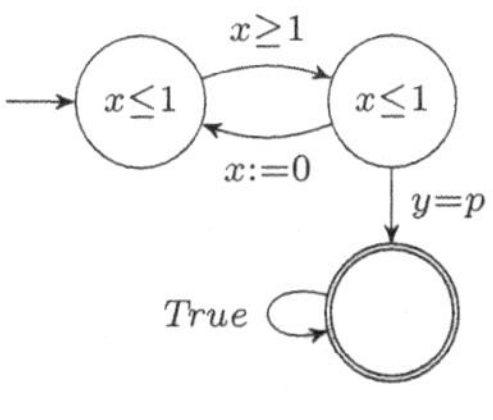

Fig. 4. This PTA has infinitely many solutions.

3 Parameter Synthesis Algorithms

For plain TA, the zone graph is finite (after applying extrapolation [8,12]), and this forms the basis of efficient model checking algorithms, both for reachability and liveness properties. In the latter case, we search for reachable accepting states and then for a nonempty cycle on those states. Accepting lassos can be detected in linear time using, for instance, the Nested Depth-First Search (NDFS) algorithm [11], or by detecting Strongly Connected Components (SCCs).

However, for PTAs the parametric zone graph is often infinite. In previous work [15], we investigated the use of NDFS as a semi-algorithm, detecting accepting lassos in a finite prefix of the PZG, and collecting all parameter values leading to such lassos. The semi-algorithm may diverge if the PZG is infinite. However, a number of techniques led to successful termination in several examples, and also increased the memory and time efficiency of the algorithm. All algorithms below have been implemented in the newest version of the tool Imitator [4] for parameter synthesis of parametric timed automata.

Cumulative Algorithm with Parameter Pruning. The cumulative algorithm (inspired by [9]), explores the PZG for accepting states (ℓ, Z) and checks if they are on a nonempty cycle. If so, we compute the parametric constraint $Z{\downarrow_P}$, which is the projection of Z on the parameters only (i.e. eliminating clock variables). These parametric constraints are accumulated in a global partial solution $\mathcal{C}$ (a finite disjunction of zones). An important insight is that the parametric zone decreases during symbolic execution, because we keep imposing constraints:

Proposition 1. *If* $(\ell_1, Z_1) \Rightarrow (\ell_2, Z_2)$ *then* $Z_2{\downarrow_P} \subseteq Z_1{\downarrow_P}$.

This provides two opportunities to prune the search. First, we can immediately backtrack from states (ℓ, Z) with $Z{\downarrow_P} \subseteq \mathcal{C}$, since (successors of) this state can never yield new solutions. Second, when checking for a nonempty cycle on an accepting state, we only need to consider transitions $(\ell_1, Z_1) \Rightarrow (\ell_2, Z_2)$ with $Z_1{\downarrow_P} = Z_2{\downarrow_P}$, since only such transitions can be a part of some cycle.

We illustrate this with the example in Fig. 1. The full PZG is infinite, but if the cumulative algorithm visits the left-most zone with ℓ_1, it finds $\mathcal{C} = (p \geq 2)$. So the dashed edges can be pruned, avoiding the infinite computation on zones with ℓ_0. Note that termination depends on the search order. We come back to this in the layering algorithm.

Subsumption. The next technique exploits the fact that a state can be subsumed by some other state that was already analysed. The subsumption relation is defined as follows: $(\ell_1, Z_1) \sqsubseteq (\ell_2, Z_2)$ if and only if $\ell_1 = \ell_2$ and $Z_1 \subseteq Z_2$. The important insight is that subsumption is a self-simulation relation, i.e.:

Proposition 2. *If* $s_1 \Rightarrow s_2$ *and* $s_1 \sqsubseteq s_1'$ *then for some* s_2', $s_1' \Rightarrow s_2'$ *and* $s_2 \sqsubseteq s_2'$.

Subsumption can be used to reduce the search space, but it must be applied with care, since the subsumption reduction can introduce spurious accepting cycles [14]. Experiments [15] showed that subsumption reduction improves the efficiency of parameter synthesis, and sometimes leads to successful termination.

Layering Heuristics. The search order influences the efficiency and even termination of parameter synthesis. One should aim at finding solutions with large parametric constraints first, since they increase the cumulative constraint $\mathcal{C}$, which leads to a more aggressive pruning of the search space.

Therefore, the *layering heuristics* first explores all states in the current parametric layer, before considering states with a smaller parametric constraint. This doesn't interfere with the accepting lasso detection algorithm, since all cycles must lie in the same parametric layer by Proposition 1. The layering strategy can be simply implemented by deferring all successors in the next layer to a so-called *pending list* for later processing. This strategy *enforces* termination of the example in Fig. 1, since zones with $p \geq 2$ are handled before $p \geq 3$.

However, the search can still get trapped in an infinite path in the current layer, since the clocks can increase without changing the parameter constraints, thus missing potential solutions in the next layer.

Breadth-First Search + SCC. A quite different algorithm, originally implemented in Imitator [4], traverses the state space in a BFS manner. This also tends to visit large parametric constraints first. Obviously, BFS is incompatible with NDFS. Instead, the algorithm uses a standard SCC decomposition algorithm to check for each state in the new layer, if it is an element of a non-trivial accepting SCC in the state space.

Bounded Model Checking with Iterative Deepening (BMC-ID). We propose a new bounded model checking (BMC) approach to avoid early divergence, as a compromise between BFS and DFS. BMC-n only computes the PZG to a certain fixed bound n and checks it for accepting lassos using NDFS. This terminates for each n. In BMC-ID, we keep increasing the bound n in an outer loop.

When checking the PZG for depth $n+1$, we reuse the computed transitions from the previous rounds (this is useful, since computing the zones requires expensive operations on polyhedra). We also keep the accumulated constraint $\mathcal{C}$ for maximal pruning. We need to perform some duplicate work though, since a state at depth less than n can be on a cycle through a state beyond depth n.

If we increase the bound by 1, BMC-ID is similar to BFS, but we can also use a larger value. The algorithm terminates when all successor states have been visited or are pruned away.

4 Completeness

We now consider the kind of completeness guarantees that semi-algorithms for parameter synthesis can provide. The results are collected in Table 1. In general, a semi-algorithm A runs on an input PTA T and yields a collection of convex zones $\mathcal{C}$ on-the-fly, specifying a set of rational parameter valuations. Semi-algorithm

A could either terminate on input T, in which case $\mathcal{C}$ must be finite, or it could diverge, yielding a (finite or infinite) stream of convex zones $\mathcal{C}$.

We consider A *sound* if $\mathcal{C} \subseteq Sol(T)$, i.e. all parameters computed by A are valid solutions. We consider A *complete* if $Sol(T) \subseteq \mathcal{C}$, i.e. A has not missed any solutions. A totally correct algorithm A, i.e. one that terminates with a sound and complete result for all T, cannot exist for two reasons: the solution is not always finite (Fig. 4), and the problem is undecidable (even for reachability, [1]).

Partial Correctness. Previous work on parameter synthesis provides the classical "partial correctness" guarantee: If the algorithm terminates, it returns a sound and complete collection of zones $\mathcal{C}$. This covers cases where the PZG is finite (since the algorithm will definitely terminate), but also some cases where the PZG is infinite for which the algorithm terminates, thanks to sufficient pruning, as in Fig. 1 (with layering heuristics). All algorithms mentioned before are partially correct, except the BMC-n approach with a *fixed* n, which would always terminate and be sound but incomplete.

Soundness. Actually, the algorithms mentioned above achieve more than advertised. They report zones on-the-fly and at all points in time, the collection of reported zones is an under-approximation of the set of solutions. So all these algorithms are sound, even if they don't terminate.

An example of an unsound algorithm would be NDFS with *unlimited* subsumption. This could detect spurious accepting runs [14], and hence report unsound zones. This algorithm is still useful for emptiness checks, since its strong abstraction leads more often to termination, and it is "partially complete": it guarantees that if it terminates then it is complete. In particular, if it terminates with $\mathcal{C} = \emptyset$, then the PTA has no accepting cycles.

Completeness for Accepting Lassos. The more interesting question is if all possible solutions will be reported eventually. A weak form of completeness would require that an algorithm reports all solutions corresponding to accepting lassos in the PZG. Actually, this is not the case for the basic cumulative algorithm, nor for the algorithms with subsumption or layering, since they could get stuck in an infinite path, missing some solutions forever.

However, the algorithm BMC-ID is complete for reachability problems: every accepting state will appear at some depth, so it would be reported eventually. More interestingly, BMC-ID even achieves completeness for accepting lassos: every accepting lasso extends to a certain depth, so it will be reported eventually.

Completeness for Accepting Runs. Note that even BMC-ID is not guaranteed to report the solutions corresponding to all accepting runs. Since the PZG is infinite, there might be accepting runs that don't correspond to an accepting lasso, as in Fig. 3. Note that for such runs, one would also need to check that the intersection of the zones is non-empty. If there is an infinite accepting run with non-empty intersection, the corresponding TA would have an accepting run, which is going to be missed by the algorithm.

Is there an semi-algorithm that is complete for accepting runs? Actually, this can be achieved by the following "naïve enumeration" algorithm, which is not based on the PZG at all: (1) enumerate all possible rational parameter valuations p; (2) for each p, decide if the TA $T[p]$ has an accepting run; (3) if so, output the singleton solution p. For Fig. 4 it could yield $p = 1$, $p = 2$, $p = 3$, ...

The naïve algorithm is sound and complete for accepting runs, but it is unsatisfactory in at least three ways: First, it is very inefficient, since it is based on "blind parameter scanning", treating each parameter value separately. Second, it doesn't provide a concise characterisation of the solutions in terms of constraints; it rather enumerates solutions one by one. Third, this algorithm would never terminate, so even for the simplest examples, one would never know that one has seen all solutions, nor that a particular value is *not* a solution.

5 Conclusion

We discussed some algorithms for parameter synthesis for liveness properties of Parametric Timed Automata. Table 1 shows the soundness and completeness results of these algorithms. The problem is undecidable, but currently there is even no algorithm that computes all the correct answers in the limit *and* terminates for cases where the set of solutions is a finite union of convex polyhedra. The algorithms based on Parametric Zone Graphs terminate in many interesting cases, but none of the variants so far is guaranteed to enumerate all solutions. On the other hand, the "trivial" parameter enumeration algorithm is complete, but never terminates (indicated by ××), so its partial correctness and completeness results are vacuous (indicated by (✓)).

Since the PZG of a PTA can be infinite, it is unclear how PZG-based algorithms could ever achieve completeness. It seems difficult to recognize infinite runs that do not correspond to lassos. This asks for new abstractions. A promising direction to increase abstraction in PZGs is parametric extrapolation [7], but this is currently limited to bounded parameter domains. Finally, since the set of solutions is not always a finite union of convex sets, this also asks for a different representation of the set of solutions.

Table 1. Soundness and completeness properties of various algorithms.

Algorithm	Terminates	Partially correct	Sound	Partially complete	Complete for lassos	Complete
Cumulative	×	✓	✓	✓	×	×
+ layering	×	✓	✓	✓	×	×
+ subsumption	×	✓	✓	✓	×	×
Full subsumption	×	×	×	✓	×	×
BFS + SCC	×	✓	✓	✓	✓	×
BMC-n	✓	×	✓	×	×	×
BMC-ID	×	✓	✓	✓	✓	×
Naïve enum.	××	(✓)	✓	(✓)	✓	✓

Acknowledgement. This work was supported by travel grants PAMPAS (Van Gogh programme, Campus France & NUFFIC), TrAVAIL (CNRS-INS2I), and SECReTS (Institut Français Danemark). We thank Étienne André and Jaime Arias for interesting discussions, and for their help with the integration of our algorithms in the Imitator tool.

References

1. Alur, R., Henzinger, T.A., Vardi, M.Y.: Parametric real-time reasoning. In: STOC, pp. 592–601. ACM (1993)
2. André, É.: What's decidable about parametric timed automata? Int. J. Softw. Tools Technol. Transfer **21**, 203–219 (2019)
3. André, É., Arias, J., Petrucci, L., van de Pol, J.: Iterative bounded synthesis for efficient cycle detection. In: Groote, J.F., Larsen, K.G. (eds.) TACAS (Part I). Lecture Notes in Computer Science, vol. 12651, pp. 311–329. Springer, Heidelberg (2021)
4. André, É., Fribourg, L., Kühne, U., Soulat, R.: IMITATOR 2.5: a tool for analyzing robustness in scheduling problems. In: Giannakopoulou, D., Méry, D. (eds.) FM 2012. LNCS, vol. 7436, pp. 33–36. Springer, Heidelberg (2012). https://doi.org/10.1007/978-3-642-32759-9_6
5. André, É., Knapik, M., Lime, D., Penczek, W., Petrucci, L.: Parametric verification: an introduction. Trans. Petri Nets Other Model. Concurr. **14**, 64–100 (2019)
6. André, É., Lime, D.: Liveness in L/U-parametric timed automata. In ACSD, pp. 9–18. IEEE Computer Society (2017)
7. André, É., Lime, D., Roux, O.H.: Integer-complete synthesis for bounded parametric timed automata. In: Bojańczyk, M., Lasota, S., Potapov, I. (eds.) RP 2015. LNCS, vol. 9328, pp. 7–19. Springer, Cham (2015). https://doi.org/10.1007/978-3-319-24537-9_2
8. Behrmann, G., Bouyer, P., Larsen, K.G., Pelánek, R.: Lower and upper bounds in zone-based abstractions of timed automata. Int. J. Softw. Tools Technol. Transf. **8**(3), 204–215 (2006)
9. Bezdek, P., Benes, N., Barnat, J., Cerná, I.: LTL parameter synthesis of parametric timed automata. In Software Engineering and Formal Methods - 14th International Conference, SEFM 2016, Proceedings, pp. 172–187 (2016)
10. Bozzelli, L., La Torre, S.: Decision problems for lower/upper bound parametric timed automata. Formal Methods Syst. Des. **35**(2), 121–151 (2009)
11. Courcoubetis, C., Vardi, M.Y., Wolper, P., Yannakakis, M.: Memory-efficient algorithms for the verification of temporal properties. Formal Methods Syst. Des. **1**(2/3), 275–288 (1992)
12. Daws, C., Tripakis, S.: Model checking of real-time reachability properties using abstractions. In: Steffen, B. (ed.) TACAS 1998. LNCS, vol. 1384, pp. 313–329. Springer, Heidelberg (1998). https://doi.org/10.1007/BFb0054180
13. Hune, T., Romijn, J., Stoelinga, M., Vaandrager, F.W.: Linear parametric model checking of timed automata. J. Log. Algebr. Program. **52–53**, 183–220 (2002)
14. Laarman, A.W., Olesen, M.C., Dalsgaard, A.E., Larsen, K.G., van de Pol, J.C.: Multi-core emptiness checking of timed Büchi automata using inclusion abstraction. In: Computer Aided Verification (CAV'13), pp. 968–983 (2013)
15. Nguyen, H.G., Petrucci, L., van de Pol, J.: Layered and Collecting NDFS with Subsumption for parametric timed automata. In: Lin, A.W., Sun, J. (eds.) 23rd IEEE IC on Engineering of Complex Computer Systems (ICECCS 2018), Melbourne, Australia, pp. 1–9. IEEE (2018)

Contributed Papers

The Wheel of Rational Numbers as an Abstract Data Type

Jan A. Bergstra[1] and John V. Tucker[2(✉)]

[1] Informatics Institute, University of Amsterdam, Science Park 904, 1098 XH Amsterdam, The Netherlands
j.a.bergstra@uva.nl

[2] Department of Computer Science, Swansea University, Bay Campus, Fabian Way, Swansea SA1 8EN, UK
j.v.tucker@swansea.ac.uk

Abstract. In an arithmetical structure one can make division a total function by defining $1/0$ to be an element of the structure, or by adding a new element such as infinity ∞ or error element $\perp$. A wheel is an algebra in which division is totalised by setting $1/0 = \infty$ but which also contains an error element $\perp$ to help control its use. We construct the wheel of rational numbers as an abstract data type $\mathbb{Q}_w$ and give it an equational specification without auxiliary operators under initial algebra semantics.

Keywords: Rational numbers · Arithmetic structures · Meadows · Wheels · Division by zero · Infinity · Error · Equational specification · Initial algebra semantics

1 Introduction

In arithmetical structures the most important operator that fails to be total is $1/x$ when $x = 0$. That division becomes a total operation is of value for the semantic modelling, specification and verification of computations with computer arithmetics. Among a number of approaches to making division total are arithmetical algebras in which:

(i) $1/0$ behaves as one of the elements in the structure, e.g., 0 or 1;
(ii) $1/0$ behaves as an error element $\perp$, additional to the structure;
(iii) $1/0$ behaves as an infinite element ∞, additional to the structure.

Meadows are an axiomatically defined class of arithmetical algebras first studied in [3,11] in which the internal option (i) was examined, especially $1/0 = 0$. Later, meadows with the external error element option (ii) were introduced in [6], where they were called common meadows. The infinity element option (iii) was discussed in the survey [2]. All three options deliver workable and interesting ways of removing partiality. In the case of (ii) and (iii), basic properties such as

$$\perp + x = \perp, \perp . x = \perp \text{ and } \infty + x = \infty, \infty . x = \infty$$

M. Roggenbach (Ed.): WADT 2020, LNCS 12669, pp. 13–30, 2021.
https://doi.org/10.1007/978-3-030-73785-6_2

begin to shape intuitions about the semantics. However, adding elements to structures commonly cause complications because the new elements must operate sensibly with all the algebraic constants and operations of the structure. For example, in the case of adding infinity, we could easily find

$$0.\infty = \infty,$$

which is unattractive and against some arithmetic intuitions. Thus, a next step in the case of infinity ∞ is to also add an error element $\perp$ so that some unwanted or suspect results can be controlled:

$$0.\infty = \perp \text{ and, indeed, } \infty + \infty = \perp .$$

The idea of adding a single infinity has several precedents, not least the Riemann sphere (from 1857 onwards); the idea of adding an error element is also older than the approach using meadows and is known as a *wheel*. Wheels are an axiomatically defined class of algebras first studied in [13,18]. Along with the key ideas of a wheel, namely, $\frac{1}{0} = \infty$ and that $\frac{1}{\infty} = 0$, come the subtle controlling properties that $0.\infty = \perp$ and $\infty + \infty = \perp$.

The viability or fitness for purpose of any method of totalising division depends upon the axioms for the structures and, subsequently, on their application to a computational problem. Both axiomatisations of meadows and wheels start with familiar axioms for commutative ring-like structures to which axioms for inverse $^{-1}$ are added. Central to both meadows, wheels and other approaches to totalisation is the field of rational numbers and the problem of totalising division; see [11] and for several other options for division by zero [2].

In the case of meadows, the development uses the theory of algebraic specifications of abstract data types, in which a central concept is axiomatisation by a finite set E of equations over a signature Σ, whose initial algebra defines the data type up to isomorphism. Thus, in [11], are finite equational specifications of the rationals with $1/0 = 0$ up to isomorphism, which defines the abstract data type $\mathbb{Q}_0$ of the meadow of rational numbers. Interestingly, the existence of a finite equational specification for the rational numbers was open until [11].

In this paper we examine the basic structure of the rational number arithmetic considered as a wheel. We will extend and adapt some of the axioms of wheels in [13] using techniques from meadows [3] to give an equational specification for the wheel of rational numbers as an abstract data type $\mathbb{Q}_w$: we give a set of equations E_w over the signature Σ_w such that under initial algebra semantics

$$I(\Sigma_w, E_w) \cong \mathbb{Q}_w.$$

The structure of the paper is as follows. In Sect. 2 we list some basic concepts and principles of our general approach, including the methodology of abstract data type theory and the focus of our interest, namely arithmetical structures. In Sect. 3 we introduce a concrete model of a wheel of rationals and in Sect. 4 we give it its initial algebra specification. Section 5 makes some concluding remarks.

We assume that the reader is familiar with the basic algebraic concepts used to model data types: *signature*, *algebra*, *expansion*, *reduct*, *congruence*, *term*, *homomorphism*, *equational theory*, *first order theory*, etc. These basics can be found in several introductions to algebraic methods and abstract data type theory [14–16, 21]. We have chosen to keep our algebraic techniques very simple to focus attention on a new topic for theoretical investigation, namely arithmetic data type theory.

2 Preliminaries on ADTs

2.1 The Approach of ADTs

The theory of abstract data types is based upon the following principle:

Principle. *In programming, data is characterised by the operations and tests we can use on the data. All the data can be constructed and accessed by applying the operations to given constants. An interface to the data type is a syntactic declaration of these constant, operator and test names. What is known to the programmer about the implementation of the data type is only a set of properties of the constants, operators and tests. The interface and set of properties is called a specification of an abstract data type.*

These ideas about programming are faithfully modelled by the algebraic and logical theories of general algebras and relational structures. In particular, the interface is modelled by a signature Σ and the properties modelled by an axiomatic theory T.

Principle. *An abstract data type is an isomorphism class of algebras of common signature. Each algebra is a possible representation or construction or implementation of the data type. The algebras for which all the data can be constructed by applying their operations to their constants are the minimal algebras.*

Thus, to specify an abstract data type is to specify an isomorphism class of algebras. In the case of the field of rational numbers, the standard notation $\mathbb{Q}$ will stand for the isomorphism type and Q will stand for a particular representative or construction or implementation of the rational isomorphism type. Thus, Q is *a* concrete data type and $\mathbb{Q}$ is *the* abstract data type.

In general, conditions are added to this idea of an abstract data type, of which finite, computable, semicomputable abstract data types are common; notice such properties must be isomorphism invariants of algebras. Computable algebras have important roles in modelling data [19], and especially in classical field theory [20].

Let us expand on the ideas introduced above.

The interface is a signature Σ and, typically, the properties is a set T of first order axioms about the constants, operations and tests in Σ. A Σ-algebra

A is Σ-minimal if all the elements of A can be constructed by applying the operations to the constants of A. The pair (Σ, T) is an axiomatic specification and $Alg(\Sigma, T)$ is the class of all Σ-structures that satisfy the axioms of T. Of particular importance is the case when the axiomatisations consist of a set E of equations only. Such an equational specification (Σ, E) has an initial algebra $I(\Sigma, E)$ in the class $Alg(\Sigma, E)$ that is unique up to isomorphism. The initial algebra has an important representative structure. Let $T(\Sigma)$ be the set of all closed terms over the signature Σ. Define a congruence on $T(\Sigma)$ for any $t_1, t_2 \in T(\Sigma)$,

$$t_1 \equiv t_2 \Longleftrightarrow E \vdash t_1 = t_2$$

Then we have

$$I(\Sigma, E) \cong T(\Sigma)/\equiv .$$

Thus the

Specification Problem. *Given a Σ-algebra A representing an implementation of an abstract data type, can we find an equational specification (Σ, E) such that $I(\Sigma, E) \cong T(\Sigma)/\equiv \cong A$.*

The general specification problem for computable, semicomputable and cosemicomputable abstract data types has been studied in depth [1,9,10]. In general, auxiliary data, operators and even sorts may be needed. For example, small equational specifications exist for *all* computable data types, provided some auxiliary operations may appear in the specification; indeed, general theory [9] shows that the rational number data types studied here are computable and, therefore, can all be specified with 6 auxiliary functions and 4 equations only! However, these general theoretical results use advanced methods from computability theory and do not yield recognisable and useable axiomatisations. Here the specifications are close to the algebra of rational numbers and do not use auxiliary operators.

2.2 Arithmetic Structures

The signature Σ_m for meadows contains the ring operations and an inverse $^{-1}$ operation. It is richer than signatures commonly used for working with fields and skew structures as often inverse $^{-1}$ is not an explicit operation having an axiomatisation. Binary division $-/-$ seems to be rarely used but is useful to have as a derived function, $\frac{x}{y} = x.y^{-1}$, that can be eliminated. In some cases of interest to us, it is convenient to add other binary operations such as subtraction as a binary operation. To give an hint of what we have in mind for the term 'arithmetic structures':

Definition 1. *Σ is an* arithmetic signature *if it extends the meadow signature, i.e., $\Sigma_m \subset \Sigma$.*

Consider the following signature for wheels which simply adds two characteristic constants, ∞ for infinity and $\perp$ for error, to the signature Σ_m for meadows:

signature Σ_w

sorts num

constants $0 :\to num$
$1 :\to num$
$\infty :\to num$
$\perp :\to num$

operations $+ : num \times num \to num$
$. : num \times num \to num$
$- : num \to num$
${}^{-1} : num \to num$
$/ : num \times num \to num$
end

Clearly, a wheel signature is an arithmetic signature.

3 The Wheel of Rationals

In working with arithmetic structures as abstract data types, the distinction between concrete constructions of algebras and their isomorphism type becomes important and subtle. There are lots of ways of constructing the rationals from the integers, and the integers from the naturals.

3.1 Basic Constructions with Rationals

We start with a specific ring Q of rational numbers with unit made from some specific copy of the integers Z. This is an algebra that is not minimal.

We begin the construction of the rationals as follows: let

$$SFP = \{(n, m) : n, m \in Z, m > 0, and\ gcd(n, m) = 1\}.$$

SFP stands for *simplified fracpairs.*[1] Note we seek to avoid equivalence classes in this construction.

The additive identity is uniquely defined by $(0, 1)$ – note that elements such as $(0, 2)$ are not in SFP. The multiplicative unit is $(1, 1)$. Note that $(1, 0)$ is not in SFP We define the operations in stages starting with addition:

$$(n, m) + (p, q) = (a, b)$$

[1] For information on fracpairs see [7].

where

$$a = \frac{np + mq}{gcd(np + mq, mq)}$$

and

$$b = \frac{mq}{gcd(np + mq, mq)}$$

Secondly, we define multiplication:

$$(n, m).(p, q) = (a, b)$$

where

$$a = \frac{np}{gcd(np, mq)}$$

and

$$b = \frac{mq}{gcd(np, mq)}$$

Thirdly, we define additive inverse:

$$-(n, m) = (-n, m).$$

Let

$$Q = (SFP \mid (0, 1), (1, 1), +, -, .)$$

3.2 A Wheel of Rationals

To build a wheel Q_w of rational numbers from Q we need to add elements that behave like infinity and error. The element $(1, 0)$ will represent infinity ∞ and the element $(0, 0)$ will represent error $\bot$.

The elements $(1, 0)$ and $(0, 0)$ are not in the set SFP and so we define

$$SFP_w = SFP \cup \{(1, 0), (0, 0)\}$$

and extend the operations of Q as follows:

For error, if $(n, m) \in SFP$ then

$$\begin{aligned}
(n, m) + (0, 0) &= (0, 0)\\
(0, 0) + (n, m) &= (0, 0)\\
(n, m).(0, 0) &= (0, 0)\\
(0, 0).(n, m) &= (0, 0)\\
-(0, 0) &= (0, 0)\\
(0, 0) + (0, 0) &= (0, 0)\\
(0, 0).(0, 0) &= (0, 0)
\end{aligned}$$

For infinity, if $(n, m) \in SFP$ and $n \neq 0$ then

$$
\begin{aligned}
(n, m) + (1, 0) &= (1, 0) \\
(1, 0) + (n, m) &= (1, 0) \\
(n, m).(1, 0) &= (1, 0) \\
(1, 0).(n, m) &= (1, 0) \\
(1, 0) + (1, 0) &= (0, 0) \\
(1, 0).(1, 0) &= (1, 0) \\
(1, 0).(0, 1) &= (0, 0) \\
(0, 1).(1, 0) &= (0, 0) \\
-(1, 0) &= (1, 0)
\end{aligned}
$$

Error and infinity combine as follows:

$$
\begin{aligned}
(1, 0) + (0, 0) &= (0, 0) \\
(0, 0) + (1, 0) &= (0, 0) \\
(1, 0).(0, 0) &= (0, 0) \\
(0, 0).(1, 0) &= (0, 0)
\end{aligned}
$$

Thus the structure Q is extended to the algebra

$$Q[(1, 1), (0, 0)] = (SFP_w \mid (0, 1), (1, 1), +, -, .)$$

The new elements are not named constants.

At this point we expand the algebra $Q[(1, 1), (0, 0)]$ with inverse operation $^{-1}$ defined by:

$$
\begin{aligned}
(n, m)^{-1} &= (m, n) \text{ for } n > 0 \\
(n, m)^{-1} &= (-m, -n) \text{ for } n < 0 \\
(0, 0)^{-1} &= (0, 0) \\
(1, 0)^{-1} &= (0, 1) \\
(0, 1)^{-1} &= (1, 0)
\end{aligned}
$$

This extended structure

$$Q_w = (SFP_w \mid (0, 1), (1, 1), (1, 0), (0, 0), +, -, ., ^{-1})$$

is a wheel of rational numbers.

Lemma 1. *The algebra Q_w is a Σ_w-minimal algebra.*

Definition 2. *The* abstract data type $\mathbb{Q}_w$ of the wheel of rational numbers *is the isomorphism class of the Σ_w-minimal algebra Q_w.*

4 Initial Algebra Specification of the Wheel of Rationals

We now give an equational specification (Σ_w, E_w) and prove that it defines our wheel of rationals.

Table 1. E_w: an initial algebra specification of the abstract data type of wheels

$x + y = y + x$	(1)
$(x + y) + z = x + (y + z)$	(2)
$x + 0 = x$	(3)
$x.y = y.x$	(4)
$x.(y.z) = (x.y).z$	(5)
$x.1 = x$	(6)
$(x.y)^{-1} = x^{-1}.y^{-1}$	(7)
$(x^{-1})^{-1} = x$	(8)
$x.x^{-1} = 1 + 0.x^{-1}$	(9)
$\frac{x}{y} = x.y^{-1}$	(10)
$(x + y).z + 0.z = x.z + y.z$	(11)
$0.0 = 0$	(12)
$0^{-1} = \infty$	(13)
$\infty + 1 = \infty$	(14)
$(-x).\infty = x.\infty$	(15)
$-\infty = \infty$	(16)
$0.\infty = \bot$	(17)
$-\bot = \bot$	(18)
$x + \bot = \bot$	(19)
$x + (-x) = 0.x$	(20)
$x^2 = x.x$	(21)
$1 + 0.(x + y + z + u) = \frac{x^2+y^2+z^2+u^2+1}{x^2+y^2+z^2+u^2+1}$	(22)
$\infty + 0.(x + y + z + u) = \frac{x^2+y^2+z^2+u^2+1}{0} + 0.(x + y + z + u)$	(23)

4.1 Axioms

The complete set of equations in E_w is in Table 1. Notice that Eqs. 1–8 are familiar; the effects of the new elements on the standard operations start to appear in Eqs. 9, 11 and 20. To get the feel of these axioms, we prove carefully some basic identities that will be needed as lemmas later on.

First, recall the properties of numerals. Let $\underline{n} = 1 + 1 + \ldots + 1$ (n-times). Then the following is easy to check:

Lemma 2. *$(\Sigma_w, E_w) \vdash \underline{n} + \underline{m} = \underline{n+m}$ and $(\Sigma_w, E_w) \vdash \underline{n}.\underline{m} = \underline{n.m}$.*

Lemma 3. *$(\Sigma_w, E_w) \vdash 0.\underline{n} = 0$.*

Proof. We do this by induction on n. As basis, note that if $n = 0$ or $n = 1$ then the lemma is true by the axioms. Suppose the lemma is true for $n = k$ and consider $n = k + 1$. Using the axioms we deduce that

$$\begin{aligned}
0.\underline{k+1} &= \underline{k+1}.0 && \text{by commutativity}\\
&= (\underline{k} + 1).0 && \text{by definition of numerals}\\
&= (\underline{k} + 1).0 + 0.0 && \text{by axioms 3 and 13}\\
&= 0.\underline{k} + 0.1 && \text{by axiom 11}\\
&= 0 + 0 && \text{by induction hypothesis}\\
&= 0.
\end{aligned}$$

□

Lemma 4. *$(\Sigma_w, E_w) \vdash \underline{m}.\underline{m}^{-1} = 1$.*

Proof. Applying Lagrange's Theorem to $m - 1$, let $m = p^2 + q^2 + r^2 + s^2 + 1$. Then:

$$\begin{aligned}
\frac{\underline{m}}{\underline{m}} &= \frac{\underline{p}^2 + \underline{q}^2 + \underline{r}^2 + \underline{s}^2 + 1}{\underline{p}^2 + \underline{q}^2 + \underline{r}^2 + \underline{s}^2 + 1}\\
&= 1 + 0.(\underline{p} + \underline{q} + \underline{r} + \underline{s}) && \text{by axiom 22}\\
&= 1 + 0.(\underline{p + q + r + s}) && \text{by Lemma 2}\\
&= 1 + 0 && \text{by Lemma 3}\\
&= 1
\end{aligned}$$

□

Lemma 5. *$(\Sigma_w, E_w) \vdash 0.\underline{m}^{-1} = 0$.*

Proof.

$$\begin{aligned}
0.\underline{m}^{-1} &= (0.\underline{m}).\underline{m}^{-1} && \text{by Lemma 3}\\
&= 0.(\underline{m}.\underline{m}^{-1}) && \text{by axiom 5}\\
&= 0.1 && \text{by Lemma 3}\\
&= 0 && \text{by axiom 6}
\end{aligned}$$

□

Lemma 6. *$(\Sigma_w, E_w) \vdash 0.(\underline{n}.\underline{m}^{-1}) = 0$.*

Proof.

$$
\begin{aligned}
0.(\underline{n}.\underline{m}^{-1}) &= (0.\underline{n}).\underline{m}^{-1}) && \text{by axiom 5}\\
&= 0.\underline{m}^{-1} && \text{by Lemma 3}\\
&= 0 && \text{by Lemma 5}
\end{aligned}
$$

□

Turning to ∞ we have these basic properties:

Lemma 7. *$(\Sigma_w, E_w) \vdash \infty - 1 = \infty$.*

Proof.

$$
\begin{aligned}
\infty - 1 &= (\infty + 1) - 1 && \text{by axiom 14}\\
&= \infty + (1 - 1) && \text{by axiom 2}\\
&= \infty + 0 && \text{by axiom 20}\\
&= \infty && \text{by axiom 3}
\end{aligned}
$$

□

Lemma 8. *$(\Sigma_w, E_w) \vdash \infty^{-1} = 0$.*

Proof. Clearly, $\infty^{-1} = (0^{-1})^{-1} = 0$ by axioms 13 and 8. □

Lemma 9. *$(\Sigma_w, E_w) \vdash \infty + \underline{m} = \infty$.*

Proof. By induction on m. If $\underline{m} = 0$ and $\underline{m} = 1$ then the lemma follows from the axioms 3 and 14, respectively. Suppose $\underline{m} = \underline{k+1}$. Then $\infty + (\underline{k+1}) = (\infty + \underline{k}) + 1$ and, by the induction hypothesis on k, we have $\infty + 1 = \infty$. □

Lemma 10. *$(\Sigma_w, E_w) \vdash \infty.\underline{m} = \infty$ and $(\Sigma_w, E_w) \vdash \infty.\underline{m}^{-1} = \infty$.*

Proof. Consider the first statement. Applying Lagrange's Theorem, let $m = p^2 + q^2 + r^2 + s^2 + 1$. Then

$$
\begin{aligned}
\infty.\underline{m} &= \frac{\underline{m}}{0} && \text{by axiom 13}\\
&= \frac{\underline{p^2 + q^2 + r^2 + s^2 + 1}}{0} && \text{by substitution}\\
&= \frac{\underline{p}^2 + \underline{q}^2 + \underline{r}^2 + \underline{s}^2 + 1}{0} + 0.(\underline{p} + \underline{q} + \underline{r} + \underline{s} + 1) && \text{by Lemma 2 and axiom 3}\\
&= \infty + 0.(\underline{p} + \underline{q} + \underline{r} + \underline{s} + 1) && \text{by axiom 23}\\
&= \infty.
\end{aligned}
$$

Next, consider the second statement.

$$\begin{aligned} \infty.\underline{m}^{-1} &= (0^{-1}.\underline{m}^{-1}) && \text{by axiom 13} \\ &= (0.0)^{-1} && \text{by axiom 7} \\ &= 0^{-1} && \text{by axiom 12} \\ &= \infty && \text{by axiom 13} \end{aligned}$$

□

Lemma 11. $(\Sigma_w, E_w) \vdash \infty.(\underline{n}.\underline{m}^{-1}) = \infty$.

Proof.

$$\begin{aligned} \infty.(\underline{n}.\underline{m}^{-1}) &= (\infty.\underline{n}).\underline{m}^{-1} && \text{by axiom 5} \\ &= \infty.\underline{m}^{-1} && \text{by Lemma 10} \\ &= \infty. && \text{by Lemma 10} \end{aligned}$$

□

Lemma 12. $(\Sigma_w, E_w) \vdash \infty.\infty = \infty$.

Proof.

$$\begin{aligned} \infty.\infty &= (0^{-1}.0^{-1}) && \text{by axiom 13} \\ &= (0.0)^{-1} && \text{by axiom 7} \\ &= 0^{-1} && \text{by Lemma 3} \\ &= \infty && \text{by axiom 13} \end{aligned}$$

□

4.2 Remarks on the Equations

The equations of E_w, displayed in Table 1, build on a number of sources and required adaptations. The basic axioms are those of commutative rings. Some of the axioms are of common meadows which introduce $\perp$: e.g., axioms 9 and 20. Axioms 22 and 23 are adaptations of the data generating axioms for the rationals in [11]. Axiom 11 was used by Setzer and Carlström [13,18].

Our set of axioms is intended to be informative and practical. It is not intended to be minimal. For instance, axiom 22 implies axiom 13 (by setting the variables = 0). As with all established axiom systems, properties that are lemmas can often also serve as axioms, whence some axioms can become lemmas.

Axioms from [13] that are true but which we do not use are:

$$\frac{x}{y} + z + 0.y = \frac{x + yz}{y} \tag{24}$$

$$(x + 0.y).z = x.z + 0.y \tag{25}$$

$$(x + 0.y)^{-1} = x^{-1} + 0.y \tag{26}$$

In the Introduction we suggested some identities about ∞ and $\perp$ were either to be expected or are desirable or undesirable. In fact, all identities involving ∞ and $\perp$ offer opportunities for mathematical investigation and possibly new technical insights and semantic perspectives.

4.3 Equational Specification Theorem

Theorem 1. *The initial algebra $I(\Sigma_w, E_w)$ of the equations in E_w is isomorphic to the wheel Q_w of rational numbers.*

Proof. We will take the standard term representation $T(\Sigma_w, E_w)$ of initial algebra $I(\Sigma_w, E_w)$ and show that $T(\Sigma_w, E_w) \cong Q_w$. Recall from 2.1 that $T(\Sigma_w, E_w) = T(\Sigma_w)/\equiv_{E_w}$ and that for $t_1, t_2 \in T(\Sigma_w)$,

$$t_1 \equiv_{E_w} t_2 \Longleftrightarrow E_w \vdash t_1 = t_2.$$

To work with the congruence we define a transversal Tr of unique representatives of the equivalence classes of $\equiv_{E_w}$. Let

$$\mathrm{Tr} = \{\underline{n}.\underline{m}^{-1}, \perp, \infty \mid (n, m) \in SFP\}.$$

Lemma 13. $(\Sigma_w, E_w) \models Q_w$

Proof. To prove soundness we inspect each axiom and show its validity in Q_w. This involves 23 equations, often with many case distinctions each. We give some examples to illustrate the pattern of reasoning.

First, consider if any one of the variables is the error element $(0, 0)$. Note that all but one of the equations have the property that the variables that appear on the left side of the equality sign also appear on the right, and vice versa. The definition of the operations in the error case of Sect. 3.2 shows that $(0, 0)$ propagates. Thus, all these equations are valid if one of the variables is $(0, 0)$. The equation left is $x + \perp = \perp$ which is valid by definition.

Thus we need only consider the equations when their variables have values that are rationals or infinity. Note that infinity does not always propagate, which can lead to many case distinctions in the equations with several variables.

1. Consider associativity: $x + (y + z) = (x + y) + z$. If all variables are rationals then the equation is easily seen to be valid. There are three cases involving infinity $(1, 0)$.

If exactly one variable is $(1,0)$ then both sides of the equation evaluate to $(1,0)$.
If exactly two variables are $(1,0)$ then both sides evaluate to $(0,0)$.
If all three variables are $(1,0)$ then both sides evaluate to $(0,0)$.

2. Consider $(x+0.y).z = x.z+0.y$. Suppose y is the infinite element $(1,0)$. Then $0.y = (0,0)$ and since error propagates both sides evaluate to $(0,0)$. Suppose $y \neq (1,0)$. Then $0.y = (0,1)$ and the equation reduces to the value of $x.z$ on both sides.
3. Consider the four squares equation. Suppose one of x, y, z, u is the infinite element $(1,0)$. Then, on the LHS, the sums of squares numerator and denominator evaluate to the infinite $(1,0)$ and their quotient is the error element $(0,0)$. On the RHS, the sum of the variables x, y, z, u is $(1,0)$ and its product with 0 is the error element $(0,0)$, and so the equation holds.

   Next suppose more than one of x, y, z, u is the infinite element $(1,0)$. Then both the sum of squares of the variables on the LHS, and the sum of the variables on the RHS, are both the error element $(0,0)$ and since error propagates the equation holds. □

Now $T(\Sigma_w, E_w)$ is the initial algebra of the class of models of (Σ_w, E_w). By Lemma 13, Q_w is such a model and so by initiality, there exists a unique surjective homomorphism $\phi : T(\Sigma_w, E_w) \longrightarrow Q_w$. We have to show that ϕ is an isomorphism. We do this by proving by induction that every term $t \in T(\Sigma_w)$ reduces to an element t_0 of the transversal Tr, i.e.,

$$(\Sigma_w, E_w) \vdash t = t_0.$$

We deal with the constants in the base case and the operator symbols in the induction step. There are several case distinctions and the argument uses the 25 equations in various subtle ways.

Basis Case: The Constants. Clearly, the transversal contains the constants $\perp$, ∞. We will show that the constant 0 is $\underline{0}.\underline{1}^{-1}$ using the axioms of $x.1 = x$ and associativity:

$$0 = 0.1 = 0.(1.1^{-1}) = 0.1^{-1}.$$

Last we show the constant 1 is $\underline{1}.\underline{1}^{-1}$ using the four squares axiom:

$$\frac{1}{1} = \frac{0^2+0^2+0^2+0^2+1}{0^2+0^2+0^2+0^2+1} = 1 + 0.(0+0+0+0) = 1$$

.

Induction Step. There are four operators $-, ^{-1}, = \, .$ to consider.

Additive Inverse. Consider the leading operator symbol $-$ and term $t = -s$. By induction, the subterm s reduces to one of three cases: $s = \infty$, $s = \perp$ and $s = \underline{n}.\underline{m}^{-1}$ in the transversal Tr. From the axioms, the first two cases of $-s$ are immediate as $-\infty = \infty$ and $-\perp = \perp$, which are in the transversal. The last case is quite involved, however.

Suppose $t = -(\underline{n}.\underline{m}^{-1})$. We will show that $t = (-\underline{n}.\underline{m}^{-1})$, which is in the transversal. We begin with some lemmas of use here and later on.

To complete the case we need these identities:

Lemma 14. $(\underline{n}.\underline{m}^{-1}) + (-(\underline{n}.\underline{m}^{-1})) = 0$ *and* $(\underline{n}.\underline{m}^{-1}) + (\underline{-n}).\underline{m}^{-1} = 0$.

Proof. First, we show that $(\underline{n}.\underline{m}^{-1}) + (-(\underline{n}.\underline{m}^{-1})) = 0$.

$$\begin{aligned}
(\underline{n}.\underline{m}^{-1}) + (-(\underline{n}.\underline{m}^{-1})) &= 0.(\underline{n}.\underline{m}^{-1}) && \text{by axiom 20}\\
&= (0.\underline{n}).\underline{m}^{-1} && \text{by axiom 5}\\
&= 0.\underline{m}^{-1} && \text{by Lemma 3}\\
&= (0.\underline{m}).\underline{m}^{-1} && \text{by Lemma 3}\\
&= 0.(\underline{m}.\underline{m}^{-1}). && \text{by axiom 5}\\
&= 0.1 && \text{by Lemma 4}\\
&= 0 && \text{by axiom 6}
\end{aligned}$$

Next we show the second identity, $(\underline{n}.\underline{m}^{-1}) + (\underline{-n}).\underline{m}^{-1} = 0$.

$$\begin{aligned}
(\underline{n}.\underline{m}^{-1}) + (-\underline{n}).\underline{m}^{-1} &= (\underline{n} + (-\underline{n})).\underline{m}^{-1} + 0.\underline{m}^{-1} && \text{by axiom 11}\\
&= (\underline{n} + (-\underline{n})).\underline{m}^{-1} && \text{by Lemma 5}\\
&= (0.\underline{n}).\underline{m}^{-1} && \text{by axiom 20}\\
&= 0.(\underline{n}.\underline{m}^{-1}) && \text{by axiom 5}\\
&= 0. && \text{by Lemma 6}
\end{aligned}$$

□

Given the Lemma 14, by subtracting the above equations, it follows that

$$-(\underline{n}.\underline{m}^{-1}) - (\underline{-n}).\underline{m}^{-1} = 0$$

and, thus,

$$-(\underline{n}.\underline{m}^{-1}) = (\underline{-n}).\underline{m}^{-1}$$

which is in the transversal. This completes the basis. □

Multiplicative Inverse. Consider the leading operator symbol $^{-1}$ and term $t = s^{-1}$. By induction, the subterm s reduces to one of four cases: $s = \infty$, $s = \perp$, $s = \underline{0}.\underline{m}^{-1}$ and $s = \underline{n}.\underline{m}^{-1}$ with $n \neq 0$ in the transversal Tr.

If $s = \perp$ then

$$\begin{aligned}
s^{-1} &= (0.\infty)^{-1} && \text{by axiom 17}\\
&= 0^{-1}.\infty^{-1} && \text{by axiom 7}\\
&= \infty.0 && \text{by axiom 17 and Lemma 8}\\
&= 0.\infty && \text{by axiom 4}\\
&= \perp && \text{by axiom 17}
\end{aligned}$$

which is in the transversal.

If $s = \infty$ then $s^{-1} = 0$ by Lemma 8.
If $s = \underline{0}.\underline{m}^{-1}$ then

$$\begin{aligned} s^{-1} &= (\underline{0}.\underline{m}^{-1})^{-1} \\ &= 0^{-1} && \text{by Lemma 5} \\ &= \infty && \text{by axiom 13} \end{aligned}$$

which is in the transversal.
If $s = \underline{n}.\underline{m}^{-1}$ for $n \neq 0$ then

$$\begin{aligned} s^{-1} &= (\underline{n}.\underline{m}^{-1})^{-1} \\ &= \underline{n}^{-1}.(\underline{m}^{-1})^{-1} && \text{by axiom 7} \\ &= \underline{n}^{-1}.\underline{m} && \text{by axiom 8} \\ &= \underline{m}.\underline{n}^{-1} && \text{by axiom 4} \end{aligned}$$

which is in the transversal.

Addition. Consider the leading operator symbol $+$ and term $t = r + s$. For notational ease, we write a for $\underline{n}$ and b for $\underline{m}$. By induction, the subterms r, s reduce to one of six cases in the table below:

r	s
$\perp$	$\perp$
$\perp$	∞
$\perp$	$a.b^{-1}$
∞	∞
∞	$a.b^{-1}$
$a.b^{-1}$	$c.d^{-1}$

The first three cases where $r = \perp$ follow from the axiom $x + \perp = \perp$ and commutativity. The next case uses axioms 20 followed by axiom 17:

$$\infty + \infty = \infty + (-\infty) = 0.\infty = \perp .$$

Now

$$\begin{aligned} \infty + a.b^{-1} &= \infty.b^{-1} + a.b^{-1} && \text{by Lemma 10} \\ &= (\infty + a).b^{-1} + 0.b^{-1} && \text{by axiom 11} \\ &= \infty.b^{-1} + 0 && \text{by Lemma 9} \\ &= \infty.b^{-1} && \text{by axiom 3} \\ &= \infty && \text{by Lemma 10} \end{aligned}$$

which is in the transversal.

Consider the last case:

$$\begin{aligned} a.b^{-1} + c.d^{-1} &= a.b^{-1}.1 + c.d^{-1}.1 && \text{by axiom 6} \\ &= a.b^{-1}.d.d^{-1} + c.d^{-1}.b.b^{-1} && \text{by Lemma 4} \\ &= a.d.b^{-1}.d^{-1} + c.b.d^{-1}.b^{-1} && \text{by axiom 4} \\ &= (a.d + c.b).b^{-1}.d^{-1} + 0.b^{-1}.d^{-1} && \text{by axiom 11} \\ &= \frac{a.d + c.b}{bd} + 0 && \text{by axiom 7} \\ &= \frac{a.d + c.b}{bd}. && \text{by axiom 3} \end{aligned}$$

To finish this deduction: let $p = gcd(a.d + c.b, bd)$. Choose p', p'' such that $p.p' = a.d + c.b$ and $p.p'' = b.d$. Then $\frac{a.d+c.b}{bd} = \frac{p.p'}{p.p''} = \frac{p'}{p''}$, which is in the transversal.

Multiplication. Consider the leading operator symbol . and term $t = r.s$. By induction, the subterms r, s reduce to one of six cases as in the table above; each case will need an argument.

$$\begin{aligned} \bot \,.\, \bot &= (\infty.0).(\infty.0) && \text{by axiom 17} \\ &= \infty.\infty.0 && \text{by axioms 5, 4, 12} \\ &= \infty.0 && \text{by lemma 12} \\ &= \bot && \text{by axiom 17} \end{aligned}$$

which is in the transversal. The next case is straightforward:

$$\begin{aligned} \bot\,.\infty &= (\infty.0).\infty && \text{by axiom 17} \\ &= (\infty.\infty).0 && \text{by axioms 5, 4} \\ &= \infty.0 && \text{by lemma 12} \\ &= \bot && \text{by axiom 17} \end{aligned}$$

which is in the transversal.

$$\begin{aligned} \bot\,.a.b^{-1} &= (\infty.0).a.b^{-1} && \text{by axiom 17} \\ &= \infty.(0.a.b^{-1}) && \text{by axioms 5} \\ &= \infty.0 && \text{by lemma 6} \\ &= \bot && \text{by axiom 17} \end{aligned}$$

which is in the transversal.

Consider $\infty.a.b^{-1}$.

$$\begin{aligned} \infty.(a.b^{-1}) &= (\infty.a).b^{-1} && \text{by axiom 5} \\ &= (\infty.b^{-1}) && \text{by lemma 10} \\ &= \infty && \text{by lemma 10} \end{aligned}$$

which is in the transversal.

Finally, the last case is this deduction: let $p = gcd(ac, bd)$

$$\begin{aligned}
a.b^{-1}.c.d^{-1} &= (a.c).(b.d)^{-1} && \text{by axioms 4 and 7}\\
&= (p.p').(p.p'')^{-1} && \text{by substitution}\\
&= (p.p').(p^{-1}.p''^{-1}) && \text{by axiom 7}\\
&= (p.p^{-1}).(p'p''^{-1}) && \text{by axiom 4}\\
&= (1.p'p''^{-1}) && \text{by Lemma 4}\\
&= p'p''^{-1} && \text{by axiom 6}
\end{aligned}$$

which is in the transversal.

This concludes the proof of the theorem. □

5 Concluding Remarks

Using a general conceptual framework for analysing numerical data types with total operations, we have given a mathematical model of the wheel of rational numbers. The concept of a wheel was introduced by Anton Setzer in unpublished notes [18]. It was motivated by Jens Blanck's lectures on exact real number computations, based on domains and rational number intervals, and Per Martin Löff's suggestion to allow 0 in denominators of elements of quotient fields. Later wheels were studied in greater generality and published by Jesper Carlström [13]. Carlström generalised the constructions to semirings, developed equations and identities, and considered the class of wheels.

The concept of a meadow emerged when we were making an algebraic specification of the rational numbers in [11]; we studied the axiomatic class of meadows in [3]. A substantial series of papers has built an algebraic theory of meadows with different properties, e.g., [4–6,8,12].

The ideas in this paper suggest problems and topics for further study. In the case of the meadow programme on totalisation, algebraic specifications for other methods of totalisation in arithmetic structures could be tackled. An obvious candidate is *transrational arithmetic* due to James Anderson, as described in [2,17]. Transrational arithmetic provides signed infinities, i.e., $+\infty$ and $-\infty$, in addition to an error element (which is called nullity and denoted by Φ instead of $\perp$). Thus, while wheels are aimed at reasoning for exact real arithmetics based on intervals, the transrationals are aimed at floating point arithmetics. Other semantic interpretations of infinities and errors are conceivable that could lead to interesting arithmetic data types.

As with most algebraic specification problems, there is also the search for new specifications with good term rewriting properties for arithmetic structures. In the specific case of wheels, can a basis theorem for the class of wheels be provided? In the case of common meadows, which feature $\perp$ but not ∞, a basis theorem has been obtained in [6]. The case of wheels seems to be much harder, however.

References

1. Bergstra, J.A., Tucker, J.V.: Algebraic specifications of computable and semicomputable data types. Theoret. Comput. Sci. **50**, 137–181 (1987)
2. Bergstra, J.A.: Division by zero: a survey of options. Transmathematica **1**(1), 1–20 (2019). https://transmathematica.org/index.php/journal/article/view/17
3. Bergstra, J.A., Hirshfeld, Y., Tucker, J.V.: Meadows and the equational specification of division. Theoret. Comput. Sci. **410**(12–13), 1261–1271 (2009)
4. Bergstra, J.A., Middelburg, C.A.: Inversive meadows and divisive meadows. J. Appl. Logic **9**(3), 203–220 (2011)
5. Bergstra, J.A., Middelburg, C.A.: Transformation of fractions into simple fractions in divisive meadows. J. Appl. Logic **16**, 92–110 (2016)
6. Bergstra, J.A., Ponse, A.: Division by zero in common meadows. In: De Nicola, R., Hennicker, R. (eds.) Software, Services, and Systems. LNCS, vol. 8950, pp. 46–61. Springer, Cham (2015). https://doi.org/10.1007/978-3-319-15545-6_6
7. Bergstra, J.A., Ponse, A.: Fracpairs and fractions over a reduced commutative ring. Indag. Math. **27**, 727–748 (2016)
8. Bergstra, J.A., Ponse, A.: Probability functions in the context of signed involutive meadows (extended abstract). In: James, P., Roggenbach, M. (eds.) WADT 2016. LNCS, vol. 10644, pp. 73–87. Springer, Cham (2017). https://doi.org/10.1007/978-3-319-72044-9_6
9. Bergstra, J.A., Tucker, J.V.: The completeness of the algebraic specification methods for computable data types. Inf. Control **54**(3), 186–200 (1982)
10. Bergstra, J.A., Tucker, J.V.: Initial and final algebra semantics for data type specifications: two characterization theorems. SIAM J. Comput. **12**(2), 366–387 (1983)
11. Bergstra, J.A., Tucker, J.V.: The rational numbers as an abstract data type. J. ACM **54**(2), 7 (2007)
12. Bergstra, J.A., Tucker, J.V.: Division safe calculation in totalised fields. Theory Comput. Syst. **43**(3–4), 410–424 (2008). https://doi.org/10.1007/s00224-007-9035-4
13. Carlstrom, J.: Wheels: on division by zero. Math. Struct. Comput. Sci. **14**, 143–184 (2004)
14. Ehrig, H., Mahr, B.: Fundamentals of Algebraic Specification 1: Equations und Initial Semantics. EATCS, vol. 6. Springer, Heidelberg (1985). https://doi.org/10.1007/978-3-642-69962-7
15. Loeckx, J., Ehrich, H., Wolf, M.: Specification of Abstract Data Types. Wiley, Hoboken (1996)
16. Meinke, K., Tucker, J.V.: Universal algebra. In: Abramsky, S., Gabbay, D., Maibaum, T. (eds.) Handbook of Logic in Computer Science. Volume I: Mathematical Structures, pp. 189–411. Oxford University Press (1992)
17. dos Reis, T., Gomide, W., Anderson, J.A.: Construction of the transreal numbers and algebraic transfields. IAENG Int. J. Appl. Math. **46**(1), 11–23 (2016)
18. Setzer, A.: Wheels (draft) (1997). http://www.cs.swan.ac.uk/~csetzer/articles/wheel.pdf
19. Stoltenberg-Hansen, V., Tucker, J.V.: Effective algebras. In: Abramsky, S., Gabbay, D., Maibaum, T. (eds.) Handbook of Logic in Computer Science. Volume IV: Semantic Modelling, pp. 357–526. Oxford University Press (1995)
20. Stoltenberg-Hansen, V., Tucker, J.V.: Computable rings and fields. In: Griffor, E. (ed.) Handbook of Computability Theory, pp. 363–447. Elsevier (1999)
21. Wechler, W.: Universal Algebra for Computer Scientists. EATCS, vol. 25. Springer, Heidelberg (1992). https://doi.org/10.1007/978-3-642-76771-5

Towards General Axiomatizations for Bisimilarity and Trace Semantics

Marco Bernardo(✉)

Dipartimento di Scienze Pure e Applicate, Università di Urbino, Urbino, Italy
marco.bernardo@uniurb.it

Abstract. We study general equational characterizations for bisimulation and trace semantics via the respective post-/pre-metaequivalences defined on the ULTraS metamodel. This yields axiomatizations encompassing those appeared in the literature, as well as new ones, for bisimulation and trace equivalences when applied to specific classes of processes. The equational laws are developed incrementally, by starting with some core axioms and then singling out additional axioms for bisimulation post-/pre-metaequivalences on the one hand, and different additional axioms for trace post-/pre-metaequivalences on the other hand. The axiomatizations highlight the fundamental differences in the discriminating power between bisimulation semantics and trace semantics, regardless of specific classes of processes. Moreover, they generalize idempotency laws of bisimilarity and choice-deferring laws of trace semantics, in addition to formalizing shuffling laws for pre-metaequivalences.

1 Introduction

Process calculi [6] constitute a foundational algebraic tool for the specification and verification of concurrent, distributed, and mobile systems. Their syntax includes operators for expressing concepts such as sequential/alternative/parallel composition, action hiding/restriction/renaming, and recursion. Their semantics is typically formalized via structural operational rules associating a labeled transition system with each process term. Many behavioral equivalences have been proposed to identify syntactically different process terms on the basis of observational criteria. Sound and complete axiomatizations have been developed to emphasize the equational laws on which the equivalences rely, which can then be exploited for the algebraic manipulation of process terms.

These axiomatizations are usually provided for a specific class of processes (e.g., nondeterministic, probabilistic, or timed), while we are interested in investigating general equational laws that are valid for multiple classes of processes. This can be accomplished by working with behavioral metamodels. On the one hand, they act as unifying theories by underpinning a deeper understanding of specific models through a uniform view of the models themselves. On the other hand, they support the study of metaresults, i.e., results that are valid for all the specific models that are embodied. Frameworks like operational

M. Roggenbach (Ed.): WADT 2020, LNCS 12669, pp. 31–53, 2021.
https://doi.org/10.1007/978-3-030-73785-6_3

semantic rule formats [1,2,19], Segala probabilistic automata [40], and weighted automata [23] can be viewed to some extent as behavioral metamodels, even though their emphasis is more on ensuring certain properties in a general setting or achieving a higher expressivity. More recently, behavioral metamodels such as WLTS – weighted labeled transition systems [31], FuTS – state-to-function labeled transition systems [20,34], and ULTraS – uniform labeled transition systems [7,10,15], have been developed with the explicit purpose of paving the way to unifying theories.

In this paper, we investigate equational characterization metaresults for the two endpoints of the branching-time – linear-time spectrum [48], i.e., bisimulation semantics and trace semantics, through the corresponding behavioral post-/pre-metaequivalences defined on ULTraS. In this metamodel – which encompasses a wide gamut of behavioral models ranging from nondeterministic transition systems to action-labeled Markov chains and several variants of automata with probability and time – every action-labeled transition goes from a state to a reachability distribution over states. We make use of this metamodel because from its inception it has been equipped with several behavioral relations. In particular, it has inspired some new relations in the probabilistic setting, whose properties have been analyzed in [11,13], and has been used in [7] to study compositionality metaresults for bisimulation and trace semantics.

The equational characterization metaresults are developed incrementally on an ULTraS-based process calculus named UProC, which contains only dynamic process operators such as action prefix and alternative composition as well as operators on state reachability distributions. This calculus provides the minimum set of operators that are necessary to highlight the fundamental differences in the discriminating power of the considered metaequivalences.

We start with some core axioms establishing associativity and commutativity of alternative composition and distribution composition, together with the existence of a neutral element for alternative composition. Then we single out additional axioms for the various semantics, by considering for each of them a post-metaequivalence and a pre-metaequivalence differring for the way in which resolutions of nondeterminism have to match each other, for a total of two bisimulation metaequivalences $\sim_{\mathrm{B}}^{\mathrm{post}}$ and $\sim_{\mathrm{B}}^{\mathrm{pre}}$ plus two trace metaequivalences $\sim_{\mathrm{T}}^{\mathrm{post}}$ and $\sim_{\mathrm{T}}^{\mathrm{pre}}$. Here is a summary of our contributions and their relationships with previous axiomatizations:

- The equational characterization of $\sim_{\mathrm{B}}^{\mathrm{post}}$ relying on *idempotency* axioms for alternative and reachability distribution compositions is the expected one, generalizes the well known ones of [4,26,27,29,36] related to various classes of specific processes, and is in agreement with the coalgebraic one of [43].
- The equational characterization of $\sim_{\mathrm{B}}^{\mathrm{pre}}$ relying on a *B-shuffling* axiom is new and yields the first axiomatization for the bisimilarities over nondeterministic and probabilistic processes of [13,45] characterized by the probabilistic modal and temporal logics of [25,33].
- The equational characterization of $\sim_{\mathrm{T}}^{\mathrm{post}}$ relying on *choice-deferring* axioms generalizes the well known ones of [18,39] for nondeterministic processes, is

in agreement with some of the axioms of the coalgebraic ones of [17,44], and provides the first axiomatization for the probabilistic trace equivalences of [29,41] given that the axiomatization in [37] holds for the simulation-like coarsest congruence [35] contained in the equivalence of [41].
- The equational characterization of $\sim_{\mathrm{T}}^{\mathrm{pre}}$ relying on a *T-shuffling* axiom is new and opens the way to the first axiomatization of the compositional trace semantics over nondeterministic and probabilistic processes of [11].

The proof of completeness of the equational characterizations of $\sim_{\mathrm{B}}^{\mathrm{post}}$ and $\sim_{\mathrm{B}}^{\mathrm{pre}}$ is based on a preliminary reduction of process terms into sum normal form [36]. In contrast, for $\sim_{\mathrm{T}}^{\mathrm{post}}$ the proof employs the technique of [5,48] by using the choice-deferring axioms as graph rewriting rules to transform the completeness problem for $\sim_{\mathrm{T}}^{\mathrm{post}}$ over arbitrary process terms into the completeness problem for $\sim_{\mathrm{B}}^{\mathrm{post}}$ over process terms in a sum normal form specific to $\sim_{\mathrm{T}}^{\mathrm{post}}$. The completeness problem for $\sim_{\mathrm{T}}^{\mathrm{pre}}$ is still open.

As mentioned above, our general axioms feature as instances the laws of bisimulation and trace semantics known from the literature for nondeterministic, probabilistic, or stochastic processes. Moreover, axioms for pre-metaequivalences have never been investigated before; similarly, the instances of those for trace post-metaequivalence were not known for certain classes of processes. To the best of our knowledge, this is the first work in which a concrete behavioral metamodel is employed in place of category theory – whose mathematics may be perceived as highly complex by researchers not familiar with it – to develop equational characterizations that are valid *regardless of specific classes of processes.*

This paper is organized as follows. In Sect. 2, we recall the ULTRAS metamodel together with its bisimulation and trace metaequivalences revisited according to [8,9]. In Sect. 3, we present the ULTRAS-inspired process calculus UPROC and show the full compositionality of the metaequivalences with respect to the selected operators thanks to the aforementioned revisitation. In Sect. 4, we incrementally develop equational characterizations over UPROC for the considered behavioral metaequivalences and discuss their relationships and limits. Finally, in Sect. 5 we provide some concluding remarks.

2 Background

We recall from [7] the ULTRAS metamodel (Sect. 2.1), reachability-consistent semirings (Sect. 2.2), bisimulation metaequivalences (Sect. 2.3), resolutions of nondeterminism (Sect. 2.4), reachability measures (Sect. 2.5), and a revisitation of trace metaequivalences based on [8,9] (Sect. 2.6).

2.1 The ULTRAS Metamodel

ULTRAS is a discrete state-transition metamodel parameterized with respect to a set D, where D-values are interpreted as degrees of *one-step reachability.* These values are assumed to be ordered according to a reflexive and transitive relation $\sqsubseteq_D$, which is equipped with minimum $\bot_D$ expressing *unreachability*. Let us denote by $(S \to D)$ the set of functions from a set S to D. When S is a set of states, every element Δ of $(S \to D)$ can be interpreted as a function that *distributes reachability* over all possible next states. We call *support* of Δ the set of states $supp(\Delta) = \{s \in S \mid \Delta(s) \neq \bot_D\}$ that are reachable according to Δ.

To represent transition targets, we use the set $(S \to D)_{\text{nefs}}$ of D-distributions Δ over S with *n*on*e*mpty and *f*inite *s*upport, i.e., satisfying $0 < |supp(\Delta)| < \omega$. The lower bound avoids distributions always returning $\bot_D$ and hence transitions leading to nowhere. The upper bound will enable a correct definition of reachability measures for trace metaequivalences in Sect. 2.5.

Definition 1. *Let* $(D, \sqsubseteq_D, \bot_D)$ *be a preordered set with minimum. A* uniform labeled transition system *on it, or* D-ULTRAS, *is a triple* $\mathcal{U} = (S, A, \longrightarrow)$ *where* $S \neq \emptyset$ *is an at most countable set of states,* $A \neq \emptyset$ *is a countable set of transition-labeling actions, and* $\longrightarrow \subseteq S \times A \times (S \to D)_{\text{nefs}}$ *is a transition relation.* ■

Every transition (s, a, Δ) of $\mathcal{U}$ is written $s \xrightarrow{a} \Delta$, where $\Delta(s')$ is a D-value quantifying the degree of reachability of s' from s via that a-transition, with $\Delta(s') = \bot_D$ meaning that s' is not reachable with that transition. In the directed graph description of $\mathcal{U}$ (see, e.g., the forthcoming Fig. 1), vertices represent states and action-labeled edges represent action-labeled transitions. Given a transition $s \xrightarrow{a} \Delta$, the corresponding a-labeled edge goes from the vertex representing state s to a set of vertices linked by a dashed line, each of which represents a state $s' \in supp(\Delta)$ and is labeled with $\Delta(s')$.

Example 1. As shown in [7,10,15], we can use the set $\mathbb{B} = \{\bot, \top\}$ with $\bot \sqsubseteq_{\mathbb{B}} \top$ for capturing labeled transition systems [30] and timed automata [3], the set $\mathbb{R}_{[0,1]}$ with the usual $\leq$ for capturing action-labeled discrete-time Markov chains [46], Markov decision processes [22], probabilistic automata [40], probabilistic timed automata [32], and Markov automata [24], and the set $\mathbb{R}_{\geq 0}$ with the usual $\leq$ for capturing action-labeled continuous-time Markov chains [46] and continuous-time Markov decision processes [38]. ■

2.2 Reachability-Consistent Semirings

To express the calculations needed by behavioral metaequivalences, we further assume that D has a *commutative semiring* structure. This means that D is equipped with two binary operations $\oplus$ and $\otimes$, with the latter distributing over the former, which satisfy the following properties:

- $\otimes$ is associative and commutative and admits neutral element 1_D and absorbing element 0_D. This multiplicative operation enables the combination of D-values of consecutive single-step reachability along the same computation.
- $\oplus$ is associative and commutative and admits neutral element 0_D. This additive operation is useful for aggregating D-values of different computations starting from the same state, as well as for shorthands like $\Delta(S') = \bigoplus_{s' \in S'} \Delta(s')$ given $s \xrightarrow{a} \Delta$.

We also assume that these two binary operations are *reachability consistent*, in the sense that they satisfy the following additional properties in accordance with the intuition behind the concept of reachability:

- $0_D = \bot_D$, i.e., the zero of the semiring denotes unreachability.
- $d_1 \otimes d_2 \neq 0_D$ if $d_1 \neq 0_D \neq d_2$, hence as expected two consecutive steps cannot result in unreachability.
- The sum via $\oplus$ of finitely many values 1_D is always different from 0_D (known as *characteristic zero*). It ensures that two nonzero values sum up to zero only if they are one the inverse of the other with respect to $\oplus$, thus avoiding inappropriate zero results when aggregating D-values of distinct computations departing from the same state.

Example 2. As shown in [7], we can use the reachability-consistent semirings $(\mathbb{B}, \vee, \wedge, \bot, \top)$ for nondeterministic models and $(\mathbb{R}_{\geq 0}, +, \times, 0, 1)$ for probabilistic and stochastic models, as well as for their respective behavioral equivalences. In contrast, characteristic zero rules out all semirings $(\mathbb{N}_n, +_n, \times_n, 0, 1)$ of the classes of natural numbers that are congruent modulo $n \in \mathbb{N}_{\geq 2}$. ■

2.3 Bisimulation Post-/Pre-metaequivalences

For bisimulation semantics we have two different variants of metaequivalence in the ULTRAS setting, $\sim_{\mathrm{B}}^{\mathrm{post}}$ and $\sim_{\mathrm{B}}^{\mathrm{pre}}$. They are both defined in the style of [33], which requires bisimulations to be equivalence relations, but deal with sets of equivalence classes, rather than only with individual classes, to avoid an undesirable decrease of the discriminating power of $\sim_{\mathrm{B}}^{\mathrm{pre}}$ in certain circumstances. The difference between the two variants lies in the position – underlined in the definition below – of the universal quantification over sets of equivalence classes.

In the first case, which is the approach of [42], the quantification occurs *after* selecting a transition from either considered state, hence for each class set the transition of the challenger state and the transition of the defender state must reach that set with the same degree (*fully matching transitions*). In the second case, inspired by [13,45,47], the quantification occurs *before* selecting transitions, so that a transition of the challenger can be matched by different transitions of the defender with respect to different class sets (*partially matching transitions*). In the definition below, given an equivalence relation $\mathcal{B}$ over a state space S together with a set of equivalence classes $\mathcal{G} \in 2^{S/\mathcal{B}}$, $\bigcup \mathcal{G} \subseteq S$ denotes the union of all the equivalence classes in $\mathcal{G}$.

Definition 2. *Let $(D, \oplus, \otimes, 0_D, 1_D)$ be a reachability-consistent semiring, $\mathcal{U} = (S, A, \longrightarrow)$ be a D-ULTRAS, and $s_1, s_2 \in S$:*

- *$s_1 \sim_{\mathrm{B}}^{\mathrm{post}} s_2$ iff there exists a post-bisimulation $\mathcal{B}$ over S such that $(s_1, s_2) \in \mathcal{B}$. An equivalence relation $\mathcal{B}$ over S is a* post-bisimulation *iff, whenever $(s_1, s_2) \in \mathcal{B}$, then for all $a \in A$ it holds that for each $s_1 \xrightarrow{a} \Delta_1$ there exists $s_2 \xrightarrow{a} \Delta_2$ such that for all $\mathcal{G} \in 2^{S/\mathcal{B}}$:*

$$\Delta_1(\bigcup \mathcal{G}) = \Delta_2(\bigcup \mathcal{G})$$

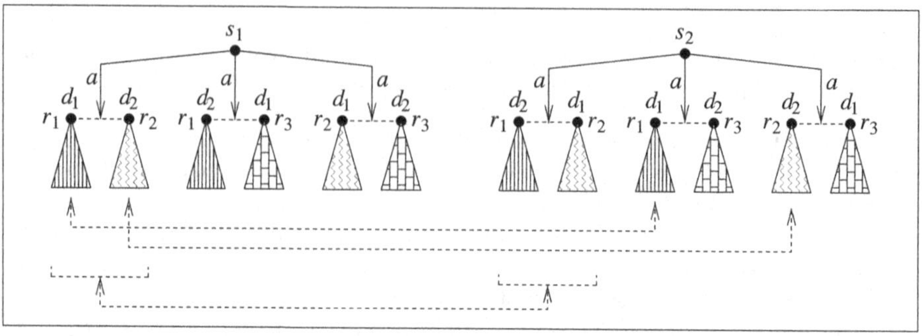

Fig. 1. Difference between bisimulation metaequivalences: $s_1 \not\sim_{\rm B}^{\rm post} s_2$, $s_1 \sim_{\rm B}^{\rm pre} s_2$

- $s_1 \sim_{\rm B}^{\rm pre} s_2$ *iff there exists a pre-bisimulation* $\mathcal{B}$ *over* S *such that* $(s_1, s_2) \in \mathcal{B}$. *An equivalence relation* $\mathcal{B}$ *over* S *is a* pre-bisimulation *iff, whenever* $(s_1, s_2) \in \mathcal{B}$*, then for all* $a \in A$ *and* for all $\mathcal{G} \in 2^{S/\mathcal{B}}$ *it holds that for each* $s_1 \xrightarrow{a} \Delta_1$ *there exists* $s_2 \xrightarrow{a} \Delta_2$ *such that:*

$$\Delta_1(\bigcup \mathcal{G}) = \Delta_2(\bigcup \mathcal{G}) \qquad \blacksquare$$

The difference between the two bisimulation metaequivalences emerges in the presence of *internal nondeterminism*, i.e., identically labeled transitions departing from the same state. Consider the two D-ULTRAS models in Fig. 1, which feature the same distinct D-values d_1 and d_2 as well as the same inequivalent continuations given by the D-ULTRAS submodels rooted at r_1, r_2, r_3. Notice that both the D-values and the continuations are *shuffled within* each model, while only the D-values are *shuffled across* the two models too. It holds that $s_1 \not\sim_{\rm B}^{\rm post} s_2$ because, e.g., the leftmost a-transition of s_1 is not matched by any of the three a-transitions of s_2. In contrast, we have that $s_1 \sim_{\rm B}^{\rm pre} s_2$. For instance, the leftmost a-transition of s_1 is matched by the central (resp. rightmost) a-transition of s_2 with respect to the equivalence class of r_1 (resp. r_2), and by the leftmost a-transition of s_2 with respect to the union of the equivalence classes of r_1 and r_2 – see the dashed arrow-headed lines at the bottom of Fig. 1.

2.4 Resolutions of Nondeterminism

When several transitions depart from the same state, they describe a nondeterministic choice among different behaviors. While in the case of bisimulation semantics nondeterminism is solved stepwise, for trace semantics overall resolutions of nondeterminism have to be made explicit.

A *resolution* of a state s of a D-ULTRAS $\mathcal{U}$ is the result of a possible way of resolving nondeterministic choices starting from s, as if a *deterministic scheduler* were applied that, at the current state s', selects one of the outgoing transitions of s', or no transitions at all thus stopping the execution. The applicability of other classes of schedulers, like randomized [40] and interpolating [21] ones and

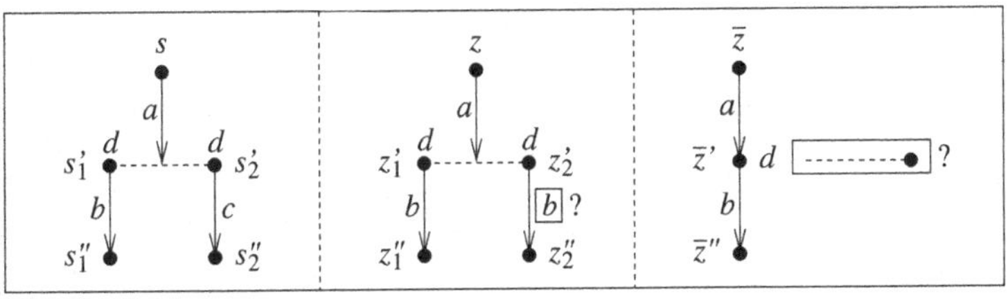

Fig. 2. Lack of bijectivity breaks structure preservation on the resolution side

combinations thereof [16], may depend on the specific D, hence we will not consider them here.

We formalize a resolution of s as a D-ULTRAS $\mathcal{Z}$ with a tree-like structure, whose branching points correspond to target distributions of transitions. It is obtained by unfolding from s the graph structure of $\mathcal{U}$ and by selecting at each reached state s' at most one of its outgoing transitions, hence it is isomorphic to a submodel of the unfolding of the original model. Following [28], we make use of a *correspondence function* from the acyclic state space of $\mathcal{Z}$ to the original state space of $\mathcal{U}$. For each transition $z \xrightarrow{a}_{\mathcal{Z}} \Delta$ in $\mathcal{Z}$, all the states in $supp(\Delta)$ must preserve the reachability degrees of the corresponding states in the support of the target of the corresponding transition in $\mathcal{U}$.

Extending [14], this function must be *bijective* between $supp(\Delta)$ and the support of the target distribution of the corresponding transition in $\mathcal{U}$. Requiring injectivity as in [7] ensures submodel isomorphism, whereas surjectivity additionally guarantees that Δ preserves the overall reachability of the target distribution of the corresponding transition in $\mathcal{U}$ (unlike number 1 in the probabilistic case, in general there is no predefined value for the total reachability of a target distribution). For instance, in Fig. 2 the association of the same value d to s_1' and s_2' allows for a function that maps z to s, z_1' and z_2' to s_1', and z_1'' and z_2'' to s_1'', which is not injective and would cause the central ULTRAS to be considered a legal resolution of the leftmost ULTRAS although the former is not isomorphic to any submodel of the latter. The situation is similar for the rightmost ULTRAS under the function that maps $\bar{z}$ to s, $\bar{z}'$ to s_1', and $\bar{z}''$ to s_1'', which is not surjective.

Definition 3. *Let* $\mathcal{U} = (S, A, \longrightarrow_{\mathcal{U}})$ *be a* D-ULTRAS *and* $s \in S$. *An acyclic* D-ULTRAS $\mathcal{Z} = (Z, A, \longrightarrow_{\mathcal{Z}})$ *is a* resolution *of* s, *written* $\mathcal{Z} \in Res(s)$, *iff there exists a correspondence function* $corr_{\mathcal{Z}} : Z \to S$ *such that* $s = corr_{\mathcal{Z}}(z_s)$, *for some* $z_s \in Z$ *acting as the initial state of* $\mathcal{Z}$, *and for all* $z \in Z$ *it holds that:*

- *If* $z \xrightarrow{a}_{\mathcal{Z}} \Delta$ *then* $corr_{\mathcal{Z}}(z) \xrightarrow{a}_{\mathcal{U}} \Gamma$, *with* $corr_{\mathcal{Z}}$ *being bijective between* $supp(\Delta)$ *and* $supp(\Gamma)$ *and* $\Delta(z') = \Gamma(corr_{\mathcal{Z}}(z'))$ *for all* $z' \in supp(\Delta)$.
- *At most one transition departs from* z. ■

2.5 Reachability Measures

The definition of trace metaequivalences requires the measurement of *multistep reachability*, i.e., the degree of reachability of a given set of states from a given state when executing a sequence of transitions labeled with a certain sequence of actions. We therefore provide a notion of *measure schema* for a D-ULTRAS $\mathcal{U}$ as a set of homogeneously defined *measure functions*, one for each resolution $\mathcal{Z}$ of $\mathcal{U}$. In the following, we denote by A^* the set of finite traces over an action set A, by ε the empty trace, and by $|\alpha|$ the length of a trace $\alpha \in A^*$.

Definition 4. *Let* $(D, \oplus, \otimes, 0_D, 1_D)$ *be a reachability-consistent semiring and* $\mathcal{U} = (S, A, \longrightarrow_{\mathcal{U}})$ *be a* D*-ULTRAS. A* D-measure schema $\mathcal{M}$ *for* $\mathcal{U}$ *is a set of* measure functions *of the form* $\mathcal{M}_{\mathcal{Z}} : Z \times A^* \times 2^Z \to D$*, one for each* $\mathcal{Z} = (Z, A, \longrightarrow_{\mathcal{Z}}) \in Res(s)$ *and* $s \in S$*, which are inductively defined on the length of their second argument as follows:*

$$\mathcal{M}_{\mathcal{Z}}(z, \alpha, Z') = \begin{cases} \bigoplus\limits_{z' \in supp(\Delta)} \Delta(z') \otimes \mathcal{M}_{\mathcal{Z}}(z', \alpha', Z') & \text{if } \alpha = a\,\alpha' \text{ and } z \xrightarrow{a}_{\mathcal{Z}} \Delta \\ 1_D & \text{if } \alpha = \varepsilon \text{ and } z \in Z' \\ 0_D & \text{otherwise} \end{cases}$$

■

In the first clause, the value of $\mathcal{M}_{\mathcal{Z}}(z, \alpha, Z')$ is built as a sum of products of D-values – a formal power series in the semiring terminology – with the summation being well defined because $supp(\Delta)$ is finite as established in Definition 1. For simplicity, we will often indicate with $\mathcal{M}$ both the measure schema and any of its measure functions $\mathcal{M}_{\mathcal{Z}}$, using $\mathcal{M}_{\mathrm{nd}}$ when the reachability-consistent semiring is $(\mathbb{B}, \vee, \wedge, \bot, \top)$ and $\mathcal{M}_{\mathrm{pb}}$ when it is $(\mathbb{R}_{\geq 0}, +, \times, 0, 1)$ as in [7].

2.6 Coherency-Based Trace Post-/Pre-metaequivalences

Also for trace semantics we have two distinct metaequivalence variants in the ULTRAS framework, $\sim_{\mathrm{T}}^{\mathrm{post}}$ and $\sim_{\mathrm{T}}^{\mathrm{pre}}$, with the difference being the position of the universal quantification over traces. In the first case, which is the approach of [41], the quantification occurs *after* selecting resolutions, hence for each trace the resolution of the challenger and the resolution of the defender must execute that trace with the same degree (*fully matching resolutions*). In the second case, inspired by [11], the quantification occurs *before* selecting resolutions, so that a resolution of the challenger can be matched by different resolutions of the defender with respect to different traces (*partially matching resolutions*).

Trace metaequivalences tend to be overdiscriminating because of the freedom of schedulers of making different decisions in states enabling the same actions. To avoid this, we limit the excessive power of schedulers by restricting them to yield *coherent resolutions*. Intuitively, this means that, if several states in the support of the target distribution of a transition are equivalent, then the decisions made by the scheduler in those states have to be coherent with each other, so that the states to which they correspond in any resolution are equivalent too.

Coherent resolutions, introduced in [8] for nondeterministic and probabilistic processes, are extended to ULTRAS in the following. They rely on coherent trace distributions, which are suitable families of sets of traces weighted with their execution degrees in a given resolution, built through the operations below.

Definition 5. *Let $A \neq \emptyset$ be a countable set and $(D, \oplus, \otimes, 0_D, 1_D)$ a reachability-consistent semiring. For $a \in A$, $d \in D$, $TD \subseteq 2^{A^* \times D}$, and $T \subseteq A^* \times D$ we define:*

$$\begin{aligned} a \,.\, TD &= \{a \,.\, T \mid T \in TD\} & a \,.\, T &= \{(a\,\alpha, d') \mid (\alpha, d') \in T\} \\ d \otimes TD &= \{d \otimes T \mid T \in TD\} & d \otimes T &= \{(\alpha, d \otimes d') \mid (\alpha, d') \in T\} \\ tr(TD) &= \{tr(T) \mid T \in TD\} & tr(T) &= \{\alpha \in A^* \mid \exists d' \in D.\, (\alpha, d') \in T\} \end{aligned}$$

while for $TD_1, TD_2 \subseteq 2^{A^* \times D}$ we define:

$$TD_1 \oplus TD_2 = \begin{cases} \{T_1 \oplus T_2 \mid T_1 \in TD_1 \wedge T_2 \in TD_2 \wedge tr(T_1) = tr(T_2)\} \\ \qquad\qquad\qquad\qquad\qquad\qquad \text{if } tr(TD_1) = tr(TD_2) \\ \{T_1 \oplus T_2 \mid T_1 \in TD_1 \wedge T_2 \in TD_2\} \\ \qquad\qquad\qquad\qquad\qquad\qquad \text{otherwise} \end{cases}$$

where for $T_1, T_2 \subseteq A^* \times D$ we define:

$$\begin{aligned} T_1 \oplus T_2 = \; & \{(\alpha, d_1 \oplus d_2) \mid (\alpha, d_1) \in T_1 \wedge (\alpha, d_2) \in T_2\} \cup \\ & \{(\alpha, d) \in T_1 \cup T_2 \mid \alpha \notin tr(T_1) \cap tr(T_2)\} \end{aligned}$$

■

Weighted trace set addition $T_1 \oplus T_2$ is commutative and associative, with degrees of identical traces in the two summands being always added up for coherency purposes. In contrast, trace distribution addition is only commutative. Essentially, the two summands in $TD_1 \oplus TD_2$ represent two families of sets of weighted traces executable in the resolutions of two states in the support of a target distribution. Every weighted trace set $T_1 \in TD_1$ is summed with every weighted trace set $T_2 \in TD_2$ – to characterize an overall resolution – unless TD_1 and TD_2 have the same family of trace sets, in which case summation is restricted to weighted trace sets featuring the same traces for the sake of coherency. Due to the lack of associativity, in the definition below all trace distributions $\Delta(s') \cdot TD^{c}_{n-1}(s')$ exhibiting the same family Θ of trace sets have to be summed up first, which is ensured by the presence of a double summation.

Definition 6. *Let $(D, \oplus, \otimes, 0_D, 1_D)$ be a reachability-consistent semiring and $(S, A, \longrightarrow)$ be a D-ULTRAS. The* coherent trace distribution *of $s \in S$ is the subset of $2^{A^* \times (D \setminus \{0_D\})}$ defined as follows:*

$$TD^{c}(s) = \bigcup\nolimits_{n \in \mathbb{N}} TD^{c}_{n}(s)$$

with the coherent trace distribution of s whose traces have length at most n being defined as:

$$TD^{\rm c}_n(s) = \begin{cases} (\varepsilon, 1_D) \dagger \bigcup_{s \xrightarrow{a} \Delta} a \,.\left(\bigoplus_{\Theta \in tr(\Delta, n-1)} \bigoplus_{s' \in supp(\Delta)}^{tr(TD^{\rm c}_{n-1}(s')) = \Theta} \Delta(s') \otimes TD^{\rm c}_{n-1}(s') \right) & \\ \qquad \text{if } n > 0 \text{ and } s \text{ has outgoing transitions} \\ \{\{(\varepsilon, 1_D)\}\} \qquad \text{otherwise} \end{cases}$$

where $tr(\Delta, n-1) = \{tr(TD^{\rm c}_{n-1}(s')) \mid s' \in supp(\Delta)\}$ *and the operator* $(\varepsilon, 1_D) \dagger \_$ *is such that* $(\varepsilon, 1_D) \dagger TD = \{\{(\varepsilon, 1_D)\} \cup T \mid T \in TD\}$. ■

As shown by several examples in [8], the coherency constraints should involve all $TD^{\rm c}_n(\_)$ distributions separately – rather than $TD^{\rm c}(\_)$ – and should not consider the degrees contained in those trace distributions, i.e., they should rely on $tr(TD^{\rm c}_n(\_))$ sets. In [9] it was further shown that the coherency constraints should be based on a monotonic construction in which any $TD^{\rm c}_n(\_)$ incrementally builds on $TD^{\rm c}_{n-1}(\_)$, in the sense that every weighted trace set in the former should include as a subset a weighted trace set in the latter. This is achieved through a variant of coherent trace distribution, called fully coherent trace distribution.

Definition 7. *Let* $(D, \oplus, \otimes, 0_D, 1_D)$ *be a reachability-consistent semiring and* $(S, A, \longrightarrow)$ *be a D-*ULTRAS. *The* fully coherent trace distribution *of* $s \in S$ *is the subset of* $2^{A^* \times (D \setminus \{0_D\})}$ *defined as follows:*

$$TD^{\rm fc}(s) = \bigcup\nolimits_{n \in \mathbb{N}} TD^{\rm fc}_n(s)$$

with the fully coherent trace distribution of s whose traces have length at most n being the subset of $TD^{\rm c}_n(s)$ *defined as:*

$$TD^{\rm fc}_n(s) = \begin{cases} \{T \in TD^{\rm c}_n(s) \mid \exists T' \in TD^{\rm fc}_{n-1}(s) .\, T' \subseteq T\} & \\ \qquad \text{if } n > 0 \text{ and } s \text{has outgoing transitions} \\ \{\{(\varepsilon, 1_D)\}\} & \\ \qquad \text{otherwise} \end{cases}$$

■

We now adapt to ULTRAS the two coherency constraints of [8,9]. The former preserves the equality of trace set families of any length n between original states and the resolutions states to which they correspond. The latter requires a complete presence in each resolution of traces of length n if any, including possible shorter maximal traces, which is looser than requiring resolution maximality.

Definition 8. *Let* $(S, A, \longrightarrow_{\mathcal{U}})$ *be a D-*ULTRAS, $s \in S$, *and* $\mathcal{Z} = (Z, A, \longrightarrow_{\mathcal{Z}}) \in Res(s)$ *with correspondence function* $corr_{\mathcal{Z}} : Z \rightarrow S$. *We say that* $\mathcal{Z}$ *is a* coherent resolution *of s, written* $\mathcal{Z} \in Res^{\rm c}(s)$, *iff for all* $z \in Z$, *whenever* $z \xrightarrow{a}_{\mathcal{Z}} \Delta$, *then for all* $n \in \mathbb{N}$:

1. $tr(TD_n^{\text{fc}}(corr_{\mathcal{Z}}(z'))) = tr(TD_n^{\text{fc}}(corr_{\mathcal{Z}}(z''))) \implies tr(TD_n^{\text{fc}}(z')) = tr(TD_n^{\text{fc}}(z''))$ *for all* $z', z'' \in supp(\Delta)$.
2. *For all* $z' \in supp(\Delta)$, *the only* $T \in TD_n^{\text{fc}}(z')$ *admits* $\bar{T} \in TD_n^{\text{fc}}(corr_{\mathcal{Z}}(z'))$ *such that* $tr(T) = tr(\bar{T})$. ■

We can now define the two trace metaequivalences by making use of coherent resolutions of nondeterminism arising from deterministic schedulers. As in the case of bisimilarity, the difference between the two emerges in the presence of internal nondeterminism and is illustrated in Fig. 3. In the definition below, z_{s_i} denotes both the initial state of $\mathcal{Z}_i$ and the state to which s_i corresponds.

Definition 9. *Let* $(D, \oplus, \otimes, 0_D, 1_D)$ *be a reachability-consistent semiring,* $\mathcal{U} = (S, A, \longrightarrow_{\mathcal{U}})$ *be a* D-ULTRAS, $\mathcal{M}$ *be a* D*-measure schema for* $\mathcal{U}$, *and* $s_1, s_2 \in S$:

- $s_1 \sim_{\text{T},\mathcal{M}}^{\text{post}} s_2$ *iff it holds that for each* $\mathcal{Z}_1 = (Z_1, A, \longrightarrow_{\mathcal{Z}_1}) \in Res^{\text{c}}(s_1)$ *there exists* $\mathcal{Z}_2 = (Z_2, A, \longrightarrow_{\mathcal{Z}_2}) \in Res^{\text{c}}(s_2)$ *such that* *for all* $\alpha \in A^*$:

$$\mathcal{M}(z_{s_1}, \alpha, Z_1) = \mathcal{M}(z_{s_2}, \alpha, Z_2)$$

and also the condition obtained by exchanging $\mathcal{Z}_1$ *with* $\mathcal{Z}_2$ *is satisfied.*
- $s_1 \sim_{\text{T},\mathcal{M}}^{\text{pre}} s_2$ *iff* *for all* $\alpha \in A^*$ *it holds that for each* $\mathcal{Z}_1 = (Z_1, A, \longrightarrow_{\mathcal{Z}_1}) \in Res^{\text{c}}(s_1)$ *there exists* $\mathcal{Z}_2 = (Z_2, A, \longrightarrow_{\mathcal{Z}_2}) \in Res^{\text{c}}(s_2)$ *such that:*

$$\mathcal{M}(z_{s_1}, \alpha, Z_1) = \mathcal{M}(z_{s_2}, \alpha, Z_2)$$

and also the condition obtained by exchanging $\mathcal{Z}_1$ *with* $\mathcal{Z}_2$ *is satisfied.* ■

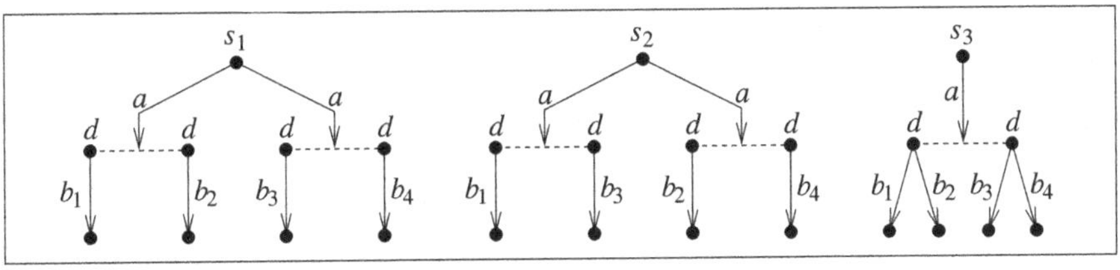

Fig. 3. Difference between trace metaequivalences: $s_i \not\sim_{\text{T},\mathcal{M}}^{\text{post}} s_j$, $s_i \sim_{\text{T},\mathcal{M}}^{\text{pre}} s_j$

The reader is referred to [7] to see that well-known specific equivalences are captured by the four metaequivalences introduced so far when instantiated with the semirings $(\mathbb{B}, \vee, \wedge, \bot, \top)$ and $(\mathbb{R}_{\geq 0}, +, \times, 0, 1)$ along with their measure functions $\mathcal{M}_{\text{nd}}$ and $\mathcal{M}_{\text{pb}}$. We finally revisit the comparison of the discriminating power of the four metaequivalences because the adoption of coherency rectifies a flaw in the proof of Prop. 3.5(3) in [7]. As shown in Fig. 4, where $s_1 \sim_{\text{B}}^{\text{post}} s_2$, the inclusion of $\sim_{\text{B}}^{\text{post}}$ in $\sim_{\text{T},\mathcal{M}}^{\text{post}}$ would be prevented by incoherent resolutions. The resolution of s_2 starting with z_2, which cannot be matched by any resolution of s_1 with respect to trace $a\,b$, is not coherent because $tr(TD_1^{\text{fc}}(s_2')) = \{\{\varepsilon, b\}, \{\varepsilon, c\}\} = tr(TD_1^{\text{fc}}(s_2''))$ whereas $tr(TD_1^{\text{fc}}(z_2')) = \{\{\varepsilon, b\}\} \neq \{\{\varepsilon, c\}\} = tr(TD_1^{\text{fc}}(z_2''))$.

Proposition 1. *Let $(D, \oplus, \otimes, 0_D, 1_D)$ be a reachability-consistent semiring, $\mathcal{U} = (S, A, \longrightarrow_{\mathcal{U}})$ be a D-ULTRAS, and $\mathcal{M}$ be a D-measure schema for $\mathcal{U}$. Then:*

1. $\sim_{\rm B}^{\rm post} \subseteq \sim_{\rm B}^{\rm pre}$, *with* $\sim_{\rm B}^{\rm post} = \sim_{\rm B}^{\rm pre}$ *if* $\mathcal{U}$ *has no internal nondeterminism.*
2. $\sim_{\rm T,\mathcal{M}}^{\rm post} \subseteq \sim_{\rm T,\mathcal{M}}^{\rm pre}$.
3. $\sim_{\rm B}^{\rm post} \subseteq \sim_{\rm T,\mathcal{M}}^{\rm post}$.
4. $\sim_{\rm B}^{\rm pre}$ *is incomparable with* $\sim_{\rm T,\mathcal{M}}^{\rm post}$ *and* $\sim_{\rm T,\mathcal{M}}^{\rm pre}$. ■

3 A Process Algebraic View of ULTRAS

We introduce a very simple process calculus inspired by the ULTRAS metamodel, which we call UPROC – uniform process calculus. In order to focus on the essence of the axiomatization for the various ULTRAS behavioral metaequivalences, we only admit dynamic process operators such as action prefix and choice.

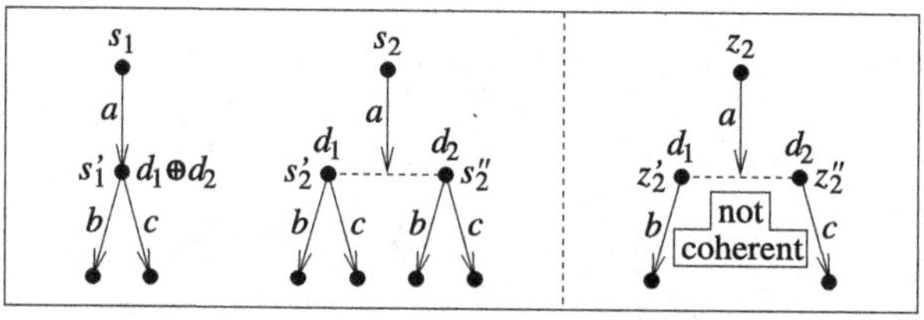

Fig. 4. Validity of the inclusion of $\sim_{\rm B}^{\rm post}$ in $\sim_{\rm T,\mathcal{M}}^{\rm post}$ thanks to coherent resolutions

Given a preordered set D equipped with minimum that yields a reachability-consistent semiring $(D, \oplus, \otimes, 0_D, 1_D)$, together with a countable set A of actions, the syntax for UPROC features two levels, one for the set $\mathbb{P}$ of process terms and one for the set $\mathbb{D}$ of reachability distribution terms:

$$P \ ::= \ \underline{0} \mid a \,.\, \mathcal{D} \mid P + P \qquad \mathcal{D} \ ::= \ d \triangleright P \mid \mathcal{D} \mathbin{\oplus\!\!\!\!+} \mathcal{D}$$

where $a \in A$, $d \in D \setminus \{0_D\}$, and unary operators take precedence over binary ones. We let $init(\underline{0}) = \emptyset$, $init(a \,.\, \mathcal{D}) = \{a\}$, and $init(P_1 + P_2) = init(P_1) \cup init(P_2)$. We denote by $d \otimes \mathcal{D}$ the distribution term obtained from $\mathcal{D}$ by $\otimes$-multiplying each of its initial D-values by d.

The operational semantic rules below generate a D-ULTRAS $(\mathbb{P}, A, \longrightarrow)$:

$$\frac{\mathcal{D} \longmapsto \Delta}{a \,.\, \mathcal{D} \xrightarrow{a} \Delta} \qquad \frac{P_1 \xrightarrow{a} \Delta}{P_1 + P_2 \xrightarrow{a} \Delta} \qquad \frac{P_2 \xrightarrow{a} \Delta}{P_1 + P_2 \xrightarrow{a} \Delta}$$

$$d \triangleright P \longmapsto \{(P, d)\} \qquad \frac{\mathcal{D}_1 \longmapsto \Delta_1 \quad \mathcal{D}_2 \longmapsto \Delta_2}{\mathcal{D}_1 \mathbin{\oplus\!\!\!\!+} \mathcal{D}_2 \longmapsto \Delta_1 \oplus \Delta_2}$$

The primary transition relation $\longrightarrow$ is defined as the smallest subset of $\mathbb{P} \times A \times (\mathbb{P} \to D)_{\text{nefs}}$ satisfying the rules in the upper part. The secondary transition relation $\longmapsto$ is the smallest subset of $\mathbb{D} \times (\mathbb{P} \to D)_{\text{nefs}}$ satisfying the rules in the lower part, with $\{(P, d)\}$ being a shorthand for the reachability distribution identically equal to 0_D except in P where its value is d; furthermore, $\oplus$ is lifted to reachability distributions by letting $(\Delta_1 \oplus \Delta_2)(P) = \Delta_1(P) \oplus \Delta_2(P)$. Whenever $\mathcal{D} \longmapsto \Delta$, we let $supp(\mathcal{D}) = supp(\Delta)$ and $\bigoplus \mathcal{D} = \bigoplus_{P \in supp(\Delta)} \Delta(P)$.

To proceed with the axiomatization of the four behavioral metaequivalences, we need to show that they are congruences with respect to all the operators of UProC. Due to the two-level format of the syntax, as a preliminary step we have to lift the metaequivalences from processes to reachability distributions over processes. Extending [33], this can be done by considering $\mathcal{D}_1, \mathcal{D}_2 \in \mathbb{D}$ related by an equivalence relation $\sim$ over $\mathbb{P}$ when they assign the same reachability degree to the same equivalence class, i.e., $\Delta_1(C) = \Delta_2(C)$ for all $C \in \mathbb{P}/\!\sim$ with $\mathcal{D}_1 \longmapsto \Delta_1$ and $\mathcal{D}_2 \longmapsto \Delta_2$.

Compositionality with respect to the two reachability distribution operators $\triangleright$ and $\oplus$ can be established by abstracting from the specific behavioral metaequivalence. As for the two process operators, we have instead different proofs for bisimulation and trace semantics. These are minor reworkings of those in [7], except for the case of action prefix under trace semantics, for which we achieve full compositionality thanks to the use of coherent resolutions.

Theorem 1. *Let* $\sim_{\mathcal{M}} \in \{\sim_{\text{B}}^{\text{post}}, \sim_{\text{B}}^{\text{pre}}, \sim_{\text{T},\mathcal{M}}^{\text{post}}, \sim_{\text{T},\mathcal{M}}^{\text{pre}}\}$ *for a measure schema* $\mathcal{M}$ *over the* D*-ULTraS semantics of* UProC. *Let* $P_1, P_2 \in \mathbb{P}$ *and* $\mathcal{D}_1, \mathcal{D}_2 \in \mathbb{D}$. *Then for all* $d \in D \setminus \{0_D\}$, $\mathcal{D} \in \mathbb{D}$, $a \in A$, $P \in \mathbb{P}$:

1. *If* $P_1 \sim_{\mathcal{M}} P_2$, *then* $d \triangleright P_1 \sim_{\mathcal{M}} d \triangleright P_2$.
2. *If* $\mathcal{D}_1 \sim_{\mathcal{M}} \mathcal{D}_2$, *then* $\mathcal{D}_1 \oplus \mathcal{D} \sim_{\mathcal{M}} \mathcal{D}_2 \oplus \mathcal{D}$ *and* $\mathcal{D} \oplus \mathcal{D}_1 \sim_{\mathcal{M}} \mathcal{D} \oplus \mathcal{D}_2$.
3. *If* $\mathcal{D}_1 \sim_{\mathcal{M}} \mathcal{D}_2$, *then* $a \,.\, \mathcal{D}_1 \sim_{\mathcal{M}} a \,.\, \mathcal{D}_2$.
4. *If* $P_1 \sim_{\mathcal{M}} P_2$, *then* $P_1 + P \sim_{\mathcal{M}} P_2 + P$ *and* $P + P_1 \sim_{\mathcal{M}} P + P_2$. ■

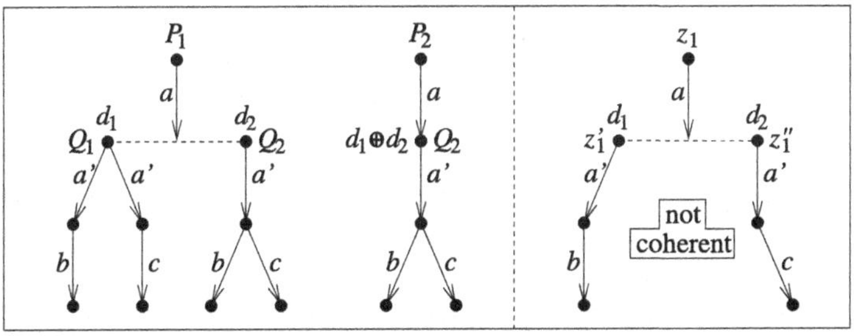

Fig. 5. Compositionality of trace semantics w.r.t. action prefix thanks to coherency

If in Definition 9 ordinary resolutions had been used instead of coherent ones, then similar to Theorem 4.2 of [7] in property 3 above we should have added "provided that all the processes in $supp(\mathcal{D}_i)$, $i \in \{1,2\}$, are pairwise $\sim_{\mathcal{M}}$-inequivalent" when $\sim_{\mathcal{M}}$ is a trace metaequivalence. In other words, compositionality of trace semantics with respect to action prefix would be partial without the restriction to coherent resolutions. The need for this trace-inequivalence constraint would emerge in our general setting because the continuation after an action is not a single process, but a reachability distribution over processes.

This can be illustrated through the following UPROC terms P_1 and P_2:

$$\begin{array}{ll} P_1 = a\,.\,(d_1 \triangleright Q_1 \oplus d_2 \triangleright Q_2) & P_2 = a\,.\,(d_1 \triangleright Q_2 \oplus d_2 \triangleright Q_2) \\ Q_1 = a'\,.\,b\,.\,\underline{0} + a'\,.\,c\,.\,\underline{0} & Q_2 = a'\,.\,(b\,.\,\underline{0} + c\,.\,\underline{0}) \end{array}$$

where a sequence of action prefixes like $a'\,.\,b\,.\,\underline{0}$ is a shorthand for $a'\,.\,(\hat{d} \triangleright b\,.\,(\hat{d} \triangleright \underline{0}))$, with the same value $\hat{d} \in D \setminus \{0_D\}$ being used here in all such sequences for simplicity. Their underlying D-ULTRAS models are shown in the leftmost part of Fig. 5. It is easy to see that Q_1 and Q_2 are trace equivalent, hence the two distributions describing the a-continuations of P_1 and P_2 are trace equivalent too. However, if we consider the resolution of P_1 starting with z_1 in the rightmost part of Fig. 5, in which trace $\alpha = a\,a'b$ is executable with degree $d_1 \otimes \hat{d} \otimes \hat{d}$, we have that no resolution of P_2 is capable of matching it, as the executability degree of α would be $(d_1 \oplus d_2) \otimes \hat{d} \otimes \hat{d}$ or 0_D, unless $D = \mathbb{B}$ in which case $d_1 = d_2 = \top$ and $d_1 \oplus d_2 = \top \vee \top = \top$. As can be noted, the considered resolution of P_1 is not coherent because $tr(TD_2^{\rm fc}(Q_1)) = \{\{\varepsilon, a', a'b\}, \{\varepsilon, a', a'c\}\} = tr(TD_2^{\rm fc}(Q_2))$ but $tr(TD_2^{\rm fc}(z_1')) = \{\{\varepsilon, a', a'b\}\} \neq \{\{\varepsilon, a', a'c\}\} = tr(TD_2^{\rm fc}(z_1''))$.

4 Axiomatizations of Behavioral Metaequivalences

In this section, we incrementally provide axioms in the UPROC language for the four behavioral metaequivalences defined over the ULTRAS metamodel. Since these axioms do not depend on any specific reachability-consistent semiring $(D, \oplus, \otimes, 0_D, 1_D)$, nor on any specific D-measure schema $\mathcal{M}$, from now on we omit $\mathcal{M}$ from trace metaequivalence symbols. Within examples, we will sometimes use subterms of the form $a\,.\,\underline{0}$ as abbreviation of $a\,.\,(\hat{d} \triangleright \underline{0})$, where the same value $\hat{d} \in D \setminus \{0_D\}$ is employed in all those subterms.

We start with the core axioms and the basic normal form used for all the metaequivalences (Sect. 4.1), then we single out additional axioms for $\sim_{\rm B}^{\rm post}$ (Sect. 4.2) and $\sim_{\rm B}^{\rm pre}$ (Sect. 4.3) on the one hand, as well as different additional axioms for $\sim_{\rm T}^{\rm post}$ (Sect. 4.4) and $\sim_{\rm T}^{\rm pre}$ on the other hand. Before presenting soundness and completeness results, each set of axioms will be either compared with those known in the literature for specific classes of processes, or mentioned to yield the first equational characterization in a certain setting. Because of the absence of a completeness result, the axioms for $\sim_{\rm T}^{\rm pre}$ require further investigation and are not shown in the paper due to lack of space.

4.1 Core Axioms: Associativity, Commutativity, Neutral Element

Thanks to the format of the semantic rules in Sect. 3 and the associativity and commutativity of $\oplus$, for each metaequivalence the two UPROC operators

$+$ and $\oplus$ turn out to be associative and commutative – hence we can use their generalized versions respectively denoted by $\sum$ and $\bigoplus$ – with $\underline{0}$ being the neutral element for operator $+$. Our starting point is thus a deduction system $\mathcal{A}$ that, in addition to reflexivity, symmetry, transitivity, and substitutivity, is based on the following core axioms:

$$\begin{array}{|lrcl|}
\hline
(\mathcal{A}_1) & (P_1 + P_2) + P_3 & = & P_1 + (P_2 + P_3) \\
(\mathcal{A}_2) & P_1 + P_2 & = & P_2 + P_1 \\
(\mathcal{A}_3) & P + \underline{0} & = & P \\
(\mathcal{A}_4) & (\mathcal{D}_1 \oplus \mathcal{D}_2) \oplus \mathcal{D}_3 & = & \mathcal{D}_1 \oplus (\mathcal{D}_2 \oplus \mathcal{D}_3) \\
(\mathcal{A}_5) & \mathcal{D}_1 \oplus \mathcal{D}_2 & = & \mathcal{D}_2 \oplus \mathcal{D}_1 \\
\hline
\end{array}$$

Axioms $\mathcal{A}_1$ to $\mathcal{A}_3$ are typical of nondeterministic process calculi [36], while axioms $\mathcal{A}_4$ and $\mathcal{A}_5$ encode those typical of probabilistic process calculi [4,29]. The latter calculi usually employ a probabilistic choice operator ${}_p+$, so that associativity is represented as $(P' \,{}_p\!+ P'') \,{}_q\!+ P''' = P' \,{}_{p \cdot q}\!+ (P'' \,{}_{(1-p) \cdot q/(1-p \cdot q)}\!+ P''')$ and commutativity is represented as $P' \,{}_p\!+ P'' = P'' \,{}_{1-p}\!+ P'$, with $p, q \in \mathbb{R}_{]0,1[}$. In $\mathcal{A}_4$ and $\mathcal{A}_5$, probabilities decorating operators like ${}_p+$ are instead expressed by degrees within distributions, which avoids calculations when moving between the two distribution terms of either axiom.

To prove the completeness of the equational characterizations for the various metaequivalences, we introduce as usual a normal form to which each term is shown to be reducible, then we work with normal forms only. Extending [36], we say that $P \in \mathbb{P}$ is in *sum normal form (snf)* iff it is equal to $\underline{0}$ or $\sum_{i \in I} a_i \,.\, (\bigoplus_{j \in J_i} d_{i,j} \rhd P_{i,j})$ where I and J_i are finite nonempty index sets and every $P_{i,j}$ is in snf. The axiom system $\mathcal{A}$ is sufficient for snf reducibility.

Lemma 1. *Let $P \in \mathbb{P}$. Then there exists $Q \in \mathbb{P}$ in snf such that $\mathcal{A} \vdash P = Q$.* ■

4.2 Equational Characterization of $\sim_{\mathrm{B}}^{\mathrm{post}}$: Idempotency

The additional laws for $\sim_{\mathrm{B}}^{\mathrm{post}}$ are given by the following *idempotency-related axioms*, where we emphasize in boldface the occurrences of identical subterms:

$$\begin{array}{|lrcl|}
\hline
(\mathcal{A}_{\mathrm{B},1}^{\mathrm{post}}) & \boldsymbol{P} + \boldsymbol{P} & = & \boldsymbol{P} \\
(\mathcal{A}_{\mathrm{B},2}^{\mathrm{post}}) & d_1 \rhd \boldsymbol{P} \oplus d_2 \rhd \boldsymbol{P} & = & (d_1 \oplus d_2) \rhd \boldsymbol{P} \\
\hline
\end{array}$$

Axiom $\mathcal{A}_{\mathrm{B},1}^{\mathrm{post}}$ expresses idempotency of choice and is typical of bisimilarity over nondeterministic process calculi [36]. Axiom $\mathcal{A}_{\mathrm{B},2}^{\mathrm{post}}$ expresses a summation-based variant of idempotency that involves operator $\rhd$ too; it encodes the axioms typical of bisimilarity over probabilistic process calculi [4,29], i.e., $P \,{}_p\!+ P = P$, and over stochastic process calculi [26,27], i.e., $\lambda_1 \,.\, P + \lambda_2 \,.\, P = (\lambda_1 + \lambda_2) \,.\, P$ with $\lambda_1, \lambda_2 \in \mathbb{R}_{>0}$ being rates of exponential distributions. The two axioms are in agreement with those developed in the coalgebraic framework of [43] for various classes of probabilistic processes possibly including nondeterminism.

It is immediate to establish the soundness with respect to $\sim_{\mathrm{B}}^{\mathrm{post}}$ of the deduction system $\mathcal{A}_{\mathrm{B}}^{\mathrm{post}}$ obtained from $\mathcal{A}$ by adding the two idempotency-related axioms $\mathcal{A}_{\mathrm{B},1}^{\mathrm{post}}$ and $\mathcal{A}_{\mathrm{B},2}^{\mathrm{post}}$.

Theorem 2. *Let $P_1, P_2 \in \mathbb{P}$. If $\mathcal{A}_{\mathrm{B}}^{\mathrm{post}} \vdash P_1 = P_2$, then $P_1 \sim_{\mathrm{B}}^{\mathrm{post}} P_2$.* ■

As far as the completeness of $\mathcal{A}_{\mathrm{B}}^{\mathrm{post}}$ with respect to $\sim_{\mathrm{B}}^{\mathrm{post}}$ is concerned, we exploit Lemma 1, i.e., reducibility to snf.

Theorem 3. *Let $P_1, P_2 \in \mathbb{P}$. If $P_1 \sim_{\mathrm{B}}^{\mathrm{post}} P_2$, then $\mathcal{A}_{\mathrm{B}}^{\mathrm{post}} \vdash P_1 = P_2$.* ■

Corollary 1. *Let $P_1, P_2 \in \mathbb{P}$. Then $P_1 \sim_{\mathrm{B}}^{\mathrm{post}} P_2$ iff $\mathcal{A}_{\mathrm{B}}^{\mathrm{post}} \vdash P_1 = P_2$.* ■

4.3 Equational Characterization of $\sim_{\mathrm{B}}^{\mathrm{pre}}$: B-Shuffling

When $P_1 \sim_{\mathrm{B}}^{\mathrm{post}} P_2$, every a-transition of either term is matched by an a-transition of the other with respect to all sets of equivalence classes, so that the target distributions Δ_1 and Δ_2 of the two a-transitions satisfy $\Delta_1 \sim_{\mathrm{B}}^{\mathrm{post}} \Delta_2$. If instead $P_1 \sim_{\mathrm{B}}^{\mathrm{pre}} P_2$, every a-transition of either term is matched by an a-transition of the other with respect to a specific set of equivalence classes, hence $\Delta_1 \sim_{\mathrm{B}}^{\mathrm{pre}} \Delta_2$ is *not* necessarily true.

This is witnessed by the example shown in Fig. 1, which yields the balanced equality $a \,.\, (d_1 \rhd P_1 \oplus d_2 \rhd P_2) + a \,.\, (d_2 \rhd P_1 \oplus d_1 \rhd P_3) + a \,.\, (d_1 \rhd P_2 \oplus d_2 \rhd P_3) = a \,.\, (d_2 \rhd P_1 \oplus d_1 \rhd P_2) + a \,.\, (d_1 \rhd P_1 \oplus d_2 \rhd P_3) + a \,.\, (d_2 \rhd P_2 \oplus d_1 \rhd P_3)$ where d_1, d_2 and P_1, P_2, P_3 are shuffled within either term, while only d_1 and d_2 are shuffled across the two terms too. An example of unbalanced equality – with unbalanced meaning that the number of $\oplus$-summands is not the same within all a-summands – is given by $a \,.\, (d_1 \rhd P_1) + a \,.\, (d_2 \rhd P_1 \oplus d_1 \rhd P_2) + a \,.\, (d_2 \rhd P_2) = a \,.\, (d_2 \rhd P_1) + a \,.\, (d_1 \rhd P_1 \oplus d_2 \rhd P_2) + a \,.\, (d_1 \rhd P_2)$.

Table 1. Axiom characterizing $\sim_{\mathrm{B}}^{\mathrm{pre}}$

$$(\mathcal{A}_{\mathrm{B},1}^{\mathrm{pre}}) \quad \sum_{i \in I_1} a \,.\, \Big(\bigoplus_{j \in J_{1,i}} d_{1,i,j} \rhd P_{1,i,j}\Big) = \sum_{i \in I_2} a \,.\, \Big(\bigoplus_{j \in J_{2,i}} d_{2,i,j} \rhd P_{2,i,j}\Big)$$

subject to:

for all $i_1 \in I_1$ and $J_1 \subseteq J_{1,i_1}$ s.t. $(j \in J_1 \wedge P_{1,i_1,k} = P_{1,i_1,j}) \Longrightarrow k \in J_1$
there exist $i_2 \in I_2$ and $J_2 \subseteq J_{2,i_2}$ s.t. $(j \in J_2 \wedge P_{2,i_2,k} = P_{2,i_2,j}) \Longrightarrow k \in J_2$
such that the following three constraints are met:

1. $\forall j_1 \in J_1 \,.\, (\exists j_2 \in J_2 \,.\, P_{1,i_1,j_1} = P_{2,i_2,j_2} \vee \nexists j_2 \in J_{2,i_2} \,.\, P_{1,i_1,j_1} = P_{2,i_2,j_2})$
2. $\{P_{1,i_1,j} \mid j \in J_1\} \supseteq \{P_{2,i_2,j} \mid j \in J_2\}$
3. $\bigoplus_{j \in J_1} d_{1,i_1,j} = \bigoplus_{j \in J_2} d_{2,i_2,j}$

and also the condition obtained by exchanging i_1, J_1 with i_2, J_2 is satisfied

In the identifications made possible by $\sim_{\mathrm{B}}^{\mathrm{pre}}$, no regularity can be assumed in general about the number of a-summands (internal nondeterminism) and the number of $\oplus$-summands inside every a-summand. The two identifications exemplified above turn out to be among the simplest instances of the *B-shuffling axiom* in Table 1 characterizing the identification power of $\sim_{\rm B}^{\rm pre}$, where I_1, $J_{1,i}$, J_1, I_2, $J_{2,i}$, J_2 are finite nonempty index sets and we emphasize in boldface the occurrences of identical actions.

All $+$-summands on both sides of the axiom start with the same action a. For each a-summand on the lefthand side indexed by i_1 and on the righthand side indexed by i_2, in the three constraints we use the *maximal* subsets J_1 of J_{1,i_1} and J_2 of J_{2,i_2} whose elements index *all* the occurrences of certain process terms, so as to consider every set of equivalence classes of process terms reached after performing a. More precisely:

1. The first constraint guarantees that, for each equivalence class C such that (i) C is reached via the a-summand on the lefthand side indexed by i_1 and (ii) the a-derivative terms in C are *all* indexed by elements of J_1, it holds that either C is reached also via the a-summand on the righthand side indexed by i_2 and the a-derivative terms in C are *all* indexed by elements of J_2, or C is not reachable at all as no P_{2,i_2,j_2} belongs to it.
2. The second constraint ensures that the elements of J_2 do not index process terms of further equivalence classes with respect to those singled out by J_1. It cannot be expressed as $\{P_{1,i_1,j} \mid j \in J_1\} = \{P_{2,i_2,j} \mid j \in J_2\}$ otherwise $a \,.\, (d \rhd P_1 \oplus d \rhd P_2) = a \,.\, (d \rhd P_1) + a \,.\, (d \rhd P_2)$ subject to $d = d \oplus d$ would not be derivable because, for J_1 indexing both P_1 and P_2, we would have J_2 indexing at most one of those two a-derivative terms.
3. The maximality of J_1 and J_2 with respect to the process terms indexed by their elements, together with the first two constraints, causes the third constraint to state that, for an arbitrary set of equivalence classes identified by J_1, this set is reached via a with the same overall D-value from both the a-summand on the lefthand side indexed by i_1 and the a-summand on the righthand side indexed by i_2.

The B-shuffling axiom $\mathcal{A}_{\rm B,1}^{\rm pre}$ subsumes the following laws that we have already encountered:

- $\mathcal{A}_{\rm B,1}^{\rm post}$, because in $P + P$ each subterm $a \,.\, \mathcal{D} + a \,.\, \mathcal{D}$ composed of two identical summands placed next to each other can be trivially equated to subterm $a \,.\, \mathcal{D}$ of P via $\mathcal{A}_{\rm B,1}^{\rm pre}$.
- $\mathcal{A}_{\rm B,2}^{\rm post}$, because $a \,.\, (d_1 \rhd P \oplus d_2 \rhd P)$ can be trivially equated to $a \,.\, ((d_1 \oplus d_2) \rhd P)$ via $\mathcal{A}_{\rm B,1}^{\rm pre}$.
- $a \,.\, \mathcal{D}_1 + a \,.\, \mathcal{D}_2 \;=\; a \,.\, (\mathcal{D}_1 \oplus \mathcal{D}_2)$ under the same conditions as $\mathcal{A}_{\rm B,1}^{\rm pre}$.

We also point out that $\mathcal{A}_{\rm B,1}^{\rm pre}$ yields the first axiomatization for the bisimilarities over nondeterministic and probabilistic processes studied in [13,45], which have the interesting property of being characterized by the probabilistic modal and temporal logics of [25,33].

We now show that $\mathcal{A}_{\rm B}^{\rm pre}$, the deduction system obtained from $\mathcal{A}$ by adding the B-shuffling axiom $\mathcal{A}_{\rm B,1}^{\rm pre}$, is sound and complete with respect to $\sim_{\rm B}^{\rm pre}$ by exploiting again Lemma 1.

Theorem 4. *Let $P_1, P_2 \in \mathbb{P}$. If $\mathcal{A}_{\mathrm{B}}^{\mathrm{pre}} \vdash P_1 = P_2$, then $P_1 \sim_{\mathrm{B}}^{\mathrm{pre}} P_2$.* ∎

Theorem 5. *Let $P_1, P_2 \in \mathbb{P}$. If $P_1 \sim_{\mathrm{B}}^{\mathrm{pre}} P_2$, then $\mathcal{A}_{\mathrm{B}}^{\mathrm{pre}} \vdash P_1 = P_2$.* ∎

Corollary 2. *Let $P_1, P_2 \in \mathbb{P}$. Then $P_1 \sim_{\mathrm{B}}^{\mathrm{pre}} P_2$ iff $\mathcal{A}_{\mathrm{B}}^{\mathrm{pre}} \vdash P_1 = P_2$.* ∎

4.4 Equational Characterization of $\sim_{\mathrm{T}}^{\mathrm{post}}$: Choice Deferral

The additional identification power of $\sim_{\mathrm{T}}^{\mathrm{post}}$ with respect to $\sim_{\mathrm{B}}^{\mathrm{post}}$ is given by the *choice-deferring axioms* in Table 2, where $\mathcal{D}$ may have an empty support (abuse of notation), J is a finite nonempty index set, and we emphasize in boldface the occurrences of noteworthy subterms, actions, and operators.

Axiom $\mathcal{A}_{\mathrm{T},1}^{\mathrm{post}}$ expresses the deferral of a nondeterministic choice. Its simplest instance $a \,.\, (d \triangleright P') + a \,.\, (d \triangleright P'') \;=\; a \,.\, (d \triangleright (P' + P''))$ is reminiscent of the axiom typical of trace equivalence over nondeterministic process calculi [18, 39] and is in agreement with axioms in the coalgebraic setting of [17]. The axiom would not be valid if several distinct terms were considered in either $\oplus$-choice, as for instance $a \,.\, (d_1 \triangleright P_1' \oplus d_2 \triangleright P_2') + a \,.\, (d_1 \triangleright P_1'' \oplus d_2 \triangleright P_2'') \not\sim_{\mathrm{T}}^{\mathrm{post}} a \,.\, (d_1 \triangleright (P_1' + P_1'') \oplus d_2 \triangleright (P_2' + P_2''))$ because on the righthand side a resolution of P_1' and a resolution of P_2'' could be jointly taken into account whereas this is not possible on the lefthand side.

Table 2. Axioms characterizing $\sim_{\mathrm{T}}^{\mathrm{post}}$

$(\mathcal{A}_{\mathrm{T},1}^{\mathrm{post}})$ $a \,.\, (\mathcal{D} \oplus d \triangleright \boldsymbol{P'}) \boldsymbol{+} a \,.\, (\mathcal{D} \oplus d \triangleright \boldsymbol{P''}) \;=\; a \,.\, (\mathcal{D} \oplus d \triangleright (\boldsymbol{P'} \boldsymbol{+} \boldsymbol{P''}))$
if $init(P' + P'') \neq init(P)$ for all $P \in supp(\mathcal{D})$, unless $init(P') = init(P'')$
$(\mathcal{A}_{\mathrm{T},2}^{\mathrm{post}})$ $a \,.\, (\mathcal{D} \oplus d_1 \triangleright (\sum_{j \in J} \boldsymbol{b_j} \,.\, \mathcal{D}_{1,j}) \boldsymbol{\oplus} d_2 \triangleright (\sum_{j \in J} \boldsymbol{b_j} \,.\, \mathcal{D}_{2,j}))$
$= a \,.\, (\mathcal{D} \oplus (d_1 \oplus d_2) \triangleright (\sum_{j \in J} \boldsymbol{b_j} \,.\, (\mathcal{D}_{1,j}' \boldsymbol{\oplus} \mathcal{D}_{2,j}')))$
if for $i = 1, 2$ there exists $d_i' \in D$ such that $(d_1 \oplus d_2) \otimes d_i' = d_i$,
where $\mathcal{D}_{i,j}' = d_i' \otimes \mathcal{D}_{i,j}$

The condition to which $\mathcal{A}_{\mathrm{T},1}^{\mathrm{post}}$ is subject is necessary because, whenever $P' + P''$ has the same initial actions as a term P in the support of $\mathcal{D}$, then all resolutions of the righthand side term of the axiom have to satisfy the first coherency constraint of Definition 8 with respect to $P' + P''$ and P, whereas this is not the case for the resolutions of the lefthand side term of the axiom, thus hampering resolution matching. This can be seen, for $\mathcal{D}$ given by $d' \triangleright (b \,.\, \underline{0} + c \,.\, \underline{0})$, by considering the two process terms $a \,.\, (\mathcal{D} \oplus d \triangleright (b \,.\, \underline{0})) + a \,.\, (\mathcal{D} \oplus d \triangleright (c \,.\, \underline{0}))$ and $a \,.\, (\mathcal{D} \oplus d \triangleright (b \,.\, \underline{0} + c \,.\, \underline{0}))$, because after performing a every resolution of the latter can execute either b or c with degree $d' \oplus d$ due to coherency, while the former has resolutions in which both b and c are executable after a, which therefore cannot be matched. The condition is not needed only if P' and P'' share the same initial actions.

Axiom $\mathcal{A}_{\mathrm{T},2}^{\mathrm{post}}$ expresses instead the deferral of a distribution choice. The degrees d_1 and d_2 in it may be different and are summed up anyhow, instead of being equal and preserved like in $\mathcal{A}_{\mathrm{T},1}^{\mathrm{post}}$. This is analogous to what happens with the two idempotency-related axioms, as $\mathcal{A}_{\mathrm{B},1}^{\mathrm{post}}$ preserves degrees while $\mathcal{A}_{\mathrm{B},2}^{\mathrm{post}}$ sums them up. The $\mathcal{A}_{\mathrm{T},2}^{\mathrm{post}}$ instance $a\,.\,(d_1 \triangleright (b\,.\,(1_D \triangleright P_1)) \mathbin{\oplus} d_2 \triangleright (b\,.\,(1_D \triangleright P_2))) = a\,.\,(1_D \triangleright b\,.\,(d_1 \triangleright P_1 \mathbin{\oplus} d_2 \triangleright P_2))$, for $d_1 \oplus d_2 = 1_D$, is reminiscent of identifications typical of trace equivalence over fully probabilistic processes [29].

We observe that there is no connection with the axiomatization of trace semantics for nondeterministic and probabilistic processes in [37], because the equivalence considered there is the simulation equivalence that turns out to be the coarsest (with respect to parallel composition) congruence [35] contained in the trace equivalence of [41]. There is some relationship with the axiomatization of trace semantics developed for fully probabilistic processes in the coalgebraic framework of [44], even though only complete traces are considered there. Since we are not aware of any other axiomatization related to probabilistic trace semantics, ours seems to be the first one that can be applied to the probabilistic trace equivalences of [29,41].

The embedding in the action prefix context $a\,.\,(\mathcal{D} \mathbin{\oplus} \_)$ of both distribution terms on the two sides of $\mathcal{A}_{\mathrm{T},2}^{\mathrm{post}}$ is due to the fact that the two distribution terms themselves are not necessarily identified by $\sim_{\mathrm{T}}^{\mathrm{post}}$. For instance, the probabilistic terms P_1', P_1'', and P_2 respectively given by $b\,.\,(0.5 \triangleright (c_1\,.\,\underline{0} + c\,.\,\underline{0}) \mathbin{\oplus} 0.5 \triangleright (c_2\,.\,\underline{0}))$, $b\,.\,(0.5 \triangleright (c_1\,.\,\underline{0}) \mathbin{\oplus} 0.5 \triangleright (c\,.\,\underline{0} + c_2\,.\,\underline{0}))$, and $b\,.\,(0.25 \triangleright (c_1\,.\,\underline{0} + c\,.\,\underline{0}) \mathbin{\oplus} 0.25 \triangleright (c_2\,.\,\underline{0}) \mathbin{\oplus} 0.25 \triangleright (c_1\,.\,\underline{0}) \mathbin{\oplus} 0.25 \triangleright (c\,.\,\underline{0} + c_2\,.\,\underline{0}))$ are pairwise $\sim_{\mathrm{T}}^{\mathrm{post}}$-inequivalent, hence so are the distribution terms $\mathcal{D}_1$ and $\mathcal{D}_2$ respectively given by $0.5 \triangleright P_1' \mathbin{\oplus} 0.5 \triangleright P_1''$ and $1 \triangleright P_2$, but $a\,.\,\mathcal{D}_1 \sim_{\mathrm{T}}^{\mathrm{post}} a\,.\,\mathcal{D}_2$ as correctly captured by $\mathcal{A}_{\mathrm{T},2}^{\mathrm{post}}$.

We now show that $\mathcal{A}_{\mathrm{T}}^{\mathrm{post}}$, the deduction system obtained from $\mathcal{A}_{\mathrm{B}}^{\mathrm{post}}$ by adding the two choice-deferring axioms $\mathcal{A}_{\mathrm{T},1}^{\mathrm{post}}$ and $\mathcal{A}_{\mathrm{T},2}^{\mathrm{post}}$, is sound with respect to $\sim_{\mathrm{T}}^{\mathrm{post}}$.

Theorem 6. *Let $P_1, P_2 \in \mathbb{P}$. If $\mathcal{A}_{\mathrm{T}}^{\mathrm{post}} \vdash P_1 = P_2$, then $P_1 \sim_{\mathrm{T}}^{\mathrm{post}} P_2$.* ∎

As far as completeness is concerned, we extend to UPROC the technique used in [5,48] for nondeterministic processes. It reduces the problem of establishing the completeness of an axiomatization on arbitrary terms with respect to some behavioral equivalence $\sim$ (which in our case is $\sim_{\mathrm{T}}^{\mathrm{post}}$) to the problem of establishing the completeness of the same axiomatization on terms in a $\sim$-specific normal form with respect to bisimilarity (which in our case is $\sim_{\mathrm{B}}^{\mathrm{post}}$).

We use each of the choice-deferring axioms $\mathcal{A}_{\mathrm{T},1}^{\mathrm{post}}$ and $\mathcal{A}_{\mathrm{T},2}^{\mathrm{post}}$ as a graph rewriting rule (applied to the ULTRAS model underlying the considered UPROC term) that transforms its lefthand side into its righthand side. Given $P \in \mathbb{P}$, we then say that it is in $\sim_{\mathrm{T}}^{\mathrm{post}}$-*snf* iff it is equal to $\underline{0}$ or $\sum_{i \in I} a_i\,.\,(\bigoplus_{j \in J_i} d_{i,j} \triangleright P_{i,j})$ where I and J_i are finite nonempty index sets, $\mathcal{A}_{\mathrm{T},1}^{\mathrm{post}}$ is not applicable to any pair of $+$-summands starting with the same action, $\mathcal{A}_{\mathrm{T},2}^{\mathrm{post}}$ is not applicable to any pair of $\mathbin{\oplus}$-summands sharing the same initial actions, and every $P_{i,j}$ is in $\sim_{\mathrm{T}}^{\mathrm{post}}$-snf.

Lemma 2. *Let $P \in \mathbb{P}$. Then there exists $Q \in \mathbb{P}$ in $\sim_{\mathrm{T}}^{\mathrm{post}}$-snf such that $\mathcal{A}_{\mathrm{T}}^{\mathrm{post}} \vdash P = Q$.* ■

The completeness of $\mathcal{A}_{\mathrm{T}}^{\mathrm{post}}$ holds only for reachability-consistent semirings whose support D always admits the existence of values d_i' that make $\mathcal{A}_{\mathrm{T},2}^{\mathrm{post}}$ applicable in the presence of any distribution term complying with the one on the lefthand side of the axiom. This is the case with $\mathbb{B}$ and $\mathbb{R}_{\geq 0}$, but not with $\mathbb{N}$, because for instance $a\,.\,(5 \triangleright (b\,.\,(2 \triangleright P_1)) \oplus 2 \triangleright (b\,.\,(3 \triangleright P_2)) \oplus 6 \triangleright (b\,.\,(5 \triangleright P_3)))$ would be equated to $a\,.\,(13 \triangleright (b\,.\,(\frac{10}{13} \triangleright P_1 \oplus \frac{6}{13} \triangleright P_2 \oplus \frac{30}{13} \triangleright P_3)))$ where $\frac{10}{13}, \frac{6}{13}, \frac{30}{13} \notin \mathbb{N}$. To achieve completeness over $\mathbb{N}$, we should add to $\mathcal{A}_{\mathrm{T}}^{\mathrm{post}}$ some further axiom equating for instance $a\,.\,(5 \triangleright (b\,.\,(2 \triangleright P_1)) \oplus 2 \triangleright (b\,.\,(3 \triangleright P_2)) \oplus 6 \triangleright (b\,.\,(5 \triangleright P_3)))$ to $a\,.\,(1 \triangleright (b\,.\,(2 \triangleright P_1)) \oplus 8 \triangleright (b\,.\,(3 \triangleright P_2)) \oplus 4 \triangleright (b\,.\,(5 \triangleright P_3)))$ for suitable P_1, P_2, P_3 such as $\underline{0}$, because in both terms the degree of executability of trace a is 13 and the one of trace $a\,b$ is 46. In the following, for the sake of brevity we denote with $D_{\mathrm{T},2}^{\mathrm{post}}$ the predicate asserting that a reachability-consistent semiring is considered whose support D always enables the applicability of $\mathcal{A}_{\mathrm{T},2}^{\mathrm{post}}$.

Lemma 3. *Let $P_1, P_2 \in \mathbb{P}$ in $\sim_{\mathrm{T}}^{\mathrm{post}}$-snf. Then $P_1 \sim_{\mathrm{T}}^{\mathrm{post}} P_2$ iff $P_1 \sim_{\mathrm{B}}^{\mathrm{post}} P_2$ under condition $D_{\mathrm{T},2}^{\mathrm{post}}$.* ■

Theorem 7. *Let $P_1, P_2 \in \mathbb{P}$. If $P_1 \sim_{\mathrm{T}}^{\mathrm{post}} P_2$, then $\mathcal{A}_{\mathrm{T}}^{\mathrm{post}} \vdash P_1 = P_2$ under condition $D_{\mathrm{T},2}^{\mathrm{post}}$.* ■

Corollary 3. *Let $P_1, P_2 \in \mathbb{P}$. Then $P_1 \sim_{\mathrm{T}}^{\mathrm{post}} P_2$ iff $\mathcal{A}_{\mathrm{T}}^{\mathrm{post}} \vdash P_1 = P_2$ under condition $D_{\mathrm{T},2}^{\mathrm{post}}$.* ■

5 Conclusions

We have incrementally developed general axiomatizations of bisimulation and trace semantics by working with the corresponding post-/pre-metaequivalences on UPROC terms. We have also revised according to [8,9] the notion of resolution of nondeterminism – originally introduced in [7] for the ULTRAS metamodel – to ensure the inclusion of $\sim_{\mathrm{B}}^{\mathrm{post}}$ in $\sim_{\mathrm{T}}^{\mathrm{post}}$ as well as the full compositionality of action prefix for both trace metaequivalences $\sim_{\mathrm{T}}^{\mathrm{post}}$ and $\sim_{\mathrm{T}}^{\mathrm{pre}}$.

We plan to expand our axiomatizations to exhibit also the general laws for static process operators, such as the expansion law for parallel composition, and recursion. It would then be interesting to search for general axiomatizations of other semantics in the branching-time – linear-time spectrum, including weak ones. However, we believe that the most challenging open problems are (i) the investigation of the completeness of the axiomatization of $\sim_{\mathrm{T}}^{\mathrm{pre}}$ and (ii) the extension of the axiomatization of $\sim_{\mathrm{T}}^{\mathrm{post}}$ for achieving completeness over reachability-consistent semirings like $\mathbb{N}$ for which axiom $\mathcal{A}_{\mathrm{T},2}^{\mathrm{post}}$ is not always applicable.

We finally observe that our general approach has allowed us to discover the first axiomatization of a behavioral equivalence in several situations. This is important because, when moving from nondeterministic processes to processes including also probabilistic and timing aspects, there are several different ways of defining the same semantics – of which the post-/pre-approaches are two notable options – and the spectrum consequently becomes much more variegated, as shown for instance in [12]. In this respect, the ULTRAS metamodel has thus proven to be a useful tool.

References

1. Aceto, L., Bloom, B., Vaandrager, F.: Turning SOS rules into equations. Inf. Comput. **111**, 1–52 (1994)
2. Aceto, L., Fokkink, W.J., Verhoef, C.: Structural operational semantics. In: Handbook of Process Algebra, pp. 197–292. Elsevier (2001)
3. Alur, R., Dill, D.L.: A theory of timed automata. Theoret. Comput. Sci. **126**, 183–235 (1994)
4. Bandini, E., Segala, R.: Axiomatizations for probabilistic bisimulation. In: Orejas, F., Spirakis, P.G., van Leeuwen, J. (eds.) ICALP 2001. LNCS, vol. 2076, pp. 370–381. Springer, Heidelberg (2001). https://doi.org/10.1007/3-540-48224-5_31
5. Bergstra, J.A., Klop, J.W., Olderog, E.R.: Readies and failures in the algebra of communicating processes. SIAM J. Comput. **17**, 1134–1177 (1988)
6. Bergstra, J.A., Ponse, A., Smolka, S.A. (eds.): Handbook of Process Algebra. Elsevier, Amsterdam (2001)
7. Bernardo, M.: ULTraS at work: compositionality metaresults for bisimulation and trace semantics. J. Log. Algebraic Methods Program. **94**, 150–182 (2018)
8. Bernardo, M.: Coherent resolutions of nondeterminism. In: Gribaudo, M., Iacono, M., Phung-Duc, T., Razumchik, R. (eds.) EPEW 2019. LNCS, vol. 12039, pp. 16–32. Springer, Cham (2020). https://doi.org/10.1007/978-3-030-44411-2_2
9. Bernardo, M.: Alternative characterizations of probabilistic trace equivalences on coherent resolutions of nondeterminism. In: Gribaudo, M., Jansen, D.N., Remke, A. (eds.) QEST 2020. LNCS, vol. 12289, pp. 35–53. Springer, Cham (2020). https://doi.org/10.1007/978-3-030-59854-9_5
10. Bernardo, M., De Nicola, R., Loreti, M.: A uniform framework for modeling nondeterministic, probabilistic, stochastic, or mixed processes and their behavioral equivalences. Inf. Comput. **225**, 29–82 (2013)
11. Bernardo, M., De Nicola, R., Loreti, M.: Revisiting trace and testing equivalences for nondeterministic and probabilistic processes. Log. Methods Comput. Sci. **10**(1:16), 1–42 (2014)
12. Bernardo, M., De Nicola, R., Loreti, M.: Relating strong behavioral equivalences for processes with nondeterminism and probabilities. Theoret. Comput. Sci. **546**, 63–92 (2014)
13. Bernardo, M., De Nicola, R., Loreti, M.: Revisiting bisimilarity and its modal logic for nondeterministic and probabilistic processes. Acta Informatica **52**(1), 61–106 (2014). https://doi.org/10.1007/s00236-014-0210-1
14. Bernardo, M., Sangiorgi, D., Vignudelli, V.: On the discriminating power of testing equivalences for reactive probabilistic systems: results and open problems. In: Norman, G., Sanders, W. (eds.) QEST 2014. LNCS, vol. 8657, pp. 281–296. Springer, Cham (2014). https://doi.org/10.1007/978-3-319-10696-0_23
15. Bernardo, M., Tesei, L.: Encoding timed models as uniform labeled transition systems. In: Balsamo, M.S., Knottenbelt, W.J., Marin, A. (eds.) EPEW 2013. LNCS, vol. 8168, pp. 104–118. Springer, Heidelberg (2013). https://doi.org/10.1007/978-3-642-40725-3_9

16. Bonchi, F., Sokolova, A., Vignudelli, V.: The theory of traces for systems with nondeterminism and probability. In: Proceedings of the 34th ACM/IEEE Symposium on Logic in Computer Science (LICS 2019), vol. 19, no. 62, pp. 1–14. IEEE-CS Press (2019)
17. Bonsangue, M.M., Milius, S., Silva, A.: Sound and complete axiomatizations of coalgebraic language equivalence. ACM Trans. Comput. Logic **14**(1:7), 1–52 (2013)
18. Brookes, S.D., Hoare, C.A.R., Roscoe, A.W.: A theory of communicating sequential processes. J. ACM **31**, 560–599 (1984)
19. D'Argenio, P.R., Gebler, D., Lee, M.D.: Axiomatizing bisimulation equivalences and metrics from probabilistic SOS rules. In: Muscholl, A. (ed.) FoSSaCS 2014. LNCS, vol. 8412, pp. 289–303. Springer, Heidelberg (2014). https://doi.org/10.1007/978-3-642-54830-7_19
20. De Nicola, R., Latella, D., Loreti, M., Massink, M.: A uniform definition of stochastic process calculi. ACM Comput. Surv. **46**(1:5), 1–35 (2013)
21. Deng, Y., van Glabbeek, R., Morgan, C., Zhang, C.: Scalar outcomes suffice for finitary probabilistic testing. In: De Nicola, R. (ed.) ESOP 2007. LNCS, vol. 4421, pp. 363–378. Springer, Heidelberg (2007). https://doi.org/10.1007/978-3-540-71316-6_25
22. Derman, C.: Finite State Markovian Decision Processes. Academic Press, Cambridge (1970)
23. Droste, M., Kuich, W., Vogler, H. (eds.): Handbook of Weighted Automata. EATCS. Springer, Heidelberg (2009). https://doi.org/10.1007/978-3-642-01492-5
24. Eisentraut, C., Hermanns, H., Zhang, L.: On probabilistic automata in continuous time. In: Proceedings of the 25th IEEE Symposium on Logic in Computer Science (LICS 2010), pp. 342–351. IEEE-CS Press (2010)
25. Hansson, H., Jonsson, B.: A logic for reasoning about time and reliability. Formal Aspects Comput. **6**, 512–535 (1994)
26. Hermanns, H.: Interactive Markov Chains. LNCS, vol. 2428. Springer, Heidelberg (2002). https://doi.org/10.1007/3-540-45804-2
27. Hillston, J.: A Compositional Approach to Performance Modelling. Cambridge University Press, Cambridge (1996)
28. Jonsson, B., Ho-Stuart, C., Yi, W.: Testing and refinement for nondeterministic and probabilistic processes. In: Langmaack, H., de Roever, W.-P., Vytopil, J. (eds.) FTRTFT 1994. LNCS, vol. 863, pp. 418–430. Springer, Heidelberg (1994). https://doi.org/10.1007/3-540-58468-4_176
29. Jou, C.-C., Smolka, S.A.: Equivalences, congruences, and complete axiomatizations for probabilistic processes. In: Baeten, J.C.M., Klop, J.W. (eds.) CONCUR 1990. LNCS, vol. 458, pp. 367–383. Springer, Heidelberg (1990). https://doi.org/10.1007/BFb0039071
30. Keller, R.M.: Formal verification of parallel programs. Commun. ACM **19**, 371–384 (1976)
31. Klin, B.: Structural operational semantics for weighted transition systems. In: Palsberg, J. (ed.) Semantics and Algebraic Specification. LNCS, vol. 5700, pp. 121–139. Springer, Heidelberg (2009). https://doi.org/10.1007/978-3-642-04164-8_7
32. Kwiatkowska, M., Norman, G., Segala, R., Sproston, J.: Automatic verification of real-time systems with discrete probability distributions. Theoret. Comput. Sci. **282**, 101–150 (2002)
33. Larsen, K.G., Skou, A.: Bisimulation through probabilistic testing. Inf. Comput. **94**, 1–28 (1991)

34. Latella, D., Massink, M., de Vink, E.: Bisimulation of labelled state-to-function transition systems coalgebraically. Log. Methods Comput. Sci. **11**(4:16), 1–40 (2015)
35. Lynch, N., Segala, R., Vaandrager, F.: Compositionality for probabilistic automata. In: Amadio, R., Lugiez, D. (eds.) CONCUR 2003. LNCS, vol. 2761, pp. 208–221. Springer, Heidelberg (2003). https://doi.org/10.1007/978-3-540-45187-7_14
36. Milner, R.: A complete inference system for a class of regular behaviours. J. Comput. Syst. Sci. **28**, 439–466 (1984)
37. Parma, A., Segala, R.: Axiomatization of trace semantics for stochastic nondeterministic processes. In: Proceedings of the 1st International Conference on the Quantitative Evaluation of Systems (QEST 2004), pp. 294–303. IEEE-CS Press (2004)
38. Puterman, M.L.: Markov Decision Processes: Discrete Stochastic Dynamic Programming. Wiley, Hoboken (1994)
39. Rabinovich, A.: A complete axiomatisation for trace congruence of finite state behaviors. In: Brookes, S., Main, M., Melton, A., Mislove, M., Schmidt, D. (eds.) MFPS 1993. LNCS, vol. 802, pp. 530–543. Springer, Heidelberg (1994). https://doi.org/10.1007/3-540-58027-1_25
40. Segala, R.: Modeling and verification of randomized distributed real-time systems. Ph.D. thesis (1995)
41. Segala, R.: A compositional trace-based semantics for probabilistic automata. In: Lee, I., Smolka, S.A. (eds.) CONCUR 1995. LNCS, vol. 962, pp. 234–248. Springer, Heidelberg (1995). https://doi.org/10.1007/3-540-60218-6_17
42. Segala, R., Lynch, N.: Probabilistic simulations for probabilistic processes. In: Jonsson, B., Parrow, J. (eds.) CONCUR 1994. LNCS, vol. 836, pp. 481–496. Springer, Heidelberg (1994). https://doi.org/10.1007/978-3-540-48654-1_35
43. Silva, A., Bonchi, F., Bonsangue, M.M., Rutten, J.J.M.M.: Quantitative Kleene coalgebras. Inf. Comput. **209**, 822–849 (2011)
44. Silva, A., Sokolova, A.: Sound and complete axiomatization of trace semantics for probabilistic systems. In: Proceedings of the 27th International Conference on the Mathematical Foundations of Programming Semantics (MFPS 2011). ENTCS, vol. 276, pp. 291–311. Elsevier (2011)
45. Song, L., Zhang, L., Godskesen, J.C., Nielson, F.: Bisimulations meet PCTL equivalences for probabilistic automata. Log. Methods Comput. Sci. **9**(2:7), 1–34 (2013)
46. Stewart, W.J.: Introduction to the Numerical Solution of Markov Chains. Princeton University Press, Princeton (1994)
47. Tracol, M., Desharnais, J., Zhioua, A.: Computing distances between probabilistic automata. In: Proceedings of the 9th International Workshop on Quantitative Aspects of Programming Languages (QAPL 2011). EPTCS, vol. 57, pp. 148–162 (2011)
48. van Glabbeek, R.J.: The linear time - branching time spectrum I. In: Handbook of Process Algebra, pp. 3–99. Elsevier (2001)

Monographs, a Category of Graph Structures

Thierry Boy de la Tour(✉)

CNRS and University Grenoble Alpes, LIG Laboratory, Grenoble, France
thierry.boy-de-la-tour@imag.fr

Abstract. Does a graph necessarily have nodes? May an edge be adjacent to itself and be a self-loop? These questions arise in the study of *graph structures*, i.e., monadic many-sorted signatures and the corresponding algebras. A simple notion of *monograph* is proposed that generalizes the standard notion of directed graph and can be drawn consistently with them. It is shown that monadic many-sorted signatures can be represented by monographs, and that the corresponding algebras are isomorphic to the monographs typed by the corresponding signature monograph. Monographs therefore provide a simple unifying framework for working with monadic algebras. Their simplicity is illustrated by deducing some of their categorial properties from those of sets.

Keywords: Universal algebra · Monadic signatures · Category theory

1 Introduction

Many different notions of graphs are used in mathematics and computer science: simple graphs, directed graphs, multigraphs, hypergraphs, etc. One favourite notion in the context of logic and rewriting is that also known as *quivers*, i.e., structures of the form (N, E, s, t) where N, E are sets and s, t are functions from E (edges) to N (nodes), identifying the source and target tips of every edge (or arrow). One reason for this is that the category of quivers is isomorphic to the category of Σ_g-algebras, where Σ_g is the signature with two sorts `nodes` and `edges` and two operator names `src` and `tgt` of type `edges` → `nodes`. In conformity with this tradition, by *graph* we mean quiver throughout this paper.

In order to conveniently represent elaborate data structures it is often necessary to enrich the structure of graphs with other objects: nodes or edges may be labelled with elements from a fixed set, or with the elements of some algebra, or graphs may be typed by another graph (i.e., a graph comes with a morphism from itself to this other graph, considered as its type). An interesting example can be found in [4] with the notion of E-graphs, since some of these new objects are also considered as edges or nodes. More precisely, an E-graph is an algebra whose signature Σ_e can be represented by the following graph:

M. Roggenbach (Ed.): WADT 2020, LNCS 12669, pp. 54–74, 2021.
https://doi.org/10.1007/978-3-030-73785-6_4

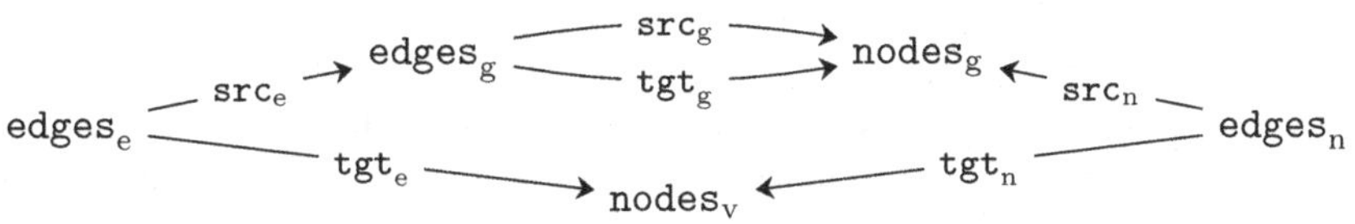

The names given to the sorts and operators help to understand the structure of the Σ_e-algebras: the $\mathtt{edges}_g$ relate the $\mathtt{nodes}_g$ among themselves, the $\mathtt{edges}_n$ relate the $\mathtt{nodes}_g$ to the $\mathtt{nodes}_v$, and the $\mathtt{edges}_e$ relate the $\mathtt{edges}_g$ to the $\mathtt{nodes}_v$. These extra edges allow values (elements of $\mathtt{nodes}_v$) to be attached to edges and nodes of the inner graph. But then we see that in E-graphs some edges can be adjacent to other edges. This is non standard, but we may still accept such structures as some form of graph, if only because we understand how they can be drawn.

Hence the way of generalizing the notion of graphs seems to involve a generalization of the signature of graphs considered as algebras. This path has been followed by Michael Löwe in [7], where a *graph structure* is defined as a monadic many-sorted signature. Indeed in the examples above, and in many examples provided in [7], all operators have arity 1 and can therefore be considered as edges from their domain to their range sort. Is this the reason why they are called graph structures? But the example above shows that, if Σ_e-algebras are interpreted as graphs of some form, these are very different from the graph Σ_e. Besides, it is not convenient that our understanding of such structures should be based on syntax, i.e., on the particular names given to objects in the signature.

Furthermore, it is difficult to see how the algebras of some very simple monadic signatures can be interpreted as graphs of any form. Take for instance Σ_g and reverse the target function to $\mathtt{tgt} : \mathtt{nodes} \to \mathtt{edges}$. Then there is a symmetry between the sorts `nodes` and `edges`, which means that in an algebra of this signature nodes and edges would be objects of the same nature. Is this still a graph? Can we draw it? Worse still, if the two sorts are collapsed into one, does it mean that a node/edge can be adjacent to itself?

We may address these problems by restricting graph structures to some class of monadic signatures whose algebras are guaranteed to behave in an orthodox way, say by exhibiting clearly separated edges and nodes. But this could be prone to arbitrariness, and it would still present another drawback: that the notion of graph structure does not easily give rise to a category. Indeed, it is difficult to define morphisms between algebras of different signatures, if only because they can have any number of carrier sets.

The approach adopted here is rather to reject any *structural* distinction between nodes and edges, to gather them all in a *single* carrier set and to rely on a *unique* function to distinguish them. For this reason, the resulting structures are called *monographs*. The definitions of monographs and their morphisms, given in Sect. 3, are thus quite simple although for reasons that will only be made clear in Sect. 5 we use sequences of ordinal length, defined in Sect. 2.

Prior to examining their mathematical properties, we show in Sect. 4 that these structures deserve to be considered as "graphs" since they can be represented by drawings, provided of course that they are finite (in a strong sense). In particular, such drawings correspond to the standard way of drawing a graph, for those monographs that can be identified with standard graphs.

The relationship between monographs and graph structures (monadic signatures) is explored in Sect. 5, using relevant notions from category theory defined in Sect. 2. This gives rise to an isomorphism-dense embedding of monographs into many-sorted monadic signatures, that will expose a fundamental difference between them. This result is used in Sect. 6 to exhibit isomorphisms between the categories of (partitioned) algebras of all graph structures and all slice categories of monographs, i.e., the categories of typed monographs.

As a result of their simplicity the category of monographs and some of its subcategories can easily be shown to share a number of properties with **Graphs**, as illustrated in Sect. 7. Concluding remarks are given in Sect. 8. The missing proofs can be found in [3].

2 Notations and Definitions

For any sets A, B, any relation $r \subseteq A \times B$ and any subset $X \subseteq A$, we write $r[X]$ for the set $\{y \in B \mid x \in X \wedge (x, y) \in r\}$. For any $x \in A$, by abuse of notation we write $r[x]$ for $r[\{x\}]$. We write r^{-1} for the relation $\{(y, x) \mid (x, y) \in r\} \subseteq B \times A$. If r is functional we write $r(x)$ for the unique element of $r[x]$, and if $q \subseteq B' \times C$ is also functional for sets B' and C such that $r[A] \subseteq B'$, we write $q \circ r$ for the functional relation $\{(x, q(r(x))) \in A \times C \mid x \in A\}$.

A *function* $f : A \to B$ is a triple (A, r, B) where A and B are sets, respectively called the *domain* and *codomain* of f, and $r \subseteq A \times B$ is a functional relation. Hence A must be the set $\{x \mid (x, y) \in r\}$ and B may be any superset of the image $r[A]$, also denoted $f[A]$ (and generally $f[X]$ and $f(x)$ stand for $r[X]$ and $r(x)$ respectively). If $A = \varnothing$ and the codomain B can be determined from the context then we write ε for $f = (\varnothing, \varnothing, B)$. If $g = (B, q, C)$ is a function, then $g \circ f \stackrel{\text{def}}{=} (A, q \circ r, C)$. We may also compose a functional relation with a function, that then denotes its underlying functional relation, so that $q \circ f = g \circ r = q \circ r$.

More generally, any object and its obvious underlying object will be written similarly, i.e., the forgetful functor will be omitted, whenever the ambiguity can easily be lifted from the context. Category theoretic concepts and notations will be consistent with [1], unless stated otherwise. In particular, id_A denotes the identity morphism of the object A in any category, except in **Sets** where it is denoted Id_A (the identity function of A) as a way of reminding the reader that A is a set. In **Sets** the standard product $\times$, projections π_1 and π_2 and coproduct $+$ are used. For functional relations f, g with the same domain A, let $\langle f, g\rangle(x) \stackrel{\text{def}}{=} (f(x), g(x))$ for all $x \in A$; if $f : A \to B$ and $g : A \to C$ are functions then $\langle f, g\rangle : A \to B \times C$ is the unique function such that $\pi_1 \circ \langle f, g\rangle = f$ and $\pi_2 \circ \langle f, g\rangle = g$.

Isomorphism between objects in a category, or between categories, is denoted by the symbol $\simeq$. For any two categories $\boldsymbol{A}$ and $\boldsymbol{B}$, a functor $F : \boldsymbol{A} \to \boldsymbol{B}$ is *faithful* (resp. *full*) if F is injective (resp. surjective) from the set of $\boldsymbol{A}$-morphisms from X to Y to the set of $\boldsymbol{B}$-morphisms from FX to FY, for all $\boldsymbol{A}$-objects X and Y. If F is faithful and injective on objects, then it is an *embedding*. F is *isomorphism-dense* if for every $\boldsymbol{B}$-object Y there exists an $\boldsymbol{A}$-object X such that $FX \simeq Y$. Categories $\boldsymbol{A}$ and $\boldsymbol{B}$ are *equivalent*, written $\boldsymbol{A} \approxeq \boldsymbol{B}$, if there is a full, faithful and isomorphism-dense functor from one to the other.

For any object T of $\boldsymbol{A}$, the *slice category*[1] $\boldsymbol{A}/T$ has as objects the morphisms of codomain T of $\boldsymbol{A}$, as morphisms from object $f : A \to T$ to object $g : B \to T$ the morphisms $k : A \to B$ of $\boldsymbol{A}$ such that $g \circ k = f$, and the composition of morphisms in $\boldsymbol{A}/T$ is defined as the composition of the underlying morphisms in $\boldsymbol{A}$. T is a *terminal object* of $\boldsymbol{A}$ if for every object A of $\boldsymbol{A}$ there is a unique $f : A \to T$. It is easy to see that id_T is a terminal object of $\boldsymbol{A}/T$, and that if T is a terminal object of $\boldsymbol{A}$ then $\boldsymbol{A} \simeq \boldsymbol{A}/T$.

Since edges will have arbitrary lengths, including infinite ones, we use the notion of ordinal and refer to [11] for their properties. An *ordinal* is a set α such that every element of α is a subset of α, and such that the restriction of the membership relation $\in$ to α is a strict well-ordering of α (every non empty subset of α has a minimal element). Every member of an ordinal is an ordinal, and we write $\lambda < \alpha$ for $\lambda \in \alpha$. For any two ordinals α, β we have either $\alpha < \beta$, $\alpha = \beta$ or $\alpha > \beta$. Every ordinal α has a successor $\alpha \cup \{\alpha\}$, denoted $\alpha + 1$. Natural numbers n are identified with finite ordinals, so that $n = \{0, 1, \ldots, n-1\}$ and $\omega = \{0, 1, \ldots\}$ is the smallest infinite ordinal.

Definition 2.1 (E-sequences s of length λ, elements s_ι, $x \mid s$). *For any set E and ordinal λ, an* E-sequence s of length λ *is an element of E^λ, i.e., a function $s : \lambda \to E$. For any $s \in E^\lambda$ and $\iota < \lambda$, the image $s(\iota)$ is written s_ι. If λ is finite and non zero then s can be described as $s = s_0 \cdots s_{\lambda-1}$. For any $x \in E$ we write $x \mid s$ and say that x* occurs in s *if there exists $\iota < \lambda$ such that $s_\iota = x$.*

Take for instance $E = \{x, y\}$, then $s = xyx$ describes the E-sequence of length $3 = \{0, 1, 2\}$ such that $s_0 = s_2 = x$ and $s_1 = y$. We have $x \mid xyx$ and $y \mid xyx$.

Note that there is no set of *all* E-sequences, hence the following notions.

Definition 2.2 (sets $E^{<\alpha}$, functions $f^{<\alpha}$). *For any set E and ordinal α, let $E^{<\alpha} \stackrel{\text{def}}{=} \bigcup_{\lambda<\alpha} E^\lambda$. For any set F and function $f : E \to F$, let $f^{<\alpha} : E^{<\alpha} \to F^{<\alpha}$ be the function defined by $f^{<\alpha}(s) \stackrel{\text{def}}{=} f \circ s$ for all $s \in E^{<\alpha}$.*

Thus $s = xyx$ is an element of $E^{<4}$, $E^{<5}$... but not of $E^{<3} = E^0 \cup E^1 \cup E^2$. If $f : E \to E$ is the function that swaps x and y ($f = (x\ y)$ in cycle notation), then $f^{<4}(s)_0 = (f \circ s)_0 = f(s_0) = y$, etc., hence $f^{<4}(s) = yxy$.

We have $E^{<0} = \varnothing$ and $E^{<1} = E^0 = \{\varepsilon\}$, i.e., the function ε (with codomain E) is the only E-sequence of length 0. It is obvious that for any $s \in E^{<\alpha}$ and any ordinal $\beta \geqslant \alpha$, we have $s \in E^{<\beta}$ and $f^{<\beta}(s) = f^{<\alpha}(s)$. If $f : E \to F$ and $g : F \to G$ then $(g \circ f)^{<\alpha} = g^{<\alpha} \circ f^{<\alpha}$.

If s and s' are respectively E- and F-sequences of length λ, then they are both functions with domain λ hence there is a function $\langle s, s' \rangle$ of domain λ.

[1] This is called the *comma category of $\boldsymbol{A}$ over T* in [5, Definition 4.19], and the *category of objects over T* in [1, Exercise 3K]. We adopt the terminology and notation of [4].

Thus $\langle s, s' \rangle$ is an $(E \times F)$-sequence of length λ, and then $\pi_1^{<\alpha}(\langle s, s' \rangle) = \pi_1 \circ \langle s, s' \rangle = s$ and similarly $\pi_2^{<\alpha}(\langle s, s' \rangle) = s'$ for all $\alpha > \lambda$.

If $f : E \to F$ and $g : E \to G$ then $\langle f, g \rangle : E \to F \times G$, hence for all $s \in E^{<\alpha}$ of length $\lambda < \alpha$ we have $\langle f, g \rangle^{<\alpha}(s) = \langle f, g \rangle \circ s = \langle f \circ s, g \circ s \rangle = \langle f^{<\alpha}(s), g^{<\alpha}(s) \rangle$ is an $(F \times G)$-sequence of length λ.

3 Categories of Monographs

We may now define the structure of monographs and some related notions. These definitions will be illustrated by a running example and will be followed by a number of basic facts on monographs and a comparison with graphs.

In graphs, edges are arbitrary objects to which are associated two arbitrary objects called nodes. We may thus associate to each edge a sequence of nodes of length 2. In monographs, the corresponding sequences may contain arbitrary edges and have arbitrary lengths.

Definition 3.1 (monographs, grade, edges E_a, length $\ell_a(x)$, trace $\mathrm{tr}(A)$). *For any ordinal α, an α-*monograph *A is a pair (E, a) where E is a set whose elements are called* edges *of A, and $a \subseteq E \times E^{<\alpha}$ is a functional relation, called the* map *of A. A pair $A = (E, a)$ is a* monograph *if it is an α-monograph for some ordinal α; we then say that α is an ordinal* for *A. The* grade *of A is the smallest ordinal for A. Monographs will usually be denoted by upper-case letters (A, B, ...), their map by the corresponding lower-case letter (a, b, ...) and their set of edges E_a, E_b, ...*

The length *$\ell_a(x)$ of an edge $x \in \mathrm{E}_a$ is the length of $a(x)$, i.e., the unique ordinal λ such that $a(x) \in \mathrm{E}_a^\lambda$. The* trace *of A is the set $\mathrm{tr}(A) \stackrel{\mathrm{def}}{=} \ell_a[\mathrm{E}_a]$. For any set O of ordinals, an O-*monograph[2] *A is a monograph such that $\mathrm{tr}(A) \subseteq O$.*

Take for instance the monograph $A = (\{x, y\}, a)$ where $a = \{(x, xyx), (y, yxy)\}$ (i.e., $a(x) = xyx$ and $a(y) = yxy$), then A is a 4-monograph and more precisely a $\{3\}$-monograph since $\mathrm{tr}(A) = \{3\}$, but A is not a 3-monograph, hence the grade of A is 4.

A monograph A is essentially defined by its map a, since $\mathrm{E}_a = \{x \mid (x, y) \in a\}$. But a is only a functional relation and not a function; there is no codomain to artificially separate monographs that have the same map. This means in particular that any α-monograph is a β-monograph for all $\beta \geqslant \alpha$. It is easy to see that there always exists an ordinal *for* any two monographs, and indeed for any set of monographs (e.g. the sum of their grades).

Definition 3.2 (adjacency, self-loops, nodes N_a, standard monographs). *For any monograph A and edges $x, y \in \mathrm{E}_a$, x is* adjacent *to y if $y \mid a(x)$. A* self-loop *is an edge x that is adjacent only to x, i.e., such that $a(x)$ is an $\{x\}$-sequence. A* node *is an edge of length 0, and the set of nodes of A is written N_a. A is* standard *if $a(x)$ is a N_a-sequence for all $x \in \mathrm{E}_a$.*

[2] Note that any ordinal α is a set of ordinals, and that a monograph A is an α-monograph iff $\mathrm{tr}(A) \subseteq \alpha$.

We see on the running example that $a(x) = xyx$, hence x is adjacent to y and to itself, but is not a self-loop. Similarly, $a(y) = yxy$ yields that y is adjacent to x and to itself, but is not a self-loop. A has two edges but no nodes, hence A is not standard.

A monograph A is not normally defined by its adjacency relation $y \mid a(x)$ on edges, since the sequences $a(x)$ may not be uniquely determined by this relation. The adjacency relation may not be symmetric: a node is never adjacent to any edge, while edges may be adjacent to nodes.

Definition 3.3 (morphisms of monographs). *A* morphism *f from monograph $A = (\mathrm{E}_a, a)$ to monograph $B = (\mathrm{E}_b, b)$, denoted $f : A \to B$, is a function $f : \mathrm{E}_a \to \mathrm{E}_b$ such that $f^{<\alpha} \circ a = b \circ f$, where α is any*[3] *ordinal for A.*

Building on the running example, we consider the function $f = (x\ y)$ from E_a to E_a, we see that $f^{<4} \circ a(x) = f^{<4}(xyx) = yxy = a(y) = a \circ f(x)$ and similarly that $f^{<4} \circ a(y) = f^{<4}(yxy) = xyx = a(x) = a \circ f(y)$, hence $f^{<4} \circ a = a \circ f$ and f is therefore a morphism from A to A. Since $f \circ f = \mathrm{Id}_{\mathrm{E}_a}$ is obviously the identity morphism of A then f is an isomorphism.

The length of edges are preserved by morphisms: if f is a morphism from A to B then for all $x \in \mathrm{E}_a$, $\ell_b(f(x))$ is the length of the E_b-sequence $b \circ f(x) = f^{<\alpha} \circ a(x)$, whose length is the same as the E_a-sequence $a(x)$, i.e., $\ell_a(x) = \ell_b(f(x))$. Hence $\mathrm{tr}(A) \subseteq \mathrm{tr}(B)$, and the equality holds if f is surjective. This means that if B is an O-monograph then so is A. This also means that the grade of B is at least that of A, hence that every ordinal for B is an ordinal for A.

Given morphisms f from A to B and g from B to C, we see that $g \circ f$ is a morphism from A to C by letting α be an ordinal for B, so that

$$(g \circ f)^{<\alpha} \circ a = g^{<\alpha} \circ f^{<\alpha} \circ a = g^{<\alpha} \circ b \circ f = c \circ g \circ f.$$

Definition 3.4 (categories of monographs). *Let* **MonoGr** *be the category of monographs and their morphisms. Let* **SMonoGr** *be its full subcategory of standard monographs. For any set O of ordinals, let O-***MonoGr** *(resp. O-***SMonoGr***) be the full subcategory of O-monographs (resp. standard O-monographs).*

A monograph A is finite *if E_a is finite. Let* **FMonoGr** *be the full subcategory of finite ω-monographs.*

It is customary in Algebraic Graph Transformation to call *typed graphs* the objects of **Graphs**$/G$, where G is a graph called *type graph*, see e.g. [4]. A type graph is therefore seen as the specification of a category of typed graphs. In particular, the terminal graph $\mathrm{G_t}$ specifies the whole category of graphs since **Graphs** $\simeq$ **Graphs**$/\mathrm{G_t}$. We will extend this terminology to monographs and refer to the objects of **MonoGr**$/T$ as the *monographs typed by T*. The monograph T is then considered as a *type monograph* and hence as a specification for a category of typed monographs.

[3] Imposing the grade of A for α here would be a useless constraint. Note that the equation $f^{<\alpha} \circ a = b \circ f$ holds for all ordinals α for A iff it holds for one.

It is obvious from the above that for any set O of ordinals, if T is an O-monograph then $\mathbf{MonoGr}/T = O\text{-}\mathbf{MonoGr}/T$. Similarly, if $f : A \to B$ then

$$f^{-1}[\mathrm{N}_b] = \{x \in \mathrm{E}_a \mid \ell_b(f(x)) = 0\} = \mathrm{N}_a,$$

hence if $b \circ f(x)$ is a N_b-sequence for some $x \in \mathrm{E}_a$ then for all $\iota < \ell_a(x)$,

$$f(a(x)_\iota) = (f \circ a(x))_\iota = (f^{<\alpha}(a(x)))_\iota = (f^{<\alpha} \circ a(x))_\iota = (b \circ f(x))_\iota \in \mathrm{N}_b,$$

hence $a(x)_\iota \in \mathrm{N}_a$ and $a(x)$ is therefore a N_a-sequence. Thus A is standard whenever B is standard. This proves that for any standard monograph (resp. standard O-monograph) T we have $\mathbf{MonoGr}/T = \mathbf{SMonoGr}/T$ (resp. $\mathbf{MonoGr}/T = O\text{-}\mathbf{SMonoGr}/T$).

The introduction of the present section suggests a similitude between graphs and standard $\{0,2\}$-monographs. It is actually easy to define a functor $\mathsf{M} : \mathbf{Graphs} \to \{0,2\}\text{-}\mathbf{SMonoGr}$ by mapping any graph $G = (N, E, s, t)$ to $\mathsf{M}G = (N + E, g)$ where $g(x) = \varepsilon$ for all $x \in N$ and $g(e) = s(e)t(e)$ for all $e \in E$ (and similarly graph morphisms are transformed into morphisms of monographs through a coproduct of functions). It is easy to see that M is an equivalence of categories[4]. This means that for any graph G we have $\mathbf{Graphs}/G \approxeq \mathbf{MonoGr}/\mathsf{M}G$, hence that typed graphs can be represented as typed monographs.

4 Drawing Monographs

Obviously we may endeavour to draw a monograph A only if E_a is finite and if its edges have finite lengths, i.e., if A is a finite ω-monograph. If we require that any monograph $\mathsf{M}G$ should be drawn as the graph G, then a node should be represented by a bullet • and an edge of length 2 by an arrow joining its two adjacent nodes. But generally the adjacent edges may not be nodes and there might be more than 2 of them, hence we adopt the following convention: an edge e of length at least 2 is represented as a sequence of connected arrows with an increasing number of tips

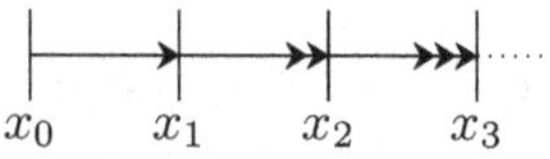

(where $a(e) = x_0 x_1 x_2 x_3 \cdots$) and such that any arrow should enter x_i at the same angle as the next arrow leaves x_i. This is important when x_i is a node since several adjacent edges may traverse the corresponding bullet, and they should not be confused. For the sake of clarity we will also represent symmetric adjacencies by a pair of crossings rather than a single one, e.g., if $a(e) = xe'y$ and $a(e') = xey$, where x and y are nodes, the drawing may be

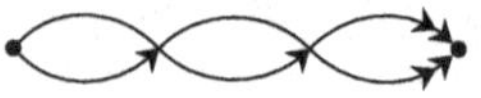 but not 

[4] This can be seen as a consequence of Corollary 6.8 below and of the isomorphism between **Graphs** and the category of Σ_{g}-algebras.

It is sometimes necessary to name the edges in a drawing. We may then adopt the convention used for drawing diagrams in a category: the bullets are replaced by the names of the corresponding nodes, and arrows are interrupted to write their name at a place free from intersection, as in

Note that no confusion is possible between the names of nodes and those of other edges, e.g., in

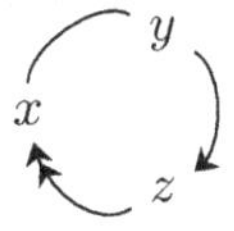

it is clear that x and z are nodes since arrow tips point to them, and that y is the name of an edge of length 3.

As is the case of graphs, monographs may not be planar and drawing them may require crossing edges that are not adjacent; in this case no arrow tip is present at the intersection and no confusion is possible with the adjacency crossings. However, it may seem preferable in such cases to erase one arrow in the proximity of the other, as in $\times$.

There remains to represent the edges of length 1. Since $a(e) = x$ is standardly written $a : e \mapsto x$, the edge e will be drawn as

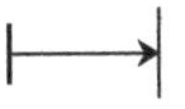

In order to avoid confusion there should be only one arrow out of the thick dash, e.g., if $a(e) = e'$ and $a(e') = ex$ where x is a node, the drawing may be

 but not 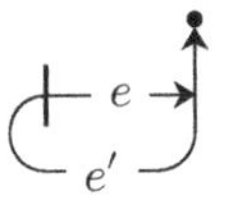

since this last drawing may be interpreted as the monograph $a(e') = x$ and $a(e) = e'e'$, that is not isomorphic to the intended monograph.

With these conventions it is only possible to read a drawing of any finite ω-monograph A as the monograph A itself if all edges are named in the drawing, or as some monograph isomorphic to A otherwise. Note that this would not be true if the map a was a function rather than a functional relation, because its codomain $\mathrm{E}_a^{<\alpha}$ is not pictured. It would of course be possible to add the ordinal α to the drawing, but then would it still qualify as a drawing?

Note that the drawing of a graph or of a standard $\{0, 2\}$-monograph can be read either as a graph G or as a monograph A, and then $\mathsf{M}G \simeq A$.

Possible drawings for the self-loops of length 1 to 4 are given below.

We may also draw typed monographs, i.e., monographs A equipped with a morphism f from A to a monograph T, considered as a type. Then every edge $e \in \mathrm{E}_a$ has a type $f(e)$ that can be written at the proximity of e. For instance, let T be the monograph

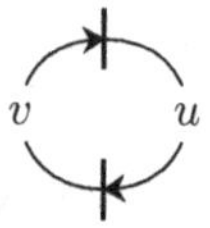

then a monograph typed by T is drawn with labels u and v as in

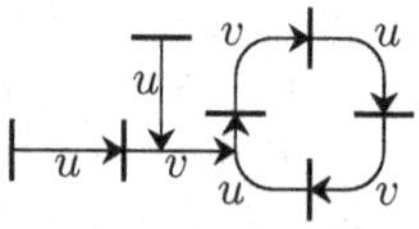

Of course, knowing that f is a morphism sometimes allows to deduce the type of an edge, possibly from the types of adjacent edges. In the present case, indicating a single type would have been enough to deduce all the others.

5 Monadic Signatures as Monographs

As mentioned in Sect. 1, graph structures, i.e., monadic many-sorted signatures, can be represented as graphs. More precisely, there is an obvious isomorphism between the category **Graphs** and the category of monadic signatures defined below[5].

Definition 5.1 (monadic signatures). *A* (monadic) signature *is a function* $\Sigma : \Omega \to S \times S$*; the elements of its domain* Ω*, that may be written* Σ_{op}*, are called* operator names *and the elements of* S*, that may be written* Σ_{srt}*, are called* sorts. Σ *is* finite *if both* Ω *and* S *are finite. Let* $\Sigma_{\mathrm{ds}} \stackrel{\mathrm{def}}{=} \pi_1 \circ \Sigma$ *and* $\Sigma_{\mathrm{rs}} \stackrel{\mathrm{def}}{=} \pi_2 \circ \Sigma$*, then* $\Sigma_{\mathrm{ds}}(o)$ *and* $\Sigma_{\mathrm{rs}}(o)$ *are respectively the* domain *and* range sorts *of* $o \in \Omega$*.*

A morphism m *from signature* Σ *to signature* Σ' *is a pair* $m = (m_{\mathrm{op}}, m_{\mathrm{srt}})$ *of functions, where* $m_{\mathrm{op}} : \Sigma_{\mathrm{op}} \to \Sigma'_{\mathrm{op}}$ *and* $m_{\mathrm{srt}} : \Sigma_{\mathrm{srt}} \to \Sigma'_{\mathrm{srt}}$*, such that*

$$\Sigma' \circ m_{\mathrm{op}} = (m_{\mathrm{srt}} \times m_{\mathrm{srt}}) \circ \Sigma.$$

[5] For the sake of simplicity, we do not allow the overloading of operator names as in [10], which would be irrelevant anyway since we wish to abstract the syntax away, hence to consider signatures only up to isomorphisms.

Let $\mathrm{id}_\Sigma \stackrel{\text{def}}{=} (\mathrm{Id}_{\Sigma_{\text{op}}}, \mathrm{Id}_{\Sigma_{\text{srt}}})$ *and given two morphisms* $m : \Sigma \to \Sigma'$ *and* $n : \Sigma' \to \Sigma''$*, let* $n \circ m \stackrel{\text{def}}{=} (n_{\text{op}} \circ m_{\text{op}}, n_{\text{srt}} \circ m_{\text{srt}})$*; then* $\mathrm{id}_\Sigma : \Sigma \to \Sigma$ *and* $n \circ m : \Sigma \to \Sigma''$ *are morphisms. Let* **MonSig** *be the category of monadic signatures and their morphisms.*

The obvious isomorphism from **MonSig** to **Graphs** maps every monadic signature $\Sigma : \Omega \to S \times S$ to the graph $(S, \Omega, \Sigma_{\text{ds}}, \Sigma_{\text{rs}})$. But we have seen in Sect. 1 on E-graphs that this representation of the monadic signature Σ_{e} bears no relation with the expected graphical representations of E-graphs. It would be more natural to represent Σ_{e} as an E-graph, or more precisely as a monograph whose drawing corresponds to that of an E-graph.

Since the image $\Sigma(\Omega)$ is a subset of $S \times S$, it can be viewed as a binary relation on S, hence there exists a monograph with S as set of edges whose adjacency relation is exactly $\Sigma(\Omega)$. However, this monograph may not be unique since, as mentioned in Sect. 3, a monograph is not generally determined by its adjacency relation. Similarly, the direction of edges in E-graphs is not determined by the signature Σ_{e}, it is only a convention given by the names of its operators.

For this reason it is more convenient to define a function *from* monographs *to* monadic signatures. Indeed, any monograph determines a unique adjacency relation that can then be interpreted as a signature. The sorts of this signature are exactly the edges of the monograph, and for every edge

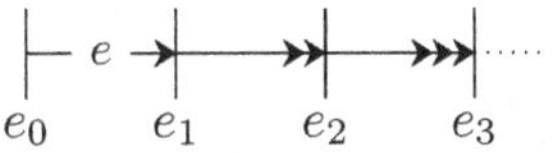

we create a first operator name from sort e to sort e_0, a second operator name from e to e_1, and so on for all elements of the sequence.

Definition 5.2 (functor S: **MonoGr** $\to$ **MonSig).** *To every monograph* $T = (\mathrm{E}_t, t)$ *we associate the set*

$$\Omega_t \stackrel{\text{def}}{=} \{(e, \iota) \mid e \in \mathrm{E}_t \wedge \iota < \ell_t(e)\}$$

of operator names, and the signature $\mathsf{S}T : \Omega_t \to \mathrm{E}_t \times \mathrm{E}_t$ *defined by*

$$\mathsf{S}T(e, \iota) \stackrel{\text{def}}{=} (e, t(e)_\iota) \text{ for all } (e, \iota) \in \Omega_t.$$

To every morphism of monographs $f : T \to U$ *we associate the morphism* $\mathsf{S}f : \mathsf{S}T \to \mathsf{S}U$ *defined by*

- $(\mathsf{S}f)_{\text{op}}(e, \iota) \stackrel{\text{def}}{=} (f(e), \iota) \in \Omega_u$ *for all* $(e, \iota) \in \Omega_t$*, and*
- $(\mathsf{S}f)_{\text{srt}} \stackrel{\text{def}}{=} f$ *(as a function from* E_t *to* E_u*).*

Note that the signature $\mathsf{S}T$ is finite iff T is a finite ω-monograph.

Lemma 5.3. S *is an embedding from* **MonoGr** *to* **MonSig**.

The next lemma uses the Axiom of Choice through its equivalent formulation known as the Numeration Theorem [11].

Lemma 5.4. S *is isomorphism-dense: for every monadic signature* Σ *there exists a monograph* T *such that* $\mathsf{S}T \simeq \Sigma$.

Proof (sketch). For any object $\Sigma : \Omega \to S \times S$ of **MonSig**, and for every sort $s \in S$ let O_s be the set of operator names in Ω whose domain sort is s. By the Numeration Theorem there exists an ordinal λ_s equipollent to O_s, i.e., such that there exists a bijection $\sigma_s : \lambda_s \to O_s$. Let $t(s)$ be the S-sequence of length λ_s such that, for all $\iota < \lambda_s$, $t(s)_\iota$ is the range sort of the operator name $\sigma_s(\iota)$, and let T be the monograph (S, t). It is then easy to see that the signature $\mathsf{S}T$ is isomorphic to Σ by mapping every operator name $(s, \iota) \in \Omega_t$ to the original operator name $\sigma_s(\iota) \in \Omega$. □

The reason why monographs require edges of ordinal length now becomes apparent: the length of an edge s is the cardinality of O_s, i.e., the number of operators whose domain sort is s, and no restriction on this cardinality is ascribed to signatures. The bijections σ_s provide linear orderings of the sets O_s.

We now show on an example that the functor S is not full, hence that S is not an equivalence between the categories **MonoGr** and **MonSig**.

Example 5.5. The monadic signature Σ_{g} has two operators `src`, `tgt`, two sorts in $\mathrm{S_g} = \{\texttt{nodes}, \texttt{edges}\}$ and is defined by $\Sigma_{\mathrm{g}} : \texttt{src}, \texttt{tgt} \mapsto (\texttt{edges}, \texttt{nodes})$. Then $O_{\texttt{nodes}} = \varnothing$ and $O_{\texttt{edges}} = \{\texttt{src}, \texttt{tgt}\}$ has 2 elements. Let $\sigma : 2 \to O_{\texttt{edges}}$ be the bijection defined by $\sigma : 0 \mapsto \texttt{src}, 1 \mapsto \texttt{tgt}$ and t be the map defined by

$$t(\texttt{nodes}) = \varepsilon,\ \ t(\texttt{edges}) = \texttt{nodes}\,\texttt{nodes}$$

then $\mathrm{T_g} = (\mathrm{S_g}, t)$ is a monograph. The signature $\mathsf{S}\mathrm{T_g}$ has the same sorts as Σ_{g}, two operators $(\texttt{edges}, 0)$, $(\texttt{edges}, 1)$ and is defined by

$$\mathsf{S}\mathrm{T_g} : (\texttt{edges}, 0), (\texttt{edges}, 1) \mapsto (\texttt{edges}, \texttt{nodes}).$$

Hence $\mathsf{S}\mathrm{T_g}$ is indeed isomorphic to Σ_{g}. However, the only automorphism of $\mathrm{T_g}$ is $\mathrm{id}_{\mathrm{T_g}}$, while Σ_{g} has a non trivial automorphism $m = ((\texttt{src}\ \texttt{tgt}), \mathrm{Id}_{\mathrm{S_g}})$ (in cycle notation), hence S is not surjective on morphisms.

This automorphism reflects the fact that Σ_{g} does not define an order between its operators `src` and `tgt`. Directing edges as arrows from `src` to `tgt` is only a matter of convention that is reflected in the choice of σ above. This contrasts with monographs, where the edges are inherently directed by the ordinals in their length. In the translation from **MonoGr** to **MonSig**, the direction of edges are necessarily lost. Note however that in this example, since `src` and `tgt` have the same range sort, the other obvious choice for σ yields the same monograph $\mathrm{T_g}$.

We therefore see that in most cases there are many distinct, non isomorphic monographs that faithfully represent a single signature, depending on the chosen direction of their edges. Monographs carry more information than signatures, but the additional information is precisely the kind of information that has to be provided by means of syntax when a monadic signature is intended as a graph structure. By observing the examples given in [7, Section 3.1], we see that this syntactic information mostly consists of an order on operators, given either by indices or by calling them "source" and "target".

More precisely, Examples 3.1 to 3.4 of [7] are monadic signatures defining graphs, edge-labelled and labelled graphs (with a possibly infinite set of labels) and hypergraphs (see Example 6.10 below). Examples 3.5 and 3.6 are special representations of signatures and terms. We observe in these examples a strict partition of sorts into domain and range sorts. It is easy to see that a monograph T is standard iff the signature ST is *separated*, i.e., no sort occurs both as a domain and a range sort. Thus the range sorts are the nodes of T and the domain sorts are edges of diverse lengths that relate nodes.

We now consider in detail Example 3.7 of [7], the only example of a monadic signature that is not separated.

Example 5.6. Let Σ_a be the monadic signature defined by the set of sorts

$$\mathrm{S_a} = \{\texttt{V}, \texttt{E}, \texttt{V-Ass}, \texttt{E-Ass}, \texttt{Graph}, \texttt{Morphism}\}$$

and the following operators:

$$\begin{array}{rrl} \Sigma_\mathrm{a}: & \texttt{s}, \texttt{t} & \mapsto (\texttt{E}, \texttt{V}) \\ & \texttt{s}_\texttt{V}, \texttt{t}_\texttt{V} & \mapsto (\texttt{V-Ass}, \texttt{V}) \\ & \texttt{s}_\texttt{E}, \texttt{t}_\texttt{E} & \mapsto (\texttt{E-Ass}, \texttt{E}) \\ & \texttt{s}_\texttt{G}, \texttt{t}_\texttt{G} & \mapsto (\texttt{Morphism}, \texttt{Graph}) \\ & \texttt{abstract}_\texttt{V} & \mapsto (\texttt{V}, \texttt{Graph}) \\ & \texttt{abstract}_\texttt{E} & \mapsto (\texttt{E}, \texttt{Graph}) \\ & \texttt{abstract}_\texttt{V-Ass} & \mapsto (\texttt{V-Ass}, \texttt{Morphism}) \\ & \texttt{abstract}_\texttt{E-Ass} & \mapsto (\texttt{E-Ass}, \texttt{Morphism}) \end{array}$$

An ALR-graph is a Σ_a-algebra. It is not very clear how such structures can be considered as graphs, especially because there is no conventional way of ordering the operator name `abstract` w.r.t. `s` and `t` (we only know that sources come before targets). Textual explanations are provided in [7] to help the reader's understanding of ALR-graphs:

> ALR-graphs not only allow to represent arbitrary labeled graphs but also morphisms between graphs. Since morphisms map vertices to vertices and edges to edges, they are represented by pairs of vertex assignments and edge assignments. In order to keep track of which assignment belongs to which morphism, an abstraction operator is introduced in ALR-graphs which allows to group vertices and edges into graphs and vertex and edge assignments into morphisms. Thus, ALR-graphs as algebras

w.r.t. the graph structure below are able to represent the diagram level (graphs and morphisms) and the object level (vertices, edges, and assignments) in a single structure.

The explanations given below on the corresponding monograph are much simpler. A choice of ordering `abstract` between `s` and `t` is made, that helps visualize the structure. The set of edges is of course $\mathrm{S_a}$, and the map $\mathrm{t_a}$ is defined by:

$\mathrm{t_a}(\texttt{Graph}) = \varepsilon$	graphs are represented by nodes
$\mathrm{t_a}(\texttt{V}) = \texttt{Graph}$	to every vertex is associated a graph
$\mathrm{t_a}(\texttt{E}) = \texttt{V}\,\texttt{Graph}\,\texttt{V}$	an edge joins two vertices through a graph
$\mathrm{t_a}(\texttt{Morphism}) = \texttt{Graph}\,\texttt{Graph}$	a morphism joins two graphs
$\mathrm{t_a}(\texttt{V-Ass}) = \texttt{V}\,\texttt{Morphism}\,\texttt{V}$	a vertex association joins two vertices through a morphism
$\mathrm{t_a}(\texttt{E-Ass}) = \texttt{E}\,\texttt{Morphism}\,\texttt{E}$	an edge association joins two edges through a morphism.

We thus see that specifying a monadic signature by a monograph may yield a better understanding of the structure of the corresponding algebras, at least if these are meant as graph structures. The next section shows that this is always possible.

6 Monadic Algebras as Typed Monographs

Now that monographs have been embedded in graph structures, the relation that the corresponding algebras bear with these monographs may be investigated. We first need a definition of Σ-algebras and Σ-homomorphisms that, for the sake of simplicity, are restricted to monadic signatures.

Definition 6.1 (Σ-algebras). *For any monadic signature $\Sigma : \Omega \to S \times S$, a* Σ-algebra *$\mathcal{A}$ is a pair $((\mathcal{A}_s)_{s\in S}, (o^{\mathcal{A}})_{o\in\Omega})$ where $(\mathcal{A}_s)_{s\in S}$ is an S-indexed family of sets and $o^{\mathcal{A}} : \mathcal{A}_{\Sigma_{\mathrm{ds}}(o)} \to \mathcal{A}_{\Sigma_{\mathrm{rs}}(o)}$ is a function for all $o \in \Omega$. $\mathcal{A}$ is* partitioned *if $s \neq s'$ entails $\mathcal{A}_s \cap \mathcal{A}_{s'} = \varnothing$ for all $s, s' \in S$.*

A Σ-homomorphism *$h : \mathcal{A} \to \mathcal{B}$ from a Σ-algebra $\mathcal{A}$ to a Σ-algebra $\mathcal{B}$ is an S-indexed family of functions $(h_s)_{s\in S}$ where $h_s : \mathcal{A}_s \to \mathcal{B}_s$ for all $s \in S$, such that*

$$o^{\mathcal{B}} \circ h_{\Sigma_{\mathrm{ds}}(o)} = h_{\Sigma_{\mathrm{rs}}(o)} \circ o^{\mathcal{A}}$$

*for all $o \in \Omega$. Let $\mathrm{id}_{\mathcal{A}} : \mathcal{A} \to \mathcal{A}$ be the Σ-homomorphism $(\mathrm{Id}_{\mathcal{A}_s})_{s\in S}$, and for any Σ-homomorphism $h : \mathcal{A} \to \mathcal{B}$ and $k : \mathcal{B} \to \mathcal{C}$, let $k \circ h : \mathcal{A} \to \mathcal{C}$ be the Σ-homomorphism $(k_s \circ h_s)_{s\in S}$. Let Σ-**Alg** be the category of Σ-algebras with Σ-homomorphisms as their morphisms, and Σ-**PAlg** be its full subcategory of partitioned algebras.*

Following Example 5.5, we notice that $\mathrm{T_g}$ =  $\simeq \mathsf{MG}_\mathrm{t}$ (where $\mathrm{G_t}$ is the terminal graph, see Sect. 3), hence we have

$$\mathbf{Graphs} \simeq \mathbf{Graphs}/\mathrm{G_t} \approxeq \mathbf{MonoGr}/\mathsf{MG}_\mathrm{t} \simeq \mathbf{MonoGr}/\mathrm{T_g}.$$

But we know that $\mathbf{Graphs} \simeq \Sigma_\mathrm{g}$-**Alg** and that $\Sigma_\mathrm{g} \simeq \mathrm{ST_g}$. The following result allows us to replace Σ_g by $\mathrm{ST_g}$.

Lemma 6.2. *If $\Sigma \simeq \Sigma'$ then Σ-**Alg** $\simeq \Sigma'$-**Alg** and Σ-**PAlg** $\simeq \Sigma'$-**PAlg**.*

Note that Σ-**Alg** is not isomorphic to Σ-**PAlg** since many distinct algebras may be Σ-isomorphic to the same partitioned algebra. There is however a trivial equivalence between these categories.

Lemma 6.3. *For every signature Σ, Σ-**PAlg** $\approxeq \Sigma$-**Alg***

By Lemma 6.2 we thus obtain $\mathbf{MonoGr}/\mathrm{T_g} \approxeq \mathrm{ST_g}$-**Alg**, the monographs typed by $\mathrm{T_g}$ are essentially the $\mathrm{ST_g}$-algebras. We are now going to generalize this property to all monographs T with the following functor from the category of monographs typed by T to the category of partitioned $\mathsf{S}T$-algebras.

Definition 6.4 (functor $\mathsf{A}_T : \mathbf{MonoGr}/T \to \mathsf{S}T$-PAlg). *Given a monograph T, we define the function A_T that maps every object $f : A \to T$ of **MonoGr**$/T$ to the partitioned $\mathsf{S}T$-algebra $\mathsf{A}_T f$ defined by*

- $(\mathsf{A}_T f)_e \stackrel{\text{def}}{=} f^{-1}[e]$ *for all* $e \in \mathrm{E}_t$, *and*
- $(e, \iota)^{\mathsf{A}_T f}(x) \stackrel{\text{def}}{=} a(x)_\iota$ *for all* $x \in f^{-1}[e]$ *and* $(e, \iota) \in \Omega_t$.

*Besides, A_T also maps every morphism $k : f \to g$ of **MonoGr**$/T$, where $f : A \to T$ and $g : B \to T$, to the $\mathsf{S}T$-homomorphism $\mathsf{A}_T k$ from $\mathsf{A}_T f$ to $\mathsf{A}_T g$ defined by*

$$(\mathsf{A}_T k)_e \stackrel{\text{def}}{=} k|_{f^{-1}[e]} \textit{ for all } e \in \mathrm{E}_t.$$

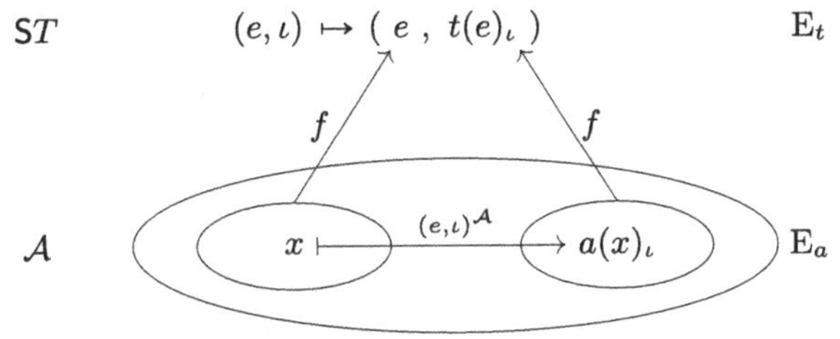

Fig. 1. The $\mathsf{S}T$-algebra $\mathcal{A} = \mathsf{A}_T f$ where $f : A \to T$

The $\mathsf{S}T$-algebra $\mathcal{A} = \mathsf{A}_T f$ can be pictured as in Fig. 1. In $\mathsf{S}T$, every operator name (e, ι) has e and $t(e)_\iota$ as domain and range sort respectively, and these two sorts are also edges in T. Hence these edges have inverse images by f in E_a (they form a partition of the set E_a). The inverse image of an edge e of T is considered as the carrier set $\mathcal{A}_e$, since e is a sort of $\mathsf{S}T$. The operator name (e, ι) is interpreted as the function $(e, \iota)^{\mathcal{A}}$ that maps every $x \in f^{-1}[e]$ to the edge $a(x)_\iota$.

Example 6.5. Consider the monograph $\mathrm{T_g}$, the corresponding signature $\mathrm{ST_g}$ from Example 5.5, and the monograph $A = (\{x, y, z\}, a)$ where $a(x) = y\,z$ and $a(y) = a(z) = \varepsilon$, i.e., x is an edge from node y to node z. There is a unique morphism $f : A \to \mathrm{T_g}$, that is $f(x) = \texttt{edges}$ and $f(y) = f(z) = \texttt{nodes}$.

Let $\mathcal{A}$ be the $\mathrm{ST_g}$-algebra $\mathsf{A}_{\mathrm{T_g}}f$. By Definition 6.4 we have

$$\mathcal{A}_{\texttt{edges}} = f^{-1}[\texttt{edges}] = \{x\} \text{ and } \mathcal{A}_{\texttt{nodes}} = f^{-1}[\texttt{nodes}] = \{y, z\}.$$

$\mathrm{ST_g}$ has two operator names $(\texttt{edges}, 0)$ and $(\texttt{edges}, 1)$, both of domain sort $\texttt{edges}$ and range sort $\texttt{nodes}$, and their interpretation in $\mathcal{A}$ is given by

$$(\texttt{edges}, 0)^{\mathcal{A}}(x) = a(x)_0 = y \text{ and } (\texttt{edges}, 1)^{\mathcal{A}}(x) = a(x)_1 = z.$$

Thus $\mathcal{A}$ is the algebra that traditionally represents A considered as a graph (more precisely, as a graph G such that $\mathsf{M}G \simeq A$).

But the important point is that not only the monograph A but also its typing $f : A \to T$ can be uniquely reconstructed from any partitioned $\mathrm{S}T$-algebra $\mathcal{A}$, and that this is also true on morphisms. In other words, A_T is not just a functor, it is an isomorphism of categories.

Theorem 6.6. *For every monograph T, $\mathsf{A}_T : \mathbf{MonoGr}/T \xrightarrow{\simeq} \mathrm{S}T\text{-}\mathbf{PAlg}$.*

Corollary 6.7. *For every monadic signature Σ there exists a monograph T such that $\Sigma\text{-}\mathbf{PAlg} \simeq \mathbf{MonoGr}/T$.*

Proof. By Lemma 5.4 there exists T such that $\Sigma \simeq \mathrm{S}T$, hence $\mathbf{MonoGr}/T \simeq \mathrm{S}T\text{-}\mathbf{PAlg} \simeq \Sigma\text{-}\mathbf{PAlg}$ by Lemma 6.2. □

We thus see that the categories of partitioned monadic algebras are isomorphic to the slice categories of monographs. Note that in the case of graphs, the partitioned Σ_{g}-algebras correspond to those graphs whose sets of vertices and edges are disjoint. This is a common restriction for graphs but not for Σ-algebras. By Lemma 6.3 we obtain a similar result for the categories $\Sigma\text{-}\mathbf{Alg}$.

Corollary 6.8. *For every monograph T, $\mathbf{MonoGr}/T \approxeq \mathrm{S}T\text{-}\mathbf{Alg}$, and for every monadic signature Σ there is a monograph T such that $\Sigma\text{-}\mathbf{Alg} \approxeq \mathbf{MonoGr}/T$.*

The first half of Corollary 6.8 also yields that $\mathbf{Graphs}/G \approxeq \mathsf{S} \circ \mathsf{M}(G)\text{-}\mathbf{Alg}$ for all graphs G, i.e., typed graphs are equivalent to algebras of monadic signatures (but not every monadic signature is isomorphic to some $\mathsf{S} \circ \mathsf{M}(G)$). Signatures are sometimes called *types* (see, e.g., [2, Chapter 9]), which leads to the following reading of Corollary 6.8:

algebras of monadic many-sorted types are essentially typed monographs.

This may seem strange since monographs may be typed in many different ways, while algebras are defined with only one type (but this type may correspond to many different type monographs). We now illustrate the corresponding equivalence between E-graphs and a category of typed monographs.

Example 6.9. The signature Σ_{e} of E-graphs from [4] has six operators $\texttt{src}_{\mathrm{g}}$, $\texttt{tgt}_{\mathrm{g}}$, $\texttt{src}_{\mathrm{n}}$, $\texttt{tgt}_{\mathrm{n}}$, $\texttt{src}_{\mathrm{e}}$, $\texttt{tgt}_{\mathrm{e}}$ and five sorts in

$$\mathrm{S_e} = \{\texttt{edges}_{\mathrm{g}}, \texttt{edges}_{\mathrm{n}}, \texttt{edges}_{\mathrm{e}}, \texttt{nodes}_{\mathrm{g}}, \texttt{nodes}_{\mathrm{v}}\},$$

and is defined by

$$\begin{array}{rll}\Sigma_e : \mathtt{src_g}, \mathtt{tgt_g} & \mapsto & (\mathtt{edges_g}, \mathtt{nodes_g}) \\ \mathtt{src_n} & \mapsto & (\mathtt{edges_n}, \mathtt{nodes_g}) \\ \mathtt{tgt_n} & \mapsto & (\mathtt{edges_n}, \mathtt{nodes_v}) \\ \mathtt{src_e} & \mapsto & (\mathtt{edges_e}, \mathtt{edges_g}) \\ \mathtt{tgt_e} & \mapsto & (\mathtt{edges_e}, \mathtt{nodes_v})\end{array}$$

hence $O_{\mathtt{edges_g}} = \{\mathtt{src_g}, \mathtt{tgt_g}\}$, $O_{\mathtt{edges_n}} = \{\mathtt{src_n}, \mathtt{tgt_n}\}$, $O_{\mathtt{edges_e}} = \{\mathtt{src_e}, \mathtt{tgt_e}\}$ and $O_{\mathtt{nodes_g}} = O_{\mathtt{nodes_v}} = \varnothing$. There are four possible monographs $T = (\mathrm{S_e}, t)$, given by

$$\begin{aligned} t(\mathtt{nodes_g}) &= t(\mathtt{nodes_v}) = \varepsilon \\ t(\mathtt{edges_g}) &= \mathtt{nodes_g}\,\mathtt{nodes_g} \\ t(\mathtt{edges_n}) &= \mathtt{nodes_g}\,\mathtt{nodes_v} \text{ or } \mathtt{nodes_v}\,\mathtt{nodes_g} \\ t(\mathtt{edges_e}) &= \mathtt{edges_g}\,\mathtt{nodes_v} \text{ or } \mathtt{nodes_v}\,\mathtt{edges_g}. \end{aligned}$$

These four monographs are depicted below.

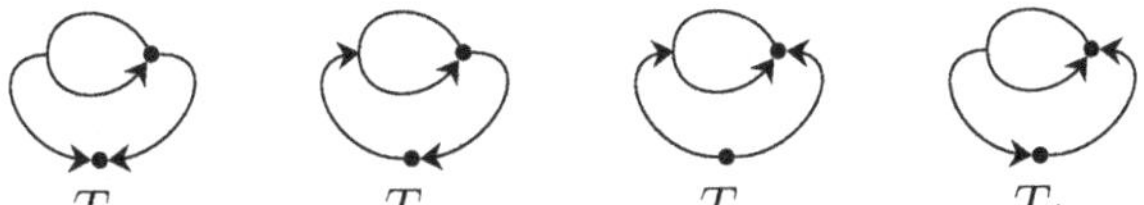

Note that, by Theorem 6.6, the categories $\mathbf{MonoGr}/T_i$ for $1 \leqslant i \leqslant 4$ are isomorphic, even though the T_i's are not. The type indicated by the syntax (and consistent with the figures in [4]) is T_1. An example of a monograph A typed by T_1 is

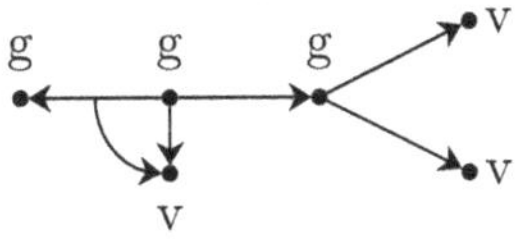

where g stands for $\mathtt{nodes_g}$ and v for $\mathtt{nodes_v}$. The types of the other edges can easily be deduced, yielding a unique typing morphism $f : A \to T_1$. This drawing can also be read as an E-graph, i.e., as a Σ_e-algebra $\mathcal{E}$ by determining the carrier sets of the five sorts and the functions interpreting the six operator names of Σ_e. This is a tedious task that corresponds to the transformation performed by the functor A_{T_1}, since $\mathcal{E} \simeq \mathsf{A}_{T_1} f$ as the reader can check.

Conversely, drawing an E-graph $\mathcal{E}$ corresponds to computing the typed monograph $\mathsf{A}_{T_1}^{-1}\mathcal{E}$ and then drawing it. Note that the operator names of Σ_e do not appear in the drawing of $\mathcal{E}$ but the sorts do, exactly as in $\mathsf{A}_{T_1}^{-1}\mathcal{E}$.

We see that E-graphs can be defined simply by drawing T_1, just as typed graphs can be defined by drawing their type graph. Of course, it is not always easy to draw a monograph, and it can be more convenient to give it explicitly as in Example 5.6, or indeed in the following example where the type monograph is infinite, though standard and with only one node. This example illustrates how a monograph may be typed in many different ways.

Example 6.10. The signature Σ_{h} of hypergraphs (see [7, Example 3.4]) is defined by the set of sorts $\mathrm{S}_{\mathrm{h}} = \{\mathtt{V}\} \cup \{\mathtt{H}_{n,m} \mid n, m \in \omega\}$ and the $n+m$ operators

$$\Sigma_{\mathrm{h}} : \mathtt{src}_i^{n,m}, \mathtt{tgt}_j^{n,m} \mapsto (\mathtt{H}_{n,m}, \mathtt{V}) \text{ for all } 1 \leqslant i \leqslant n,\ 1 \leqslant j \leqslant m.$$

For any hypergraph $\mathcal{H}$ (i.e., any Σ_{h}-algebra) and $n, m \in \omega$, let us call (n,m)-hyperedges the elements of the set $\mathcal{H}_{\mathtt{H}_{n,m}}$; these are the hyperedges with n sources and m targets. The corresponding type monograph $\mathrm{T}_{\mathrm{h}} = (\mathrm{S}_{\mathrm{h}}, \mathrm{t}_{\mathrm{h}})$ is defined by

$\mathrm{t}_{\mathrm{h}}(\mathtt{V}) = \varepsilon$ vertices are nodes

$\mathrm{t}_{\mathrm{h}}(\mathtt{H}_{n,m}) = \mathtt{V}^{n+m}$ (n,m)-hyperedges are edges joining $n+m$ vertices

for all $n, m \in \omega$. Hypergraphs are therefore isomorphic to monographs typed by T_{h}, i.e., every edge is typed by some $\mathtt{H}_{n,m}$ (or $\mathtt{V}$ if it is a node). An edge of length 2 can therefore be typed either by $\mathtt{H}_{2,0}$, $\mathtt{H}_{1,1}$ or $\mathtt{H}_{0,2}$ and thus represent either a $(2,0)$-, a $(1,1)$- or a $(0,2)$-hyperedge.

7 Some Properties of MonoGr

Depending on the signature Σ, working with Σ-algebras can be cumbersome. For instance, the proofs given in [4, Chapter 11] have to deal with the five carrier sets and six operators of E-graphs. With only one carrier set and one map, monographs allow simpler notations and proofs. This can be illustrated by establishing a few fundamental properties of **MonoGr** (see e.g. [5] or [1] for the following notions from Category Theory that are not defined in Sect. 2).

By Corollary 6.8 it would be surprising if **MonoGr** had a terminal object, since such a monograph would be a type for all monographs, hence the corresponding signature would be in a sense universal. A more direct argument is given below.

Definition 7.1 (monographs M_α). *For every ordinal $\alpha > 0$ let a_α be the functional relation that to every $\lambda < \alpha$ associates the unique $\{0\}$-sequence of length λ. Let $\mathrm{M}_\alpha \stackrel{\text{def}}{=} (\alpha, \mathrm{a}_\alpha)$.*

It is clear that M_α is a standard α-monograph, since $\mathrm{a}_\alpha \subseteq \alpha \times \alpha^{<\alpha}$ and $\mathrm{a}_\alpha(0) = \varepsilon$, i.e., 0 is a node of M_α.

Lemma 7.2. *For all ordinals $\alpha > 0$, β and every β-monograph B, if there is a morphism $f : \mathrm{M}_\alpha \to B$ then $\alpha \leqslant \beta$.*

Proof. α is the grade of M_α, since for any $\lambda < \alpha$ there is an edge of length λ, that is $\ell_{\mathrm{a}_\alpha}(\lambda) = \lambda$, hence $\mathrm{a}_\alpha(\lambda) \notin \alpha^{<\lambda}$, and therefore M_α is not a λ-monograph. By the existence of f the grade α of M_α is less than the grade of B, hence $\alpha \leqslant \beta$. □

Theorem 7.3. **MonoGr**, **SMonoGr** *and* **FMonoGr** *have no terminal object.*

Proof. Suppose that B is a terminal monograph, then there is an ordinal β such that B is a β-monograph, and there is a morphism from $\mathrm{M}_{\beta+1}$ to B. By Lemma 7.2 this implies that $\beta+1 \leqslant \beta$, a contradiction. This still holds if B is standard since $\mathrm{M}_{\beta+1}$ is standard. And it also holds if B is a finite ω-monograph, since then β can be chosen finite, and then $\mathrm{M}_{\beta+1}$ is also a finite ω-monograph. □

This of course is a major difference between **MonoGr** and **Graphs**, but also with the category **Sets** (whose terminal object is 1). Other properties derive directly from those of **Sets**. This can be illustrated by using the standard construction of pullbacks in **Sets** for building pullbacks of monographs.

Lemma 7.4. *Let B, C, D be α-monographs and $f : B \to D$, $g : C \to D$ be morphisms, then there exists an α-monograph A and morphisms $g' : A \to B$, $f' : A \to C$ such that (A, f', g') is a pullback of (f, g, D) in* **MonoGr**.

Proof. Let $E = \{(y,z) \in \mathrm{E}_b \times \mathrm{E}_c \mid f(y) = g(z)\}$, $g' = \pi_1|_E$, $f' = \pi_2|_E$ and $A = (E, a)$, where a maps every $x \in E$ to $\langle b \circ g'(x), c \circ f'(x)\rangle$.

We first prove that A is an α-monograph, i.e., that $a(x) \in E^{<\alpha}$ for all $x \in E$. Let $y = g'(x)$ and $z = f'(x)$ (so that $x = (y,z)$), then $\ell_b(y) = \ell_d(f(y)) = \ell_d(g(z)) = \ell_c(z)$, i.e., $b \circ g'(x)$ and $c \circ f'(x)$ have the same length $\lambda < \alpha$. Then, for all $\iota < \lambda$,

$$\begin{aligned} f((b \circ g'(x))_\iota) = (f^{<\alpha} \circ b(y))_\iota &= (d \circ f(y))_\iota \\ &= (d \circ g(z))_\iota = (g^{<\alpha} \circ c(z))_\iota = g((c \circ f'(x))_\iota), \end{aligned}$$

hence $a(x)_\iota = ((b \circ g'(x))_\iota, (c \circ f'(x))_\iota) \in E$, so that $a(x) \in E^\lambda \subseteq E^{<\alpha}$.

It is obvious that $g'^{<\alpha} \circ a(x) = b \circ g'(x)$ and $f'^{<\alpha} \circ a(x) = c \circ f'(x)$, hence $g' : A \to B$ and $f' : A \to C$ are morphisms. There remains to prove that (A, g', f') is a pullback of (f, g, D).

Let A' be a monograph and $g'' : A' \to B$, $f'' : A' \to C$ be morphisms such that $f \circ g'' = g \circ f''$. Since (E, f', g') is a pullback of (f, g, E_d) in **Sets** (see [4]) then there exists a unique function h from $\mathrm{E}_{a'}$ to E such that $g'' = g' \circ h$ and $f'' = f' \circ h$. Then, for all $x \in \mathrm{E}_{a'}$,

$$\begin{aligned} a \circ h(x) &= \langle b \circ g' \circ h(x), c \circ f' \circ h(x)\rangle \\ &= \langle b \circ g''(x), c \circ f''(x)\rangle \\ &= \langle g''^{<\alpha} \circ a'(x), f''^{<\alpha} \circ a'(x)\rangle \\ &= \langle g'^{<\alpha} \circ h^{<\alpha} \circ a'(x), f'^{<\alpha} \circ h^{<\alpha} \circ a'(x)\rangle \\ &= \langle \pi_1 \circ (h^{<\alpha} \circ a'(x)), \pi_2 \circ (h^{<\alpha} \circ a'(x))\rangle \\ &= h^{<\alpha} \circ a'(x) \end{aligned}$$

hence $h : A' \to A$ is a morphism in **MonoGr**. □

Theorem 7.5. *The categories* **MonoGr**, **SMonoGr**, **FMonoGr**, O-**MonoGr** *and* O-**SMonoGr** *have pullbacks for every set O of ordinals.*

Proof. By Lemma 7.4 and since A is finite (resp. standard, resp. an O-monograph) if so are B and C. □

Corollary 7.6. *The monomorphisms in* **MonoGr** *are the injective morphisms.*

Proof. Assume $f : B \to D$ is a monomorphism and let $C = B$, $g = f$ and (A, f', g') be the pullback of (f, g, D) defined in the proof of Lemma 7.4, then $f \circ g' = f \circ f'$ hence $\pi_1|_{\mathrm{E}_a} = g' = f' = \pi_2|_{\mathrm{E}_a}$. For all $x, y \in \mathrm{E}_b$, if $f(x) = f(y)$ then $(x, y) \in \mathrm{E}_a$ and $x = g'(x, y) = f'(x, y) = y$, hence f is injective. The converse is obvious. □

Another way of stating this last property is that the forgetful functor from **MonoGr** to **Sets** reflects monomorphisms (and since it is faithful it obviously preserves them as well).

Similarly the standard construction of pushouts in **Sets** can be used to build pushouts in **MonoGr** (see [3]). Since $(\varnothing, \varnothing)$ is an initial object in **MonoGr** (as in all the considered subcategories), we get the following property.

Theorem 7.7. *The categories* **MonoGr**, **SMonoGr**, **FMonoGr**, O-**MonoGr** *and* O-**SMonoGr** *are finitely co-complete for every set* O *of ordinals.*

Note that the categories mentioned in Theorem 7.3 are not finitely complete since limits of empty diagrams are terminal objects.

As above, the construction of pushouts can be used to establish that the epimorphisms in **MonoGr** are exactly the surjective morphisms (i.e., the forgetful functor also reflects epimorphisms). But then it is easy to see that the isomorphisms in **MonoGr** are exactly the bijective morphisms: if $f : A \to B$ and $g : B \to A$ are such that $g \circ f = \mathrm{id}_A$ and $f \circ g = \mathrm{id}_B$, then f is bijective since the underlying functions of id_A and id_B are $\mathrm{Id}_{\mathrm{E}_a}$ and $\mathrm{Id}_{\mathrm{E}_b}$. Hence **MonoGr** is obviously *balanced*, i.e., its isomorphisms are exactly the morphisms that are both mono and epimorphisms.

Since the forgetful functor reflects both mono and epimorphisms, this obviously means that it reflects isomorphisms. This has an interesting consequence.

Lemma 7.8. *The forgetful functor from* **MonoGr** *preserves and reflects pullbacks and pushouts.*

Proof. We first see that the forgetful functor preserves pullbacks. Let (f, g, D) be a sink in **MonoGr** and (A', f'', g'') be a pullback of (f, g, D). Let (A, f', g') be the pullback of (f, g, D) constructed in the proof of Lemma 7.4, then there is an isomorphism $i : A' \to A$ such that $f'' = f' \circ i$ and $g'' = g' \circ i$. Since (E_a, f', g') is a pullback of (f, g, E_d) in **Sets**, then so is $(\mathrm{E}_{a'}, f'', g'')$.

Since the forgetful functor is faithful, reflects isomorphisms and preserves pullbacks, then [5, Theorem 24.7] it also reflects them. The case for pushouts is similar. □

This means that properties of pullbacks and pushouts in **Sets** can easily be transfered to **MonoGr**. Of particular importance in the Double Pushout approach to Algebraic Graph Transformation is the notion of *adhesive* category from [6].

Definition 7.9. *A pushout square* (A, B, C, D) *is a* van Kampen square *if for any commutative cube*

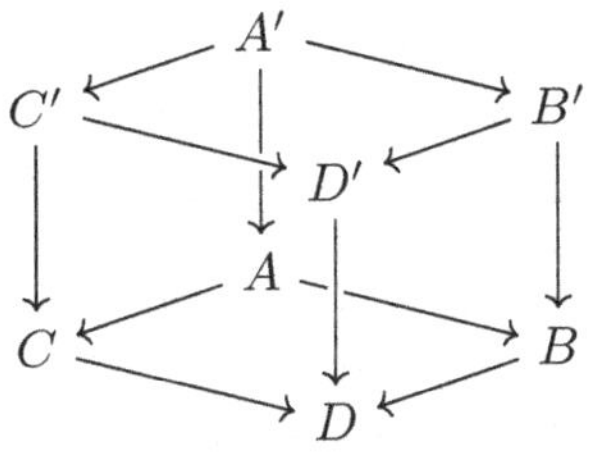

where the back faces (A', A, B', B) *and* (A', A, C', C) *are pullbacks, it is the case that the top face* (A', B', C', D') *is a pushout iff the front faces* (B', B, D', D) *and* (C', C, D', D) *are both pullbacks.*

A category has pushouts along monomorphisms *if all sources* (A, f, g) *have pushouts whenever* f *or* g *is a monomorphism.*

A category is adhesive *[6] if it has pullbacks, pushouts along monomorphisms and all such pushouts are van Kampen squares.*

Theorem 7.10. *The categories* **MonoGr**, **SMonoGr**, **FMonoGr**, O-**MonoGr** *and* O-**SMonoGr** *are adhesive for every set* O *of ordinals.*

Proof. In any of these categories a commutative cube built on a pushout along a monomorphism as bottom face and with pullbacks as back faces, has an underlying cube in **Sets** that has the same properties by Lemma 7.8 and Corollary 7.6. Since **Sets** is an adhesive category (see [6]) the underlying bottom face is a van Kampen square, hence such is the bottom face of the initial cube by Lemma 7.8. We conclude with Theorems 7.5 and 7.7. □

Note that their slice categories are therefore also adhesive by [4, Theorem 4.15]. Other properties can be found in [3], in particular a gluing condition that characterizes the existence of a pushout complement, and a construction of a product for some pairs of monographs.

8 Conclusion

Monographs generalize standard notions of directed graphs in the following ways.

1. Nodes are considered as a special kind of edges, namely the edges of length zero.
2. Edges can be adjacent to any edges and not only to nodes. This means that a monograph may contain edges but no nodes. This also means that edges can loop on themselves.
3. Edges can have any length, including infinite ones. Similarly (but this is not a special feature) monographs can be infinite.
4. Edges are well-ordered, hence they generalize directed arrows.

The prefix of "monograph" is justified by this unified view of nodes as edges and indiscriminate adjacency that provide formal conciseness; the suffix is justified by the correspondence (up to isomorphism) between finite ω-monographs and their drawings.

Monographs are universal with respect to monadic many sorted signatures (or graph structures) and the corresponding algebras, in the sense that monographs are equivalent to graph structures extended with suitable ordering conventions on their operator names, and that categories of typed monographs are equivalent to the corresponding categories of algebras. Since many standard or exotic notions of directed graphs can be represented as monadic algebras, they can also be represented as typed monographs.

Drawing a typed monograph appears to be a much easier task than drawing an algebra whose signature is a graph structure. This suggests that working directly with typed monographs rather than monadic algebras would be closer to graphical intuition as well as formally simpler.

Future work includes determining further properties of categories of monographs, especially in relation with the Double-Pushout approach to Algebraic Graph Transformation, studying submonographs and partial morphisms [9], attributed monographs as a way of generalizing the notion of attributed graphs based on E-graphs (see [4, Definition 8.4], see also [8]), and their relations with the Single-Pushout approach [7].

References

1. Adámek, J., Herrlich, H., Strecker, G.E.: Abstract and Concrete Categories - The Joy of Cats. Online Edition. John Wiley & Sons, Inc., Hoboken (1990)
2. Bergman, G.M.: An Invitation to General Algebra and Universal Constructions. U. Springer, Cham (2015). https://doi.org/10.1007/978-3-319-11478-1
3. Boy de la Tour, T.: On monographs, monadic many-sorted algebras and graph structures. HAL:02428793 (2020)
4. Ehrig, H., Ehrig, K., Prange, U., Taentzer, G.: Fundamentals of Algebraic Graph Transformation. MTCSAES. Springer, Heidelberg (2006). https://doi.org/10.1007/3-540-31188-2
5. Herrlich, H., Strecker, G.E.: Category Theory, 3rd edn. Heldermann Verlag, Berlin (2007)
6. Lack, S., Sobocinski, P.: Adhesive and quasiadhesive categories. Informatique Théorique et Applications **39**(3), 511–545 (2005)
7. Löwe, M.: Algebraic approach to single-pushout graph transformation. Theoret. Comput. Sci. **109**, 181–224 (1993)
8. Löwe, M., Korff, M., Wagner, A.: An algebraic framework for the transformation of attributed graphs. In: Sleep, R., Plasmeijer, R., van Eekelen, M. (eds.) Term Graph Rewriting: Theory and Practice, pp. 185–199. Wiley, New York (1993)
9. Robinson, E., Rosolini, G.: Categories of partial maps. Inf. Comput. **79**(2), 95–130 (1988)
10. Sannella, D., Tarlecki, A.: Foundations of Algebraic Specification and Formal Software Development. EATCS. Springer, Heidelberg (2012). https://doi.org/10.1007/978-3-642-17336-3
11. Suppes, P.: Axiomatic Set Theory. Dover Publications Inc., New York (1972)

Parallel Coherent Graph Transformations

Thierry Boy de la Tour(✉) and Rachid Echahed

LIG Laboratory, CNRS and University Grenoble Alpes, Grenoble, France
{thierry.boy-de-la-tour,rachid.echahed}@imag.fr

Abstract. Cellular automata as well as simultaneous assignments in Python can be understood as the parallel application of local rules to a grid or an environment that can be easily represented as an attributed graph. Since the result of such transformations cannot generally be obtained by a sequential application of the involved rules, this situation infringes the standard notion of parallel independence. An algebraic approach with production rules of the form $L \leftarrow K \leftarrow I \rightarrow R$ is adopted and a condition of *parallel coherence* more general than parallel independence is formulated, that enable the definition of the *Parallel Coherent Transformation* (PCT). This transformation supports a generalisation of the Parallelism Theorem in the theory of adhesive HLR categories, showing that the PCT yields the expected result of sequential rewriting steps when parallel independence holds. Categories of *finitely attributed structures* are proposed, in which PCTs are guaranteed to exist. These notions are introduced and illustrated on several detailed examples.

1 Introduction

Graph transformations [28] constitute a natural extension of string rewriting [3] and term rewriting [2]. Due to the visual and intuitive appearance of their structures, graph rewrite systems play an important role in the modeling of complex systems in various disciplines including computer science, mathematics and biology.

Computing with graphs as first-class citizens requires the use of advanced graph-based computational models. Several approaches to graph transformations have been proposed in the literature, divided in two lines of research: the algebraic approaches (e.g. [17,28]) where transformations are defined using notions of category theory, and the algorithmic approaches (e.g. [14,20]) where graph transformations are defined by means of the involved algorithms.

In this context of graph transformations by means of production rules, parallelism is generally understood as the problem of performing in one step what is normally achieved in two or more sequential steps. This is easy when these steps happen to be independent, a situation analogous to the expression $x := z + 1;\ y := z + 2$ that could be executed in any order, hence also in parallel, yielding exactly the same result in each case. If the two steps are not sequentially independent, it may also be possible to synthesize a new production rule that accounts for the sequence of transformations in one step (see the Concurrency

M. Roggenbach (Ed.): WADT 2020, LNCS 12669, pp. 75–97, 2021.
https://doi.org/10.1007/978-3-030-73785-6_5

Theorem in, e.g., [17]). This parallel rule obviously depends on the order in which this sequence in considered, if more than one is possible. As long as parallelism refers to a sequence of transformations, this synthesis can only be commutative if the order of the sequence is irrelevant, i.e., in case of sequential independence.

We can also understand parallelism as a way of expressing a transformation as the *simultaneous* execution of two (or more) basic transformations. To see how this could be meaningful even when independence does not hold, let us consider a transformation intended to compute the next item in the Fibonacci sequence, given by $u_{n+1} = u_{n-1} + u_n$. Since it depends on the two previous items u_{n-1} and u_n, they need to be saved in two placeholders, say x and y respectively. As the new value $x + y$ of y is computed the old value of y must be simultaneously transfered to x. This can be elegantly specified as a multiple assignment $x, y := y, x + y$ in Python, which can be understood as the parallel evaluation

$$x := y \mid\mid y := x + y \tag{1}$$

It is clear that executing these expressions in sequence in one or the other order yields two different results, hence they are not independent, and that both results are incorrect w.r.t. the intended meaning. This notion of parallelism ought to be commutative in the sense that (1) is equivalent to $y := x + y \mid\mid x := y$, hence it cannot refer to a sequence of transformations.

Of course (1) can be computed by a sequence of expressions using an extra placeholder (though this breaks the symmetry between the two expressions), or as a single graph transformation rule (see Sect. 6). The point of the present paper is to define the simultaneous application of possibly non independent graph transformation rules, and to identify the situations in which this is possible.

For the sake of generality a new algebraic approach based on enriched rules is adopted. The motivation of this extension is demonstrated on a detailed example in Sect. 2. In Sect. 3, the notion of parallel coherence is introduced, that allows the construction of parallel coherent transformations (PCTs). Section 4 is devoted to the study of PCTs in the theory of adhesive HLR categories. In Sect. 5, a family of categories is defined in which PCTs are guaranteed to exist. In Sect. 6, all these notions are illustrated on detailed examples, including a cellular automaton. Related work and concluding remarks are given in Sect. 7. The missing proofs can be found in [5,6].

2 Weak Spans

In order to represent the expressions given in (1) as graph transformation rules, the state of the system must be represented as some form of graph. Since we need to hold (and compute with) natural numbers, this obviously requires the use of attributes. A precise definition of attributed graphs is postponed to Sect. 6, Example 2. Placeholders x and y may be represented as nodes with an arrow from x to y, so that placeholder x is identified as the source and y as the sink, hence no confusion is possible between the two. The contents of the placeholders are represented as attributes of the corresponding nodes, e.g., 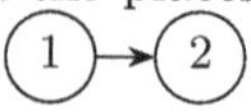

represents

the state $(x, y) = (1, 2)$. This state is *correct* in the sense that $(x, y) = (u_{n-1}, u_n)$ for some n.

The left-hand side of a production rule corresponding to $y := x + y$ should then be the graph $L =$ 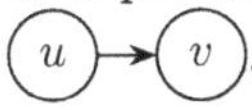, where u and v are the contents of placeholders x and y respectively. The right-hand side should ideally be restricted to $R =$ , to be matched to placeholder y, since $y := x + y$ has no effect on x; the only effect is on y's content, that should be replaced by $u + v$. In the Double-Pushout approach [11,19], a rule is expressed as a span $L \xleftarrow{l} K \xrightarrow{r} R$, where l specifies what should be removed and r what should be added. Obviously, the content of y, and nothing else, has to be removed. This means that $K =$ 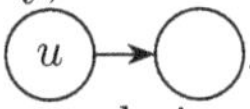.

But then there is no morphism from K to R, hence if a span rule is used to express $y := x + y$ then its right-hand side has to be 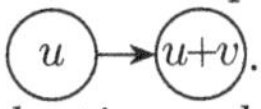. Since there must be a matching from the right-hande side of a production rule to the result of the transformation, this means that the value of x *cannot* change and therefore $x := y$ cannot be applied simultaneously.

It is therefore necessary to express the lack of effect on x in a weaker sense than as the lack of change (the preservation) of x's content. Thus, the morphism r should add the content $u + v$ to y, and *say nothing* of x's content. This is specified by making r match an intermediate graph $I =$  into $R =$ . And to make sure that I and R both match to placeholder y, a morphism i from I to K that maps I's node to K's sink (that stands for y) is also needed. This leads to the rule below, where i is specified by a dotted arrow in order to avoid any ambiguity.

$(y := x + y)$ 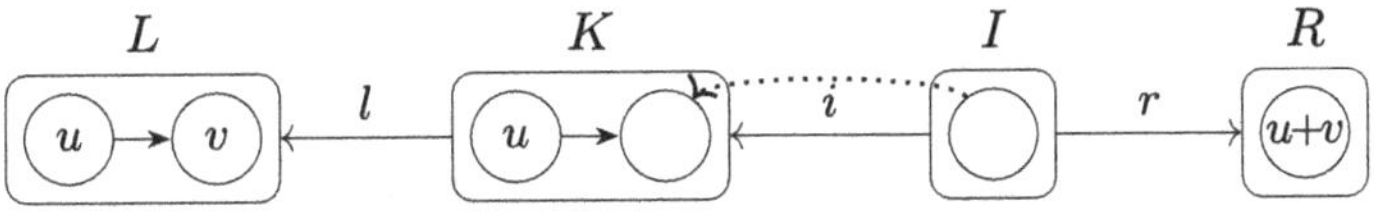

We thus see that the part of K that is not matched by I, that can be informally described as $K \setminus i(I)$, is not modified by this rule but can still be modified by another rule, while the part of K that is matched by I, i.e., node y, is here required to be preserved and therefore cannot be removed by another rule.

Similarly, the rule corresponding to the expression $x := y$ should be

$(x := y)$ 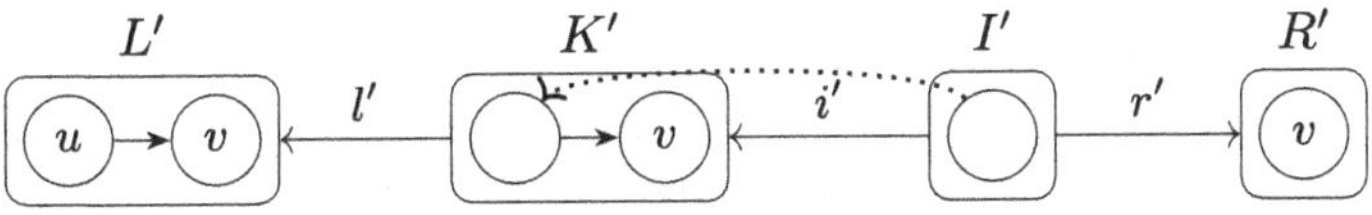

where i' maps the node of I' to the source node of K', that stands for x.

A general definition can now be ventured, assuming a suitable category $\mathcal{C}$.

Definition 1. *A* weak span *is a diagram* $L \xleftarrow{l} K \xleftarrow{i} I \xrightarrow{r} R$ *in* $\mathcal{C}$. *Given an object* G *of* $\mathcal{C}$ *and a weak span* ρ, *a* direct transformation γ *of* G *by* ρ *is a commuting diagram*

$$\begin{array}{ccccccc} L & \xleftarrow{l} & K & \xleftarrow{i} & I & \xrightarrow{r} & R \\ \quad\searrow^{m} & & \quad\searrow^{k} & & \swarrow^{k\circ i} \quad PO & & \swarrow^{n} \\ & G & \xleftarrow{f} & D & \xrightarrow{g} & H & \end{array}$$

such that (g, n, H) is a pushout of $(I, r, k \circ i)$; we then write $G \overset{\gamma}{\Rightarrow} H$. The object H is called the result *and D the* context *of γ. Let $\Delta(G, \rho)$ be the set of all direct transformations of G by ρ. For a set $\mathcal{R}$ of weak spans, let $\Delta(G, \mathcal{R}) \overset{\text{def}}{=} \biguplus_{\rho\in\mathcal{R}} \Delta(G, \rho)$.*

If (f, m, G) is a pushout of (K, l, k), then γ is called Weak Double-Pushout. *Let $\Delta^{\mathrm{PO}}(G, \mathcal{R})$ be the set of Weak Double-Pushouts in $\Delta(G, \mathcal{R})$.*

As ρ is part of any diagram $\gamma \in \Delta(G, \rho)$, it is obvious that $\Delta(G, \rho) \cap \Delta(G, \rho') = \varnothing$ whenever $\rho \neq \rho'$. A span can be seen as a weak span where $I = K$ and $i = \mathrm{id}_K$, and then a Weak Double-Pushout is a standard Double-Pushout.

Not all elements of $\Delta(G, \rho)$ are usually considered as valid transformations. Many approaches exist to compute the context D from ρ, G and m, e.g. [8,10,19]. Each approach corresponds to a particular subset of $\Delta(G, \rho)$ that confers a particular semantics to the production rule ρ. Since the parallel transformation defined in Sect. 3 applies uniformly to all these approaches, it is simply assumed that any element of $\Delta(G, \rho)$ may participate in a parallel transformation.

In the rest of the paper, when we refer to some weak span ρ, possibly indexed by a natural number, we will also assume the objects and morphisms L, K, I, R, l, i and r, indexed by the same number, as given in the definition of weak spans. The same schema will be used for direct transformations and indeed for all diagrams given in future definitions.

3 Parallel Coherent Transformations

If we assume direct transformations γ_1 of $G = \textcircled{1}\rightarrow\textcircled{2}$ by $(x := y)$ and γ_2 of G by $(y := x + y)$ as in Fig. 1, we may then refer to the objects and morphisms involved as I_1, I_2, D_1, D_2, i_1, i_2, etc. As stated above, the node that is matched by I_2, i.e., node y, cannot be removed by another rule, hence must belong to D_1. A parallel transformation is not possible without this condition. This means that there must be a morphism $j_2^1 : I_2 \to D_1$ that maps I_2's node to the sink in D_1. Symmetrically, node x matched by I_1 must belong to D_2 and there must be a morphism $j_1^2 : I_1 \to D_2$ that maps I_1's node to the source in D_2.

Definition 2. *Given an object G of $\mathcal{C}$, two weak spans ρ_1 and ρ_2, and direct transformations $\gamma_1 \in \Delta(G, \rho_1)$ and $\gamma_2 \in \Delta(G, \rho_2)$, we say that γ_1 and γ_2 are* parallel coherent *if there exist two morphisms $j_1^2 : I_1 \to D_2$ and $j_2^1 : I_2 \to D_1$ such that the following diagram commutes, i.e., $f_2 \circ j_1^2 = f_1 \circ k_1 \circ i_1$ and $f_1 \circ j_2^1 = f_2 \circ k_2 \circ i_2$.*

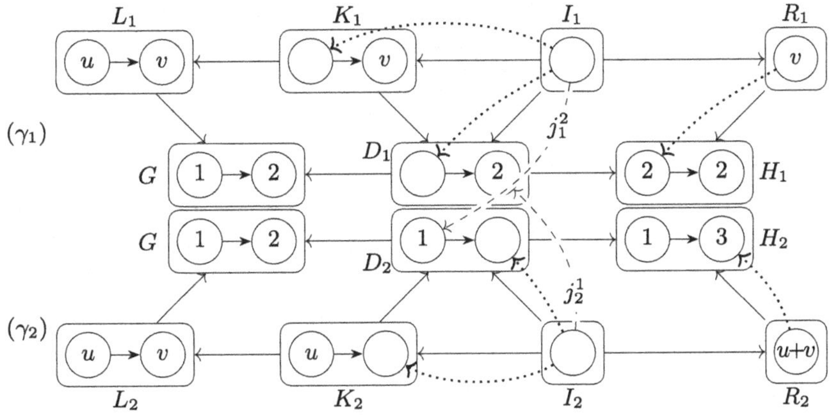

Fig. 1. The direct transformations γ_1 and γ_2

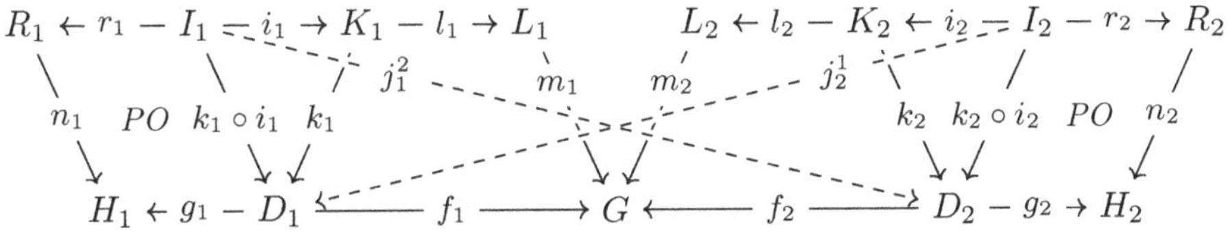

A parallel coherent diagram for G *is a commuting diagram* Γ *in* $\mathcal{C}$ *constituted of diagrams* $\gamma_1, \ldots, \gamma_p \in \Delta(G, \mathcal{R})$ *for some* $p \geqslant 1$, *and morphisms* $j_a^b : I_a \to D_b$ *for all* $1 \leqslant a, b \leqslant p$.

Since $\gamma_1, \ldots, \gamma_p$ are commuting diagrams, the commuting property of Γ amounts to $f_b \circ j_a^b = f_a \circ k_a \circ i_a$ for all $1 \leqslant a, b \leqslant p$. Note that for any $\gamma \in \Delta(G, \mathcal{R})$, the diagram Γ constituted of γ and morphism $j = k \circ i$ is parallel coherent. For any parallel coherent diagram Γ, it is obvious that γ_a and γ_b are parallel coherent for all $1 \leqslant a, b \leqslant p$, and that

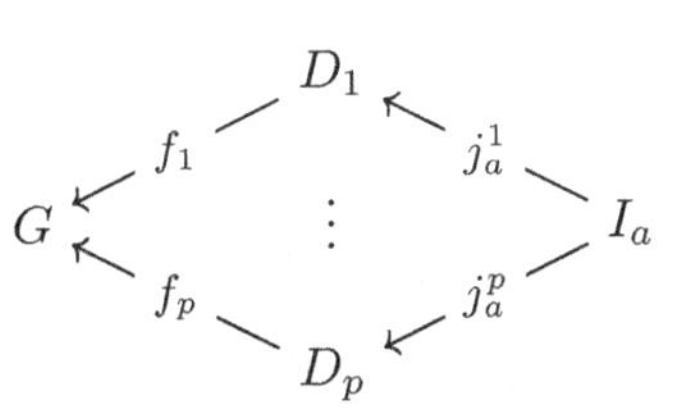

is a sub-diagram of Γ for all $1 \leqslant a \leqslant p$, hence commutes.

The transformation of an object by a parallel coherent diagram Γ may now be endeavoured. In order to preserve the semantics of the rules, as defined by the direct transformations in Γ, anything that is removed by some direct transformation should be removed from the input G, and everything that is added to G by some direct transformation should still be added to G.

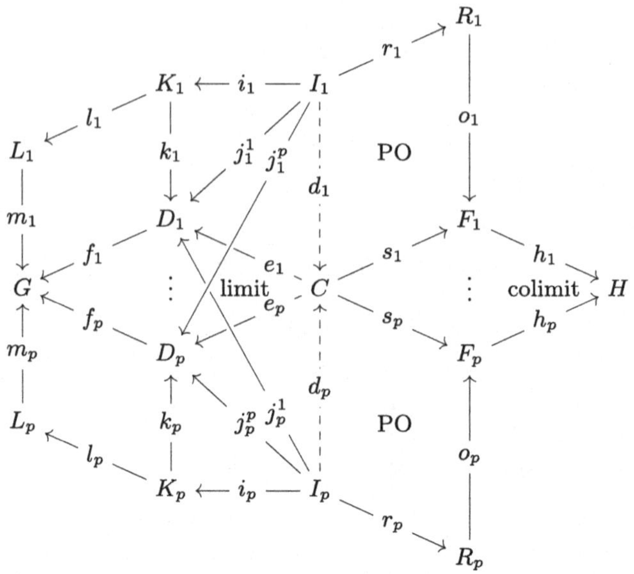

Fig. 2. A parallel coherent transformation (or PCT)

Definition 3. *For any object G of $\mathcal{C}$ and Γ a parallel coherent diagram for G,* a parallel coherent transformation (or PCT) *of G by Γ is a diagram as in Fig. 2 where:*

- $(C, e_1, \ldots, e_p)$ *is a limit of* $(f_1, \ldots, f_p, G)$*; C is called the* common context *of the PCT,*
- *for all* $1 \leqslant c \leqslant p$, $d_c : I_c \to C$ *is the unique morphism such that for all* $1 \leqslant a \leqslant p$, $j_c^a = e_a \circ d_c$,
- *for all* $1 \leqslant a \leqslant p$, (s_a, o_a, F_a) *is a pushout of* (I_a, r_a, d_a),
- $(h_1, \ldots, h_p, H)$ *is a colimit of* $(C, s_1, \ldots, s_p)$*; H is called the* result *of the PCT.*

If such a diagram exists we write $G \overset{\Gamma}{\Rightarrow} H$.

It is easy to see that H can actually be defined as the colimit of the diagram $(C \xleftarrow{d_a} I_a \xrightarrow{r_a} R_a)_{a=1}^{p}$, hence the objects F_a could be dispensed with.

If $p = 1$ then C is isomorphic to D_1 and therefore F_1 and H are isomorphic to H_1 (the result of the direct transformation γ_1). This means that the PCT is a conservative extension of direct transformations, which is obviously a necessary property of parallelism.

When $p > 1$, the left part of the direct transformations γ_a are preserved, but generally not their results H_a. This is not surprising since the results of the direct transformations cannot generally be preserved in a parallel transformation (unless they all yield the same result, a rather dull restriction). However, the result H of a PCT does contain images of the right-hand sides R_a, and more precisely of pushouts along morphisms r_a, as is the case in direct transformations. Hence the semantics of the individual rules is preserved as much as possible in PCTs: this is why these rules can be said to be applied *in parallel.* This also means that in practice it is not necessary to compute the pushouts H_a.

Example 1. Let us consider the following span in the category of graphs

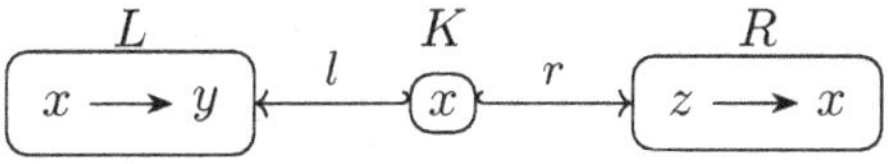

where the hooked arrows are canonical injections, x and y are vertices and the graph arrows are not named since their image by graph morphisms will be uniquely determined by the image of their adjacent vertices. As mentioned in Sect. 2, this span is a weak span ρ with $K = I$ and $i = \mathrm{id}_K$. The left-hand side L has exactly two matches in the graph $G = b \longrightarrow a \longleftarrow c$. Consider the following direct transformation γ_1 of G by ρ:

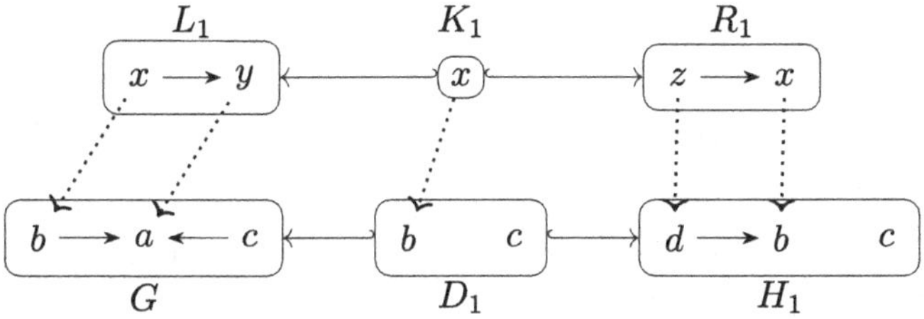

where the dotted arrows indicate the images of vertices by the morphisms that are not canonical injections, i.e., m_1, k_1 and n_1. In the left part, the vertex a and its two adjacent arrows are removed, in the right part a vertex d and an arrow from d to b are added. This direct transformation is a Sesqui-pushout [10].

Let us next consider the following direct transformation γ_2 of G by ρ:

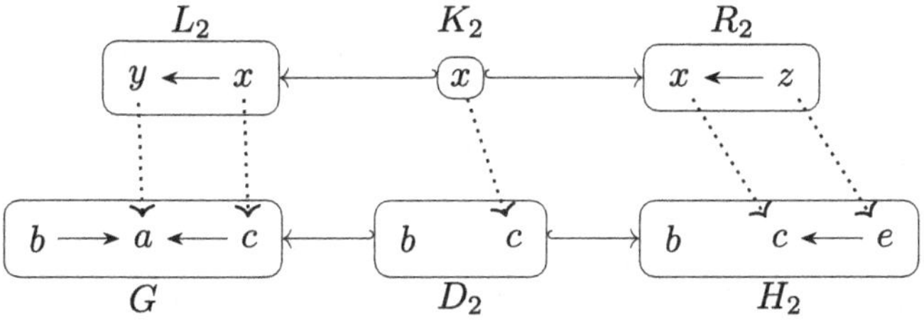

Let $j_1^2 : K_1 \to D_2$ defined by $j_1^2(x) = b$, then $f_2 \circ j_1^2(x) = b = f_1 \circ k_1(x)$. Similarly, let $j_2^1 : K_2 \to D_1$ defined by $j_2^1(x) = c$, then $f_1 \circ j_2^1(x) = c = f_2 \circ k_2(x)$, hence γ_1 and γ_2 are parallel coherent. The following diagram is a PCT of G by γ_1, γ_2.

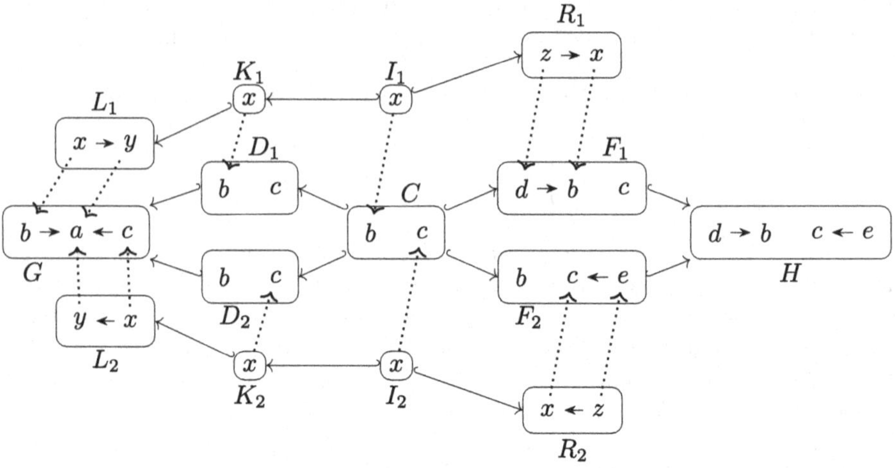

Since $D_1 = D_2 = C$ then $F_1 = H_1$ (the result of γ_1) and $F_2 = H_2$.

Note that in Definition 3, Γ being given, the existence of a PCT diagram depends on the existence of the limit C, the pushouts F_a and the colimit H. Since H may not exist, the existence of a parallel coherent diagram Γ is a necessary but by no means a sufficient condition for the existence of a PCT. Two direct derivations may be parallel coherent and still be incompatible, say by writing two different labels on a node that can take at most one. Parallel coherence only involves the left-hand parts of the input derivations.

4 PCTs in the Theory of Adhesive HLR Categories

In this section we assume a class of monomorphisms $\mathcal{M}$ of $\mathcal{C}$ that confers $(\mathcal{C}, \mathcal{M})$ a structure of adhesive HLR category. The rather long definition of this concept is not given here; it can be found in [17]. In the results below only the following properties of adhesive HLR categories are used. (Others are used in the missing proofs that can be found in [5].)

1. $\mathcal{M}$ contains all isomorphisms, is closed under composition and under decomposition, i.e., if $g \circ f \in \mathcal{M}$ and $g \in \mathcal{M}$ then $f \in \mathcal{M}$.
2. There are pushouts and pullbacks along morphisms in $\mathcal{M}$, and $\mathcal{M}$ is closed under pushouts and pullbacks, i.e., if $f \in \mathcal{M}$ then there is a pushout square

$$\begin{array}{ccc} A & \xrightarrow{f} & B \\ \downarrow & & \downarrow \\ C & \xrightarrow{f'} & D \end{array}$$

and for all such pushout squares we have $f' \in \mathcal{M}$; similarly if $f' \in \mathcal{M}$ then there is a pullback square and $f \in \mathcal{M}$ for all such squares.

In this theory, the morphisms in production rules are elements of $\mathcal{M}$, and the direct derivations are Double Pushouts.

Definition 4. *An* $\mathcal{M}$-weak span ρ *is a weak span whose morphisms* l, i, r *belong to* $\mathcal{M}$. *Similarly, an* $\mathcal{M}$-span *is a span where* $l, r \in \mathcal{M}$. *The* associated span $\check{\rho}$ *of* ρ *is the diagram* $L \xleftarrow{l} K \xrightarrow{r'} R'$ *where* (i', r', R') *is a pushout of* (I, i, r).

The associated span always exists and is an $\mathcal{M}$-span by the closure properties of $\mathcal{M}$. This association is reflected in the following equivalence of direct derivations.

Lemma 1. *For all objects* G, H *of* $\mathcal{C}$ *and* $\mathcal{M}$*-weak span* ρ*, we have*

$$\exists \gamma \in \Delta^{\mathrm{PO}}(G, \rho) \text{ s.t. } G \overset{\gamma}{\Rightarrow} H \quad \text{iff} \quad \exists \delta \in \Delta^{\mathrm{PO}}(G, \check{\rho}) \text{ s.t. } G \overset{\delta}{\Rightarrow} H.$$

Proof. Only if part. Since $r \in \mathcal{M}$ there exists a pushout (g, n, H) of $(I, r, k \circ i)$, then $n \circ r = g \circ k \circ i$, hence there is a unique morphism $n' : R' \to H$ such that $n' \circ i' = n$ and $n' \circ r' = g \circ k$. By pushout decomposition (g, n', H) is a pushout of (K, r', k).

$$\begin{array}{ccccc}
 & & I & \xrightarrow{r} & R \\
 & & \downarrow{\scriptstyle i} & & \downarrow{\scriptstyle i'} \\
L & \xleftarrow{l} & K & \xrightarrow{r'} & R' \quad n \\
\downarrow{\scriptstyle m} & & \downarrow{\scriptstyle k} & & \downarrow{\scriptstyle n'} \\
G & \xleftarrow{f} & D & \xrightarrow{g} & H
\end{array}$$

If part. Since $r \in \mathcal{M}$ then $r' \in \mathcal{M}$ and hence there exists a pushout (g, n', H) of (K, r', k), then by pushout composition $(g, n' \circ i', H)$ is a pushout of $(I, r, k \circ i)$. □

This lemma suggests that weak spans can be analyzed with respect to the properties of their associated spans, on which a wealth of results is known.

Definition 5. *For any* $\mathcal{M}$*-weak span* ρ*, object* G *and* $\gamma \in \Delta^{\mathrm{PO}}(G, \rho)$*, let* $\check{\gamma} \in \Delta^{\mathrm{PO}}(G, \check{\rho})$ *be the diagram built from* γ *in the proof of Lemma 1.*

Given $\mathcal{M}$*-weak spans* ρ_1 *and* ρ_2*, an object* G *of* $\mathcal{C}$ *and direct transformations* $\gamma_1 \in \Delta^{\mathrm{PO}}(G, \rho_1)$ *and* $\gamma_2 \in \Delta^{\mathrm{PO}}(G, \rho_2)$*,* γ_1 *and* γ_2 *are* parallel independent *if* $\check{\gamma}_1$ *and* $\check{\gamma}_2$ *are parallel independent, i.e., if there exist morphisms* $j_1 : L_1 \to D_2$ *and* $j_2 : L_2 \to D_1$ *such that* $f_2 \circ j_1 = m_1$ *and* $f_1 \circ j_2 = m_2$.

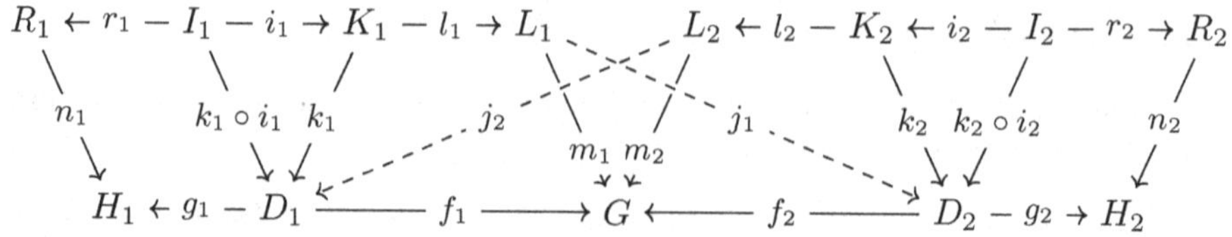

Given direct transformations $\gamma_1 \in \Delta^{\mathrm{PO}}(G, \rho_1)$ *such that* $G \overset{\gamma_1}{\Longrightarrow} H_1$ *and* $\gamma_2 \in \Delta^{\mathrm{PO}}(H_1, \rho_2)$ *(with* $H_1 \overset{\gamma_2}{\Longrightarrow} H_2$*),* γ_1 *and* γ_2 *are* sequential independent *if* $\check{\gamma}_1$ *and* $\check{\gamma}_2$ *are sequential independent, i.e., if there exist morphisms* $j_1' : R_1' \to D_2$ *and* $j_2' : L_2 \to D_1$ *such that* $f_2 \circ j_1' = n_1$ *and* $g_1 \circ j_2' = m_2$*.*

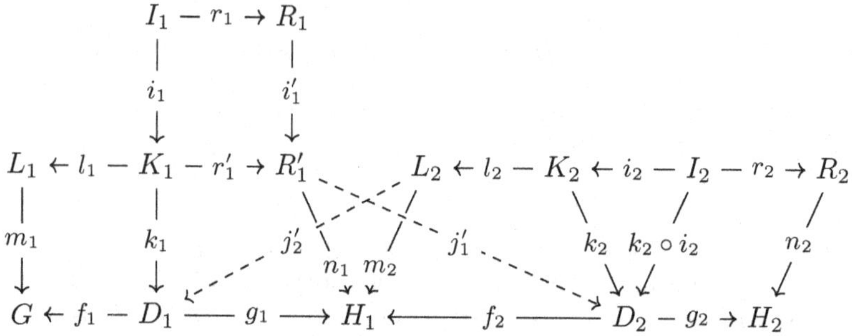

It is obvious that if $\gamma_1 \in \Delta^{\mathrm{PO}}(G, \rho_1)$ and $\gamma_2 \in \Delta^{\mathrm{PO}}(G, \rho_2)$ are parallel independent then they are also parallel coherent, and therefore there is a parallel coherent diagram Γ corresponding to γ_1 and γ_2 with $j_1^2 = j_1 \circ l_1 \circ i_1$ and $j_2^1 = j_2 \circ l_2 \circ i_2$. In the sequel, such diagram Γ will be written (γ_1, γ_2).

Theorem 1 (Independent Parallelism Theorem). *For any* $\mathcal{M}$*-weak spans* ρ_1*,* ρ_2*, objects* G*,* H_1*,* H *and direct transformation* $\gamma_1 \in \Delta^{\mathrm{PO}}(G, \rho_1)$ *such that* $G \overset{\gamma_1}{\Longrightarrow} H_1$*, then*

1. *(analysis) to any* $\gamma_2 \in \Delta^{\mathrm{PO}}(G, \rho_2)$ *such that* γ_1, γ_2 *are parallel independent and* $G \overset{(\gamma_1,\gamma_2)}{\Longrightarrow} H$*, is associated a* $\gamma_2' \in \Delta^{\mathrm{PO}}(H_1, \rho_2)$ *such that* $G \overset{\gamma_1}{\Longrightarrow} H_1 \overset{\gamma_2'}{\Longrightarrow} H$ *is sequential independent,*
2. *(synthesis) to any* $\gamma_2' \in \Delta^{\mathrm{PO}}(H_1, \rho_2)$ *such that* $G \overset{\gamma_1}{\Longrightarrow} H_1 \overset{\gamma_2'}{\Longrightarrow} H$ *is sequential independent is associated a* $\gamma_2 \in \Delta^{\mathrm{PO}}(G, \rho_2)$ *such that* γ_1, γ_2 *are parallel independent and* $G \overset{(\gamma_1,\gamma_2)}{\Longrightarrow} H$*,*
3. *and these two correspondences are inverse to each other up to isomorphism.*

This means that a PCT of G by two parallel independent direct transformations yields a result that can be obtained by a sequence of two direct transformations, in any order (they are sequential independent). This can be interpreted as a result of correctness of PCTs w.r.t. the standard approach to (independent) parallelism of algebraic graph transformations. In this sense, parallel coherence is a conservative extension of parallel independence. Note that Theorem 1 generalizes the standard Parallelism Theorem [17] in two ways: it applies to Weak Double-Pushouts and, by using PCTs rather than coproducts, it dispenses with the hypothesis that $\mathcal{C}$ has coproducts compatible with $\mathcal{M}$, i.e., such that $f + g \in \mathcal{M}$ whenever $f, g \in \mathcal{M}$.

The next result is connected to the notions of *derived span* of a sequence of direct transformations, that is a shortcut for the sequence (see, e.g., [11, Theorem 3.6.3]). Similarly, it is possible to give a shortcut for a PCT as defined below.

Definition 6. *For all objects G, H and weak-spans ρ, we write $G \vdash_\rho H$ if there exists a diagram $\gamma \in \Delta^{\mathrm{PO}}(G, \rho)$ such that $G \overset{\gamma}{\Rightarrow} H$. We write $G \Vdash_{\mathcal{R}} H$ if there exists a parallel coherent diagram Γ with $\gamma_1, \ldots, \gamma_p \in \Delta^{\mathrm{PO}}(G, \mathcal{R})$ such that $G \overset{\Gamma}{\Rightarrow} H$.*

*Given a binary relation $\vdash$ between objects of $\mathcal{C}$ and G, H such that $G \vdash H$, we call $\vdash$-*derived rule *of G, H any span σ in $\mathcal{C}$ such that $G \vdash_\sigma H$ and for all objects G', H' of $\mathcal{C}$, if $G' \vdash_\sigma H'$ then $G' \vdash H'$.*

Note that if σ is an $\mathcal{M}$-span then it is also an $\mathcal{M}$-weak span since id_K is an isomorphism and hence belongs to $\mathcal{M}$.

By Lemma 1, for every $\mathcal{M}$-weak span ρ and every objects G, H such that $G \vdash_\rho H$, the associated span $\check{\rho}$ is a $\vdash_\rho$-derived rule of G, H. The span $\check{\rho}$ does not depend on G or H, but this is not generally true for derived rules.

Theorem 2. *For all sets $\mathcal{R}$ of $\mathcal{M}$-weak spans, all objects G, H, all parallel coherent diagrams Γ and parallel coherent transformations $G \overset{\Gamma}{\Rightarrow} H$, the $\mathcal{M}$-span $G \xleftarrow{f_1 \circ e_1} C \xrightarrow{h_1 \circ s_1} H$ is a $\Vdash_{\mathcal{R}}$-derived rule of G, H.*

Hence to any Double-Pushout direct transformation of any object G' by this derived rule corresponds a PCT of G' that yields the same result.

5 Finitely Attributed Structures

The problem of the construction of a category suitable for the example of Sects. 1 and 2 is now addressed, and more generally the construction of categories where PCTs are guaranteed to exist and can effectively be computed.

This example requires a category of graphs whose nodes can be labelled by zero or one attribute, namely a natural number. More importantly, we saw in Sect. 2 that morphisms l and r of both rules $(x := y)$ and $(y := x + y)$ map an unlabelled node to a labelled node, hence the notion of morphism cannot be strict on labels. This means that the notion of comma category, which is a standard tool for building categories of attributed structures, cannot be used. Another candidate is to use the notion of partially attributed structures, see [13], but the resulting category has few pushouts or colimits. The notion of attributes as special nodes of so-called E-graphs in [17] would better fit our purpose, but PCTs may add an uncontrollable number of edges to an attribute. A more convenient notion of labels as *sets* of attributes is therefore adopted. This notion encodes in a natural way partial attribution as empty sets and ensures the existence of pushouts and pullbacks (see Lemmas 2 and 3).

Another concern is the effective construction of PCTs, hence of finite limits and colimits, which requires to be scrupulous about the finiteness of all structures involved. This is particularly important since the attributes belong to infinite sets (e.g. natural numbers), which means that pullbacks of finite attributed graphs may require infinitely many nodes. The proofs of this section can be found in [6].

Definition 7. *Let $\mathcal{F}$ be a category with pushouts, pullbacks and a pushout-preserving functor $V : \mathcal{F} \to$ **FinSets**, where **FinSets** is the category of finite sets. Let $\mathcal{A}$ be a category with a functor $U : \mathcal{A} \to$ **Sets**. Let $\mathscr{P}_{<\omega} :$ **Sets** $\to$ **Sets** be the functor which to every set maps the set of its finite subsets. Let $\mathscr{I} :$ **FinSets** $\to$ **Sets** be the canonical injective functor. We write $\mathscr{E} \stackrel{\text{def}}{=} \mathscr{I} \circ V$ and $\mathscr{S} \stackrel{\text{def}}{=} \mathscr{P}_{<\omega} \circ U$.*

A finitely attributed structure *is a triple (F, A, f) where F, A are objects in $\mathcal{F}, \mathcal{A}$ respectively and $f : \mathscr{E}F \to \mathscr{S}A$ is a function (a morphism in* **Sets***). A* morphism of finitely attributed structures *from (F, A, f) to (G, B, g) is a pair (σ, α) where $\sigma : F \to G$ is a morphism in $\mathcal{F}$ and $\alpha : A \to B$ is a morphism in $\mathcal{A}$ such that $\forall u \in \mathscr{E}F, \mathscr{S}\alpha \circ f(u) \subseteq g \circ \mathscr{E}\sigma(u)$; it is* neutral *if $A = B$ and $\alpha = \mathrm{id}_A$. The identity morphism on (F, A, f) is the morphism $(\mathrm{id}_F, \mathrm{id}_A)$. The composition of morphisms $(\sigma, \alpha) : (F, A, f) \to (G, B, g)$ and $(\tau, \beta) : (G, B, g) \to (H, C, h)$ is $(\tau, \beta) \circ (\sigma, \alpha) \stackrel{\text{def}}{=} (\tau \circ \sigma, \beta \circ \alpha)$, that is easily seen to be a morphism from (F, A, f) to (H, C, h). We denote* **FinAttr**(V, U) *the category of finitely attributed structures.*

$$\begin{array}{ccccc}
\mathscr{E}F & \xrightarrow{\mathscr{E}\sigma} & \mathscr{E}G & \xrightarrow{\mathscr{E}\tau} & \mathscr{E}H \\
\downarrow f & \subseteq & \downarrow g & \subseteq & \downarrow h \\
\mathscr{S}A & \xrightarrow[\mathscr{S}\alpha]{} & \mathscr{S}B & \xrightarrow[\mathscr{S}\beta]{} & \mathscr{S}C
\end{array}$$

For all $v \in \mathscr{E}G$, we write $\mathscr{E}\sigma^{-1}(v) \stackrel{\text{def}}{=} \{u \in \mathscr{E}F \mid \mathscr{E}\sigma(u) = v\}$.

For instance, $\mathcal{F}$ can be the category of finite graphs and V be the functor that maps any finite graph $G = (V, E, s, t)$ to the direct sum $V + E$ in **FinSets**, hence $\mathscr{E}G$ is the set of "elements" of G. $\mathcal{A}$ can be the category of Σ-algebras for some signature Σ, and U the functor that maps any Σ-algebra A to its carrier set, hence $\mathscr{S}A$ contains the finite subsets of UA.

Lemma 2. *Let $(\sigma, \mathrm{id}_A) : (F, A, f) \to (G, A, g)$ be a neutral morphism and $(\tau, \alpha) : (F, A, f) \to (H, B, h)$ a morphism with the same domain, let (σ', τ', E) be a pushout of (F, σ, τ) in $\mathcal{F}$, then $((\tau', \alpha), (\sigma', \mathrm{id}_B), (E, B, e))$ is a pushout of $((F, A, f), (\sigma, \mathrm{id}_A), (\tau, \alpha))$, where for all $x \in \mathscr{E}E$,*

$$e(x) = \left(\bigcup_{v \in \mathscr{E}\tau'^{-1}(x)} \mathscr{S}\alpha \circ g(v) \right) \cup \left(\bigcup_{w \in \mathscr{E}\sigma'^{-1}(x)} \mathscr{S}\mathrm{id}_B \circ h(w) \right).$$

Corollary 1. *For all integers* $p \geqslant 1$, *if* $s_a : C \to F_a$ *is a neutral morphism for all* $1 \leqslant a \leqslant p$, *then there exists a colimit* $(h_1, \ldots, h_p, H)$ *of* $(C, s_1, \ldots, s_p)$ *such that* $h_1, \ldots, h_p$ *are neutral morphisms.*

Contrary to pushouts, the construction of pullbacks has to be restricted to the case where both morphisms are neutral.

Lemma 3. *Let* $(\sigma, \mathrm{id}_A) : (G, A, g) \to (F, A, f)$ *and* $(\tau, \mathrm{id}_A) : (H, A, h) \to (F, A, f)$ *be morphisms and let* (E, σ', τ') *be a pullback of* (σ, τ, F) *in* $\mathcal{F}$, *then* $((E, A, e), (\sigma', \mathrm{id}_A), (\tau', \mathrm{id}_A))$ *is a pullback of* $((\sigma, \mathrm{id}_A), (\tau, \mathrm{id}_A), (F, A, f))$, *where for all* $x \in \mathscr{E}E$, $e(x) = g \circ \mathscr{E}\tau'(x) \cap h \circ \mathscr{E}\sigma'(x)$.

Corollary 2. *For all integers* $p \geqslant 1$, *if* $f_a : D_a \to G$ *is a neutral morphism for all* $1 \leqslant a \leqslant p$, *then there exists a limit* $(C, e_1, \ldots, e_p)$ *of* $(f_1, \ldots, f_p, G)$ *such that* $e_1, \ldots, e_p$ *are neutral morphisms.*

With these constructions and their restrictions on morphisms, only transformations of finitely attributed structures that preserve the object A in which the labels are chosen (e.g. the set of natural numbers) can be achieved. This is of course convenient to the example of Sect. 2, and could be considered sensible in practice.

Definition 8. *A weak span* ρ *in* $\mathbf{FinAttr}(V, U)$ *is* neutral *if its morphisms* l, i *and* r *are neutral. For any object* G, *a direct transformation* $\gamma \in \Delta(G, \rho)$ *is* neutral *if* ρ *and its morphisms* f *and* g *are neutral. Let* $\Delta_{\mathrm{n}}(G, \rho)$ *be the set of neutral direct transformations of* G *by* ρ.

Note that it is not required of l, i and r to be monomorphisms as in Sect. 4.

Theorem 3. *For any set* $\mathcal{R}$ *of neutral weak spans in* $\mathbf{FinAttr}(V, U)$, *for any object* G *and parallel coherent diagram* Γ *where* $\gamma_1, \ldots, \gamma_p \in \Delta_{\mathrm{n}}(G, \mathcal{R})$, *there exists an object* H, *unique up to isomorphism, such that* $G \overset{\Gamma}{\Longrightarrow} H$.

Proof. Let us prove that a PCT of G by Γ can be constructed (see Definition 3). By hypothesis the f_a's are neutral for all $1 \leqslant a \leqslant p$, hence by Corollary 2 there exists a limit $(C, e_1, \ldots, e_p)$ of $(f_1, \ldots, f_p, G)$, unique up to isomorphism. As r_a is neutral, by Lemma 2 there exist pushouts (s_a, o_a, F_a) of (I_a, r_a, d_a) where the s_a's are neutral for all $1 \leqslant a \leqslant p$, and they are unique up to isomorphism. By Corollary 1 there exists a colimit $(h_1, \ldots, h_p, H)$ of $(C, s_1, \ldots, s_p)$, and it is unique up to isomorphism. □

A related issue relevant to the Double-Pushout approach is the existence of pushout complements. Provided that a pushout complement exist in $\mathcal{F}$, it is easy to compute at least one pushout complement in $\mathbf{FinAttr}(V, U)$, as seen in the following result.

Theorem 4. *Let $(\sigma, \mathrm{id}_A) : (F, A, f) \to (G, A, g)$ and $(\tau', \alpha) : (G, A, g) \to (E, B, e)$ be two morphisms in* $\mathbf{FinAttr}(V, U)$*, if the left square below is a pushout in $\mathcal{F}$ then so is the right square in* $\mathbf{FinAttr}(V, U)$*, where for all $w \in \mathscr{E}H$*

$$h(w) = (e \circ \mathscr{E}\sigma'(w) \setminus k(w)) \cup \bigcup_{u \in \mathscr{E}\tau^{-1}(w)} \mathscr{S}\alpha \circ f(u)$$

$$\text{with } k(w) \subseteq \bigcup_{v \in \mathscr{E}\tau'^{-1} \circ \mathscr{E}\sigma'(w)} \mathscr{S}\alpha \circ g(v).$$

$$\begin{array}{ccc} F & \xrightarrow{\sigma} & G \\ {\scriptstyle\tau}\downarrow & & \downarrow{\scriptstyle\tau'} \\ H & \xrightarrow{\sigma'} & E \end{array} \qquad \begin{array}{ccc} (F, A, f) & \xrightarrow{(\sigma, \mathrm{id}_A)} & (G, A, g) \\ {\scriptstyle(\tau, \alpha)}\downarrow & & \downarrow{\scriptstyle(\tau', \alpha)} \\ (H, B, h) & \xrightarrow{(\sigma', \mathrm{id}_B)} & (E, B, e) \end{array}$$

In practice it seems sensible to choose the smallest possible sets for $h(w)$, and hence to take $k(w) = \bigcup_{v \in \mathscr{E}\tau'^{-1} \circ \mathscr{E}\sigma'(w)} \mathscr{S}\alpha \circ g(v)$. This result also shows that $\mathbf{FinAttr}(V, U)$ may not be an adhesive HLR category (where pushout complements are unique), hence that PCTs exist in a larger class of categories than those considered in Sect. 4.

6 Examples

All the necessary tools are now available to develop in detail the example of Sects. 1 and 2.

Example 2. As suggested above, let $\mathcal{F}$ be the category of finite graphs and $\mathcal{A}$ be the category of Σ-algebras, where $\Sigma = \{+\}$ and $+$ is a binary function symbol. Among the objects of $\mathcal{A}$ only the standard Σ-algebra $\mathbb{N}$ and the algebra of Σ-terms on the set of variables $\{u, v\}$, here denoted T, need to be considered. The objects (F, A, f) of $\mathbf{FinAttr}(V, U)$ will be depicted as graphs indexed by A, and since the attributes of nodes will only be $\varnothing$ or singletons[1], and the attributes of arrows always $\varnothing$, nodes will be represented by circles containing either nothing or an element of A (as in Sect. 2). The morphisms (σ, α) will only be specified as α since the graph morphism σ from the domain to the codomain's graphs will either be unique or specified by a dotted arrow (except for the j morphisms). Let $m : T \to \mathbb{N}$ be the morphism in $\mathcal{A}$ such that $m(u) = 1$ and $m(v) = 2$.

The finitely attributed graph $G = (1) \to (2)_{\mathbb{N}}$ corresponds to a correct state, and the transformations γ_1 and γ_2 of Fig. 1 can be interpreted as diagrams in $\mathbf{FinAttr}(V, U)$. They are obviously parallel coherent, hence a PCT of G by $\{\gamma_1, \gamma_2\}$ can be constructed, as illustrated in Fig. 3 top. The pushouts and pullbacks are computed as in Lemmas 2 and 3. The result of this transformation is the finitely attributed graph $(2) \to (3)_{\mathbb{N}}$ that corresponds to a correct state.

[1] This property is not generally true, but happens to be true in this example.

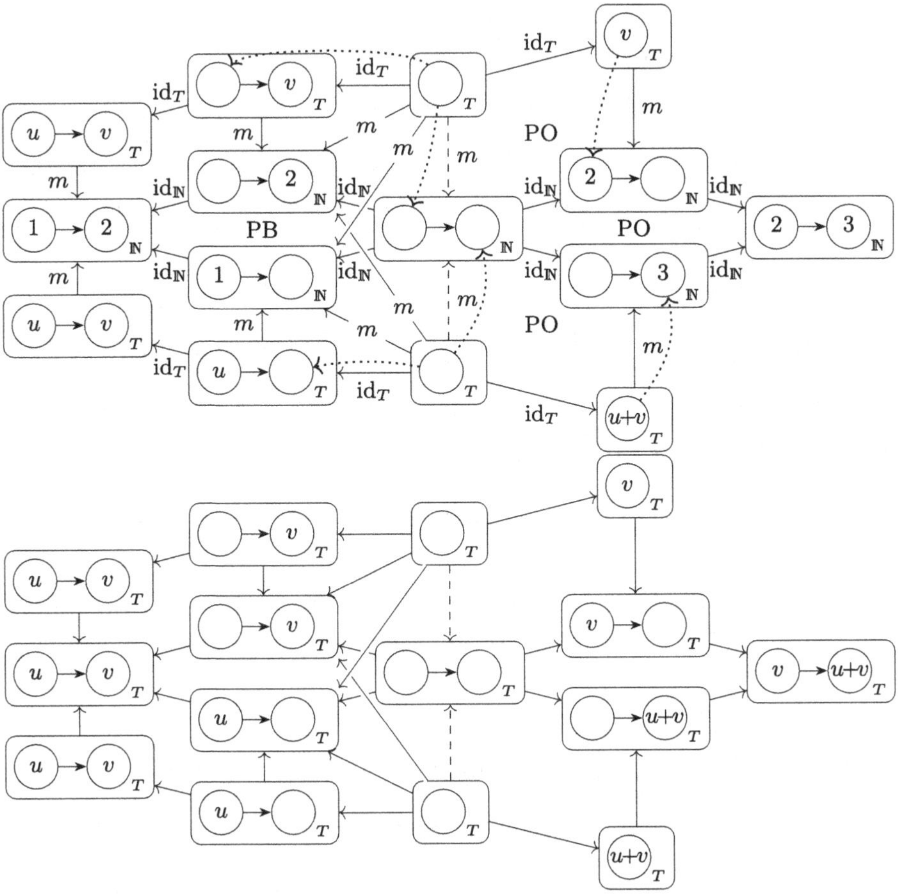

Fig. 3. Two parallel coherent transformations

Observe that these rules (weak spans) have the same left-hand side L. The generality of the algebraic approach thus allows us to apply both rules to L, which again yields parallel coherent direct transformations and hence the PCT given in Fig. 3 bottom (all morphisms are labelled by id_T, hence are omitted, as are dotted arrows since they are the same as above). From this PCT the following derived rule can be extracted, which describes the PCT as a single graph transformation rule, already mentioned in Sect. 1. Note however that Theorem 2 has been proven in the theory of adhesive HLR categories and not in $\mathbf{FinAttr}(V, U)$.

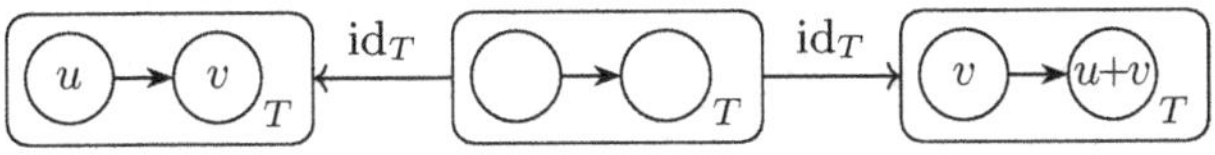

Another important class of examples is provided by cellular automata, where the states of cells at a given generation are computed in parallel from the states of the previous generation. The local transitions may not be independent from each other, as the following example illustrates.

Example 3. The Hex-Ulam-Warburton automaton, see [22], has the same rule as the Ulam-Warburton automaton, namely that a new cell is born if it is adjacent to exactly one live cell, but it grows in the hexagonal grid. The first generations are depicted in Fig. 4, and give rise to nice fractal structures as shown in [22].

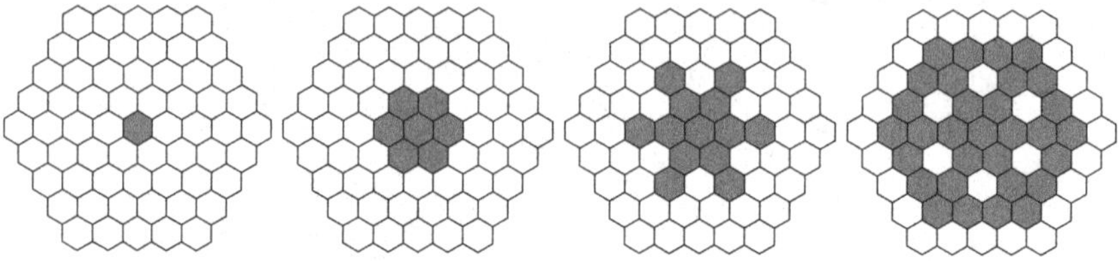

Fig. 4. Generations 0, 1, 2 and 3 of the Hex-Ulam-Warburton automaton

The six transitions that yield Generation 1 and the 24 that yield Generation 3 are not independent since they cannot be obtained sequentially. In contrast, the 6 transitions that yield Generation 2 are independent and can be produced in any order.

In this framework the dead cells are labelled by a singleton, say $\{0\}$ (represented by ⬡), live cells by another singleton, say $\{1\}$ (represented by ⬢), and cells labelled by $\varnothing$ (represented by ⬡) are also needed, hence let $\mathcal{A}$ be the category with one object $\{0,1\}$ and its identity morphism (all morphisms of finitely attributed structures are therefore neutral). Assuming for $\mathcal{F}$ a category of finite hexagonal grids where morphisms map adjacent cells to adjacent cells (or equivalently, a morphism is a translation followed by a rotation of $\frac{k\pi}{3}$ for some $k \in \mathbb{Z}_6$), the state transitions can be represented by the following weak span

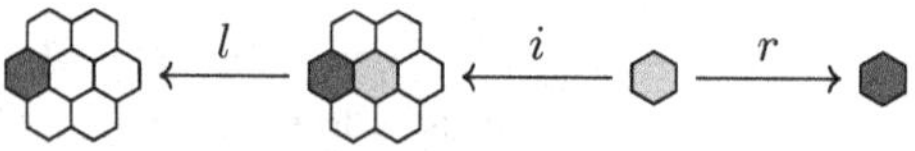

where i maps the cell of I to the center cell of K. There are exactly 6 matchings $m_1, \ldots, m_6$ of L in Generation 0, centered on the 6 cells adjacent to the live cell and rotated by $\frac{k\pi}{3}$ for $k = 0, \ldots, 5$ respectively. Hence there are 6 direct transformations $\gamma_1, \ldots, \gamma_6$ (not depicted) of Generation 0 that yield the PCT in Fig. 5 (where only the matchings m_1 and m_6 are depicted).

Note that morphism j_1^6 maps the cell of I to the dead cell (not the empty cell) of D_6 adjacent to the east border of its live cell, and similarly j_6^1 maps the cell of I to the cell of D_1 adjacent to the south east border of its live cell, which proves that the pair γ_1, γ_6 is parallel coherent, and for reasons of symmetry the diagram constituted of $\gamma_1, \ldots, \gamma_6$ and the morphisms j_a^b is parallel coherent.

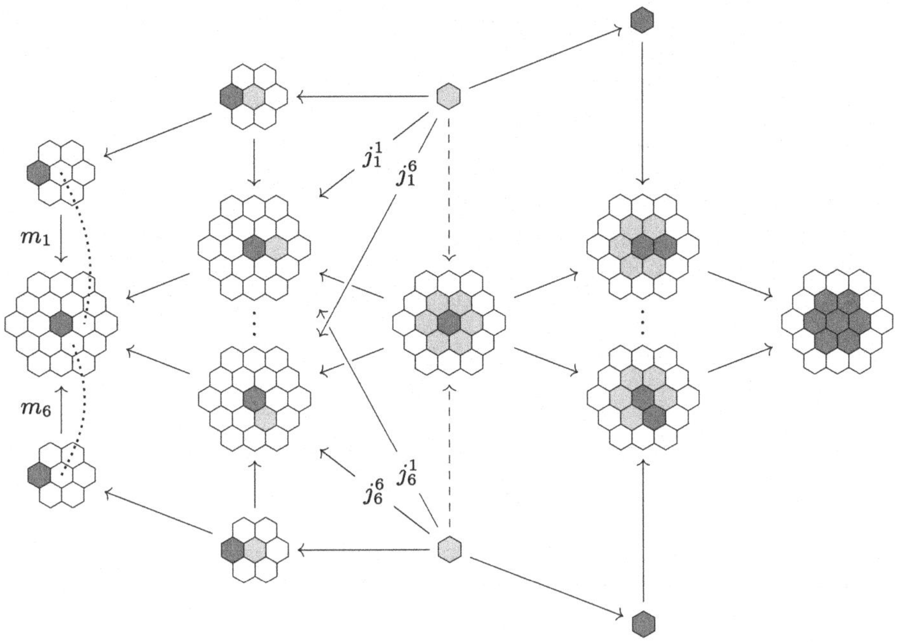

Fig. 5. The parallel coherent transformation of Generation 0

Cellular automata are models of computation that involve infinite cells (located on an infinite grid $\mathbb{Z}^d$) and each configuration involves infinite transitions. Representing such transformations by means of PCTs implies infinite parallel coherent diagrams. It is of course possible to extend Definition 3 accordingly (see [1, 11.3] for the general definition of a limit). It would then be easy to prove that cellular automata can be represented by PCTs, with a single production rule (see also [4, Theorem 6.3]).

A similar idea has been proposed in [25] by using edge-labelled graphs and rules with positive context where the state of cells are encoded by the label of loops. Rules with positive context seem very close to weak-spans, the only difference is the way direct transformations are defined. We consider here only the DPO approach.

Definition 9. *A* rule with positive context *(or* PC-rule*) is a diagram*

$$P \xleftarrow{p} L \xleftarrow{l} K \xrightarrow{r} R$$

in $\mathcal{C}$. Given an object G of $\mathcal{C}$ and a PC-rule π, a direct transformation of G *by π is a commuting diagram*

$$\begin{array}{ccccccc}
P & \xleftarrow{p} & L & \xleftarrow{l} & K & \xrightarrow{r} & R \\
& \searrow^{m'} & \downarrow m & PO & \downarrow k & PO & \downarrow n \\
& & G & \xleftarrow{f} & D & \xrightarrow{g} & H
\end{array}$$

One benefit of PC-rules is that they can be seen as standard span rules together with a very simple form of positive application condition, for which a wealth of results are known, see, e.g., [17, chapter 7]. However, the positive context P may prevent a pushout complement to exist, as we now illustrate.

Example 4. Consider the following weak span

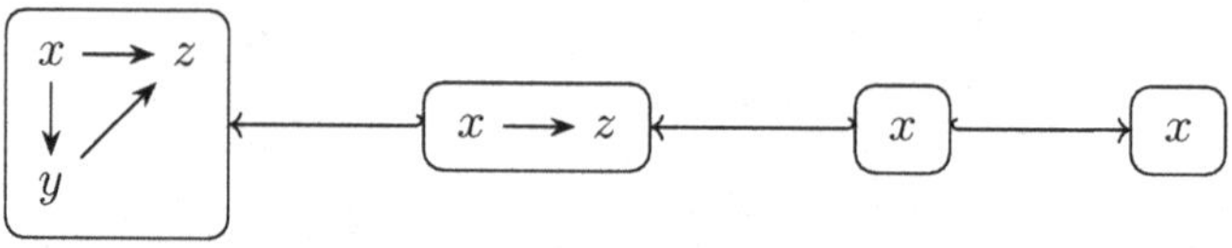

that deletes y (and its two adjacent arrows) and preserves x, leaving z to be possibly deleted by another rule. The corresponding PC-rule should be

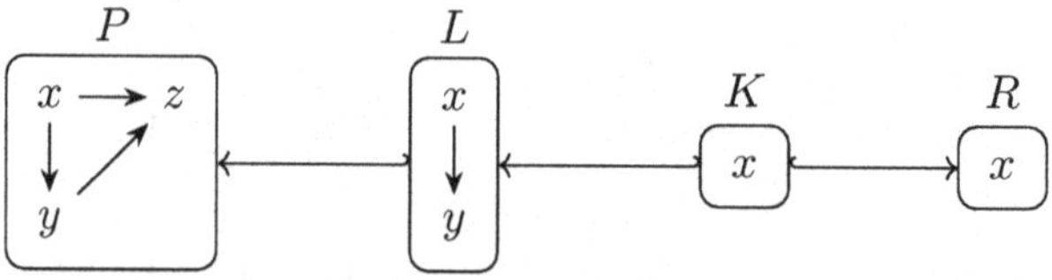

since the deletion of y is enforced by the middle morphism. But this PC-rule can only be applied to a graph G that has an arrow leaving the node matched to y, which therefore cannot be deleted according to the *gluing condition* (see e.g. [17]) by which nodes can only be deleted if *all* adjacent arrows are explicitly deleted. In fact, this PC-rule cannot by applied to P with the matching id_P (for lack of a pushout complement), a problem that never happens with weak-spans, nor indeed with spans.

We therefore see that PCTs generalize cellular automata by allowing not only to modify the state of cells but also their neighborhood frame, and also to delete, merge, create cells, and even to clone cells, as we now illustrate.

Example 5. In the previous examples the morphisms involved in weak spans are always monomorphisms. Non injective morphisms can be used for cloning vertices, and this can also be parallelized as is now illustrated. Let γ_1 be the following direct transformation,

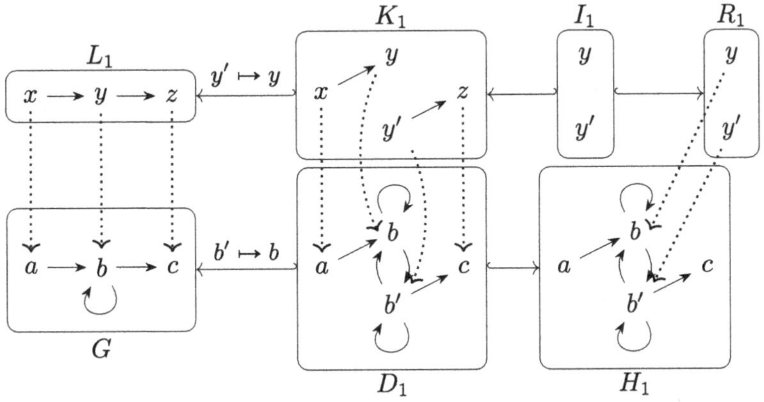

where canonical injections are extended by the indicated function, e.g., $l_1(x) = x$, $l_1(y) = y$, $l_1(z) = z$ and $l_1(y') = y$. This transformation is a Sesqui-pushout, see [10]: D_1 is the final pullback complement of $G \xleftarrow{m_1} L_1 \xleftarrow{l_1} K_1$, which means that it is the largest graph such that the left square is a pullback.

Let γ_2 be the following direct transformation of G.

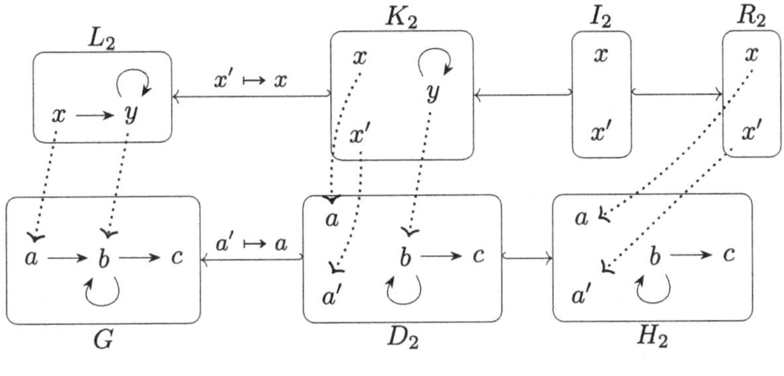

It is easy to see that there is no morphism $j_1 : L_1 \to D_2$ such that $f_2 \circ j_1 = m_1$, hence γ_1 and γ_2 are not parallel independent. But they are parallel coherent: let $j_1^2 : I_1 \to D_2$ be defined by $j_1^2(y) = j_1^2(y') = b$, and let $j_2^1 : I_2 \to D_1$ be defined by $j_2^1(x) = j_2^1(x') = a$, we have $f_2 \circ j_1^2 = f_1 \circ k_1 \circ i_1$ and $f_1 \circ j_2^1 = f_2 \circ k_2 \circ i_2$. A PCT can therefore be built from $\gamma_1, \gamma_2, j_1^2, j_2^1$. Since $I_1 = R_1$ and $r_1 = \mathrm{id}_{I_1}$, then $o_1 = d_1$, $F_1 = C$ and $s_1 = \mathrm{id}_C$. Similarly $s_2 = \mathrm{id}_C$ and therefore $H = C$; the result of the PCT is the common context and is easy to compute as the pullback of (f_1, f_2, G).

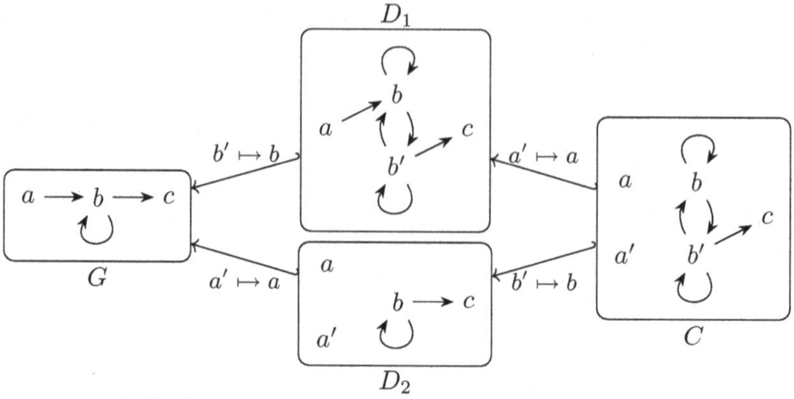

We therefore see that the cloning of a performed by one rule and the cloning of b performed by the other rule can be performed in parallel by means of a PCT.

We also see that, with $j_2 : L_2 \to D_1$ defined by $j_2(x) = a$ and $j_2(y) = b$ we have $f_1 \circ j_2 = m_2$. This means that the second rule can be applied to the result H_1 of γ_1; this yields a direct transformation γ_2'. The reader may check that the result of γ_2' is exactly the result of the PCT. In this sense, this PCT yields a correct result.

7 Conclusion and Related Work

Parallel graph rewriting has already been considered in the literature. In the mid-seventies, H. Ehrig and H.-J. Kreowski [18] tackled the problem of parallel graph transformations and introduced the notion of parallel independence. This pioneering work has been considered for several algebraic graph transformation approaches, see [16] as well as the more recent contributions [7,25,26]. At almost the same period, parallel graph transformations has been used as an extension of L-systems [29,31] as was proposed in, e.g., [12]. This stream of work departs drastically from the present one, where parallel derivations are not meant to be sequentialized.

In [27, chapter 14], parallel graph transformations have been studied in order to improve the operational semantics of the functional programming language CLEAN [21], where parallelism is considered under an interleaving semantics of parallelism. Such is the case of other frameworks [15,24,25] where massive parallel graph transformations are defined in order to simulate sequential rewriting.

Non independent parallelism has been considered in the Double-Pushout approach, see e.g. [30] where rules can be amalgamated by agreeing on common deletions and creations. This approach is formulated on span rules where the notion of parallel coherence loses much of its expressive power. Besides, amalgamation may not preserve the semantics of the rules that are amalgamated, in the sense that an item that should be deleted according to an input rule and a matching may not be deleted by an amalgamated rule.

In [23], a framework based on the algebraic Single-Pushout approach has been proposed where conflicts between parallel transformations are allowed but requires the user to solve them by providing the right control flow.

The present work stems from [4] where an algorithmic framework is proposed for rule-based deterministic parallel transformations of graphs whose vertices and arrows are mapped to sets of attributes. The rules are triples (L, K, R) where K is a subgraph of L and the intersection of L and R (that stands for the object I in a weak span) is a subgraph of K. Parallel coherence is replaced with a more general *effective deletion property* that distinguishes graph items (vertices and arrows) from attributes. It is shown that every cellular automaton can be represented by a single rule and a class of infinite graphs that correspond to configurations of the automaton (where cells are vertices attributed with a state), so that the parallel transformations of these graphs is the transition function of the automaton.

The introduction of the notion of weak span is key in our contribution which gives a new insight in the study of parallel graph transformation. Particularly, the object D in Definition 1 could be constructed following different algebraic methods such as DPO [19] or SqPO [10]. Extension to recent approaches such as AGREE [8] or PBPO [9] is rather straightforward. This opens the possibility to integrate, in one parallel step, rules written in different approaches. Future work include further analysis of PCTs and particularly the development of dedicated verification techniques.

References

1. Adámek, J., Herrlich, H., Strecker, G.E.: Abstract and Concrete Categories - The Joy of Cats. John Wiley & Sons, Inc., Hoboken (1990)
2. Baader, F., Nipkow, T.: Term Rewriting and All That. Cambridge University Press, Cambridge (1998)
3. Book, R.V., Otto, F.: String-Rewriting Systems. Texts and Monographs in Computer Science, Springer (1993). https://doi.org/10.1007/978-1-4613-9771-7_3
4. Boy de la Tour, T., Echahed, R.: Parallel rewriting of attributed graphs. Theor. Comput. Sci. **848**, 106–132 (2020)
5. Boy de la Tour, T.: Parallelism theorem and derived rules for parallel coherent transformations. arXiv:1907.06585 (2019)
6. Boy de la Tour, T., Echahed, R.: True parallel graph transformations: an algebraic approach based on weak spans. arXiv:1904.08850 (2019)
7. Corradini, A., et al.: On the essence of parallel independence for the double-pushout and sesqui-pushout approaches. In: Heckel, R., Taentzer, G. (eds.) Graph Transformation, Specifications, and Nets. LNCS, vol. 10800, pp. 1–18. Springer, Cham (2018). https://doi.org/10.1007/978-3-319-75396-6_1
8. Corradini, A., Duval, D., Echahed, R., Prost, F., Ribeiro, L.: AGREE – algebraic graph rewriting with controlled embedding. In: Parisi-Presicce, F., Westfechtel, B. (eds.) ICGT 2015. LNCS, vol. 9151, pp. 35–51. Springer, Cham (2015). https://doi.org/10.1007/978-3-319-21145-9_3
9. Corradini, A., Duval, D., Echahed, R., Prost, F., Ribeiro, L.: The pullback-pushout approach to algebraic graph transformation. In: de Lara, J., Plump, D. (eds.) ICGT 2017. LNCS, vol. 10373, pp. 3–19. Springer, Cham (2017). https://doi.org/10.1007/978-3-319-61470-0_1

10. Corradini, A., Heindel, T., Hermann, F., König, B.: Sesqui-pushout rewriting. In: Corradini, A., Ehrig, H., Montanari, U., Ribeiro, L., Rozenberg, G. (eds.) ICGT 2006. LNCS, vol. 4178, pp. 30–45. Springer, Heidelberg (2006). https://doi.org/10.1007/11841883_4
11. Corradini, A., Montanari, U., Rossi, F., Ehrig, H., Heckel, R., Löwe, M.: Algebraic approaches to graph transformation - part I: basic concepts and double pushout approach. In: Rozenberg [28], pp. 163–246 (1997)
12. Culik II, K., Lindenmayer, A.: Parallel graph generating and recurrence systems for multicellular development. Int. J. Gen. Syst. **3**(1), 53–66 (1976)
13. Duval, D., Echahed, R., Prost, F., Ribeiro, L.: Transformation of attributed structures with cloning. In: Gnesi, S., Rensink, A. (eds.) FASE 2014. LNCS, vol. 8411, pp. 310–324. Springer, Heidelberg (2014). https://doi.org/10.1007/978-3-642-54804-8_22
14. Echahed, R.: Inductively sequential term-graph rewrite systems. In: Ehrig, H., Heckel, R., Rozenberg, G., Taentzer, G. (eds.) ICGT 2008. LNCS, vol. 5214, pp. 84–98. Springer, Heidelberg (2008). https://doi.org/10.1007/978-3-540-87405-8_7
15. Echahed, R., Janodet, J.-C.: Parallel admissible graph rewriting. In: Fiadeiro, J.L. (ed.) WADT 1998. LNCS, vol. 1589, pp. 122–138. Springer, Heidelberg (1999). https://doi.org/10.1007/3-540-48483-3_9
16. Ehrig, H., Kreowski, H.J., Montanari, U., Rozenberg, G. (eds.): Handbook of Graph Grammars and Computing by Graph Transformation, Volume 3: Concurrency, Parallelism and Distribution. World Scientific (1999)
17. Ehrig, H., Ehrig, K., Prange, U., Taentzer, G.: Fundamentals of Algebraic Graph Transformation. MTCSAES. Springer, Heidelberg (2006). https://doi.org/10.1007/3-540-31188-2
18. Ehrig, H., Kreowski, H.: Parallelism of manipulations in multidimensional information structures. In: Mathematical Foundations of Computer Science. LNCS, vol. 45, pp. 284–293. Springer (1976). https://doi.org/10.1007/3-540-07854-1
19. Ehrig, H., Pfender, M., Schneider, H.J.: Graph-grammars: an algebraic approach. In: 14th Annual Symposium on Switching and Automata Theory, pp. 167–180 (1973)
20. Engelfriet, J., Rozenberg, G.: Node replacement graph grammars. In: Rozenberg [28], pp. 1–94 (1997)
21. Group, S.T.R.: The Clean Home Page. Radboud University, Nijmegen, https://clean.cs.ru.nl/Clean
22. Khovanova, T., Nie, E., Puranik, A.: The Sierpinski triangle and the Ulam-Warburton automaton (2014)
23. Kniemeyer, O., Barczik, G., Hemmerling, R., Kurth, W.: Relational growth grammars - a parallel graph transformation approach with applications in biology and architecture. In: Third International Symposium AGTIVE, Revised Selected and Invited Papers, pp. 152–167 (2007)
24. Kreowski, H., Kuske, S.: Graph multiset transformation: a new framework for massively parallel computation inspired by DNA computing. Nat. Comput. **10**(2), 961–986 (2011)
25. Kreowski, H.-J., Kuske, S., Lye, A.: A simple notion of parallel graph transformation and its perspectives. In: Heckel, R., Taentzer, G. (eds.) Graph Transformation, Specifications, and Nets. LNCS, vol. 10800, pp. 61–82. Springer, Cham (2018). https://doi.org/10.1007/978-3-319-75396-6_4
26. Löwe, M.: Characterisation of parallel independence in AGREE-rewriting. In: Lambers, L., Weber, J. (eds.) ICGT 2018. LNCS, vol. 10887, pp. 118–133. Springer, Cham (2018). https://doi.org/10.1007/978-3-319-92991-0_8

27. Plasmeijer, R., Eekelen, M.V.: Functional Programming and Parallel Graph Rewriting. Addison-Wesley Longman Publishing Co., Inc., Boston, MA, USA, 1st edn. (1993)
28. Rozenberg, G. (ed.): Handbook of Graph Grammars and Computing by Graph Transformation, Volume 1: Foundations. World Scientific (1997)
29. Rozenberg, G., Salomaa, A.: The Book of L. Springer (1986). https://doi.org/10.1007/978-3-642-95486-3
30. Taentzer, G.: Parallel high-level replacement systems. Theoret. Comput. Sci. **186**, 43–81 (1997)
31. Wolfram, S.: A New Kind of Science. Wolfram-Media (2002)

𝕂 and KIV: Towards Deductive Verification for Arbitrary Programming Languages

Dominik Klumpp[1(✉)] and Philip Lenzen[2]

[1] University of Freiburg, Freiburg, Germany
klumpp@informatik.uni-freiburg.de
[2] Augsburg University, Augsburg, Germany
lenzen@isse.de

Abstract. Deductive program verification is a powerful tool to gain confidence in the correctness of software. However, its application to real programs faces a major hurdle: Each programming language requires development of dedicated verification tool support. In this work, we aim to advance deductive software verification to arbitrary programming languages. We developed a tool that derives algebraic specifications for the deductive proof assistant KIV from the syntax and operational semantics of a programming language specified in the 𝕂 semantic framework. We adapt and implement the generic One-Path Reachability calculus and provide instant tool support for deductive proofs. Through a sophisticated automation approach, we drastically reduce the manual proof steps.

Keywords: K framework · Reachability logic · Interactive verification

1 Introduction

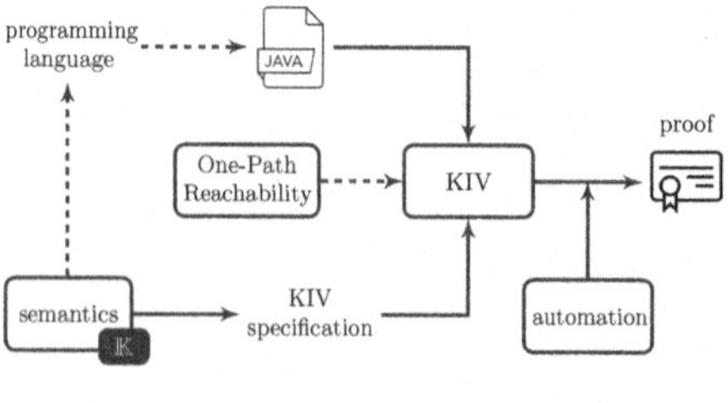

Fig. 1. Schematic view of our approach

Formal verification provides strong correctness guarantees for programs. In particular, interactive verification supported by a deductive proof assistant combines the guarantees of a machine-checked proof with the deductive power of the human mind, circumventing undecidability results applying to purely automated verification. However, it is paramount to minimize the cognitive effort placed on the human to the essential proof steps in order to be practicable, performing simple proof steps automatically. By verifying concrete software implementations – in addition to abstract algorithms – we can rule out errors introduced by the implementation process, giving a strong

M. Roggenbach (Ed.): WADT 2020, LNCS 12669, pp. 98–119, 2021.
https://doi.org/10.1007/978-3-030-73785-6_6

correctness guarantee for actual software products. However, in order to support and check proofs of implementations, a deductive proof assistant must be aware of the semantics of the used programming language, and implement a proof calculus for this language. Separate development, implementation and maintenance of proof assistants for many different languages requires an enourmous amount of work. The approach presented in this paper aims to reduce this workload, by implementing a generic solution that can be instantiated for many programming languages. Figure 1 illustrates our approach: We take as input the definition of a programming language's syntax and semantics specified using the 𝕂 semantics framework [16]. 𝕂 is a powerful specification framework, which allows one to modularly specify complex language features such as concurrency, inheritance or exception handling. Several real-life programming languages (based on different programming paradigms) such as Java [1], C [9], JavaScript [13] or Scheme [11] have been specified in 𝕂. Given such a definition, we generate algebraic specifications for the deductive proof assistant KIV [14]. The translation process is described in Sect. 2. We adapt the One-Path Reachability Calculus [15], a generic program verification calculus parametrized in an operational semantics, to the KIV setting (Sect. 3). This allows us to verify programs in the given language using KIV. An automation approach based on symbolic execution (Sect. 4) reduces the manual proof effort. Our prototype tool implementing this approach is available online (https://git.io/Jvl4x).

1.1 Related Work

The 𝕂 framework and reachability logic have previously been combined with different reasoning backends. The 𝕂 framework itself offers a verification tool [2,5] that, given a property to be verified, performs symbolic rewrites by applying rules of the proof system for One-Path or for All-Path Reachability Logic [19]. It relies on SMT solvers for reasoning about first- and second-order formulae. However, since the configuration theory is typically undecidable, they may fail to prove or disprove a formula. In the interactive setting, we side-step undecidability issues and rely on the human user. Furthermore, Şerbanuţă and Roşu implemented 𝕂 [4] on top of the Maude System [3]. Their tool translates language definitions from 𝕂 to Maude rewrite theories. Programs can then be analyzed and verified using Maude's formal verification tools. Finally, reachability logic has been formalized in the proof assistant Coq [20] to prove its soundness [17]. For demonstration purposes, a language definition for an exemplary imperative language together with a simple program were translated to Coq and proven based on the OPR proof system. However, 𝕂's Coq backend is still experimental.

Other interactive and automated verifiers targeting multiple input languages are typically built around an intermediate verification language such as Boogie [10], Viper [12] or Why3 [7]. Input programs are translated to the intermediate language, the resulting program is verified, and the resulting proof (or possibly counterexample) is transferred back to the input program. In this approach, the formal semantics of the high-level input language is not explicit: Rather, it is implicitly encoded in the tool-specific translation code, combined with the semantics of the intermediate language. Each verifier thus has its own understanding of the language semantics, and the translation of complex language constructs to an intermediate language with different constructs can introduce subtle and hard-to-find bugs. In contrast, our approach is based on a machine-readable specification of the input language's operational semantics. From this, we automatically infer all the necessary constructs and instantiate a generic calculus parametrized in a semantics. The $\mathbb{K}$ semantics definition is clearly separated from any tool-specific concepts and data structures, and can serve as a gold standard for the formal semantics of the language, used by many different tools and different analyses. While intermediate language-based tools can optimize their proof automation for the particular language, automation poses a challenge for our approach due to the necessary generality. However, we believe that the solid foundation of the verification directly on a formal semantics makes the effort to adapt (as seen in Sect. 4) and implement automation techniques worthwhile.

2 From $\mathbb{K}$ to KIV

Our approach combines the $\mathbb{K}$ semantic framework [16], which allows one to intuitively specify syntax and semantics of a programming language in a uniform and modular way, and the deductive proof assistant KIV [6], an interactive verification system that offers partial proof automation based on a powerful simplifier and heuristics. Language semantics in $\mathbb{K}$ are given as small-step operational semantics based on term rewriting, as described in Sect. 2.1. KIV works on algebraic data types defined in structured algebraic specifications, introduced in Sect. 2.2. Therefore, we translate $\mathbb{K}$ language definitions to KIV's internal representations: In Sect. 2.3 we describe the translation of program syntax and state into KIV's specifications. Based on these, we show how we generate axioms from rewrite rules to describe the program semantics in Sect. 2.4. Throughout this paper we illustrate our approach using the example program in Fig. 2a: This program (written in a newly invented language) calculates the factorial of x for a numerical input $x \geq 0$. We define the language in $\mathbb{K}$, translate it to KIV and then specify and prove correctness of the program.

2.1 The $\mathbb{K}$ Framework

The $\mathbb{K}$ semantic framework[1] is a definitional framework based on context insensitive term rewriting [16], developed by Roşu et al. It allows defining operational semantics for programming languages using *rewrite rules* between terms describing the program state, called *configurations*. A configuration contains the current $\mathbb{K}$ Abstract Syntax Tree (KAST) of the program and additional semantic data. The syntax of programs and configurations is defined by a context-free grammar.

[1] http://www.kframework.org.

```
f := 1

// terminates once x=0
while (x) {
  f *= x
  x--
}
```

(a) A simple program which computes the factorial of a variable x and stores the result in f.

```
syntax Stmt ::= Id ":=" Int
  | Id "*=" Id
  | Id "--"
  | "while" "(" Id ")" "{" Stmt "}"
  | Stmt Stmt
```

(b) A context-free grammar for the syntax of the programming language used in fig. 2a.

Fig. 2. An example program and the syntax of the used programming language

To specify the programming language of our program in Fig. 2a, we first define the syntax as a context-free grammar in 𝕂. 𝕂 provides several built-in sorts we can use: Besides the basic types *Int*, *Bool* and *String*, and sorts for untyped collections like *List* or *Map*, 𝕂 also offers a special sort *Id* for identifiers, defined using a regular expression. Using these, we define a 𝕂 sort *Stmt* and construct our language grammar as shown in Fig. 2b.

𝕂 can then parse our program into the 𝕂 *Abstract Syntax Tree* (KAST), which consists of so-called *computations*. A computation is a sequence of extended syntax terms which represent computational tasks. Its structure reflects the intuition of step-by-step program execution and allows an elegant handling of evaluating contexts or continuations [18]: A computation $v \curvearrowright C$ with terms v, C and list constructor $\_ \curvearrowright \_$ (read "followed-by") can be thought of as $C[v]$, which means evaluating v with context C, or passing v to the continuation C. 𝕂 transforms the language syntax to multiple *syntax productions* defining subsorts of the sort of computations K. For example, our grammar is transformed to the following syntax productions:

$$\mathit{Stmt} ::= \_\texttt{:=}\_(\mathit{Id}, \mathit{Int}) \qquad \mathit{Stmt} ::= \texttt{while(}\_\texttt{)\{}\_\texttt{\}}(\mathit{Id}, \mathit{Stmt})$$
$$\mathit{Stmt} ::= \_\texttt{*=}\_(\mathit{Id}, \mathit{Id}) \qquad \mathit{Stmt} ::= \_\texttt{--}(\mathit{Id}) \qquad \mathit{Stmt} ::= \_\_(\mathit{Stmt}, \mathit{Stmt})$$

Further, 𝕂 maintains subsort relationships, and each sort is a subsort of the sort K. Given these productions, 𝕂 can parse our program in Fig. 2a into a KAST – we leave it as an exercise for the reader to derive it.

Now we have a sufficient description of our language syntax, we move on to telling 𝕂 about the structures describing our program state, the *configurations*. Configurations of sort *cfg* are hierarchically structured representations of the current KAST and additional semantic data, such as variable environments for mapping variables to memory locations, stores for mapping locations to values, program stacks, thread collections, and others. To distinguish the algebraic structures of this data, 𝕂 applies constructor operations called *cells* to them. A special cell **k** which contains the abstract program syntax must always be defined within a configuration. Other cells can further be marked as optional or cell bag (which can dynamically contain zero, one or more cell instances and can e.g. be used for thread handling). For our running example, we define a configuration cell T holding the abstract syntax tree of our program and a mapping defining the current values of defined program variables:

$$\texttt{k}: \ K \to \mathit{cfgItem}_{\texttt{k}} \qquad \texttt{state}: \mathit{Map}[\mathit{Id} \mapsto \mathit{Int}] \to \mathit{cfgItem}_{\texttt{state}}$$
$$\texttt{T}: \ \mathit{cfgItem}_{\texttt{k}} \times \mathit{cfgItem}_{\texttt{state}} \to \mathit{cfg}$$

where $\mathit{Map}[\mathit{Id} \mapsto \mathit{Int}]$ is the sort of map structures from variable names to their current integer values. Typically, the *initial configuration* that declares the cell contents prior to program execution is given in-place when defining the configuration structure. In our case, the initial configuration is given (using 𝕂's XML notation for cells) as:

<T><k> $\$PGM$ </k><state> .Map </state></T>

The `k` cell contains a special placeholder $\$PGM$ where the program KAST is inserted, and the `state` cell initially contains an empty map. 𝕂 converts the initial configuration to multiple *initializer rules*, one for each cell.

After defining the syntax and configuration, we give the semantics of our language in the form of rewrite rules. 𝕂's rewrite rules rely on semantic data as well as the program syntax. Thus, the program state in which the rewrite rule is applicable must be specified. Therefore, 𝕂 extends the conventional rewrite form $t \Rightarrow t'$ by wrapping rewrites in (potentially nested) cell operations:

$$\eta ::= x \mid f(\eta_1, \dots, \eta_n) \mid t \Rightarrow t'$$

where x is a cell variable and f is a cell constructor. This allows an *in-place* style for rewrite rules. To avoid having to note irrelevant parts of the configuration in a rewrite rule, 𝕂 offers *context transformation* [16]. This allows to specify only relevant cells while the rest of the context is inferred from the defined configuration structure. For our programming language, the rule for compound assignment is written as:

<k> (X:Id *= Y:Id ⇒ .) ...</k><state>... (Y ↦ J) X ↦ (I ⇒ I $*_{Int}$ J) ...</state>

The single dot denotes the empty computation (i.e. the compound assignment has been completely executed) and ... denotes the existence of additional but irrelevant parts of the configuration. $*_{Int}$ is a built-in 𝕂 operation for the multiplication of integer values. Intuitively, the rule states that if our program reaches a configuration in which the `k` cell starts with a computation of the form `X *= Y` (where `X` and `Y` are variables of sort *Id*) and the `state` cell includes a mapping for both variables, then we can simultaneously perform rewrites in both cells: The compound assignment computation is removed from the `k` cell (replaced by the empty computation) and the value of `X` is multiplied with the value of `Y` and assigned to `X` inside the `state` cell. 𝕂 replaces irrelevant configuration parts with free variables, infers the missing cells and transform this rule to:

$$\texttt{T}\Big(\texttt{k}\big((\texttt{X *= Y} \Rightarrow \texttt{.}) \curvearrowright K\big), \texttt{state}\big(\texttt{Y} \mapsto \texttt{J} \oplus \texttt{X} \mapsto (\texttt{I} \Rightarrow \texttt{I} \ *_{\mathit{Int}} \ \texttt{J}) \oplus \mathit{map}\big)\Big)$$

where K, *map* are free variables of the respective sort, . is the empty computation and $\oplus$ is map concatenation. $\mathbb{K}$ allows preconditions ϕ to restrict rule applications, resulting in rules of the form η **requires** ϕ. We use this for instance in one of the rules for the `while`-loop:

```
<k> while (X) { S } ⇒ S while (X) { S } ...</k><state>... X ↦ I ...</state>
                                                    requires 0 ≠_Int I
```

The rule states that if our `k` cell starts with the `while` statement and the loop condition variable `X` is non-zero (as indicated by the precondition which restricts the value of our `state` mapping for `X`), we can replace the `while` statement with the actual loop body `S` followed by the original `while` statement.

$\mathbb{K}$ automatically parses and transforms the syntax, configuration and rules and generates a language-specific parser for programs. This parser can convert programs into KASTs and embed them in the configuration structure.

2.2 KIV Proof Assistant

KIV is an interactive verification system developed by Reif et al. [14] based on higher-order logic (HOL). The logical foundation is a simply-typed lambda calculus and structured algebraic specifications, which can be used to build a hierarchy of data type definitions. Syntax is defined by signatures consisting of sorts and function symbols, whereas the meaning is determined by axioms, i.e., HOL-formulae. We assume the usual notions of HOL signatures Σ, algebras $\mathcal{A}$ and variable valuations ρ. Given a signature Σ and a set of variables Var, we write $\mathcal{T}_{\Sigma,s}(Var)$ for the set of terms of a sort s, $\mathcal{E}_{\Sigma,\tau}(Var)$ for the HOL-expressions of a type τ, and $\mathcal{F}_{\Sigma}(Var)$ for the HOL-expressions of type *bool*, i.e. the HOL-formulae. Further, we write $[\![e]\!]_{\mathcal{A},\rho}$ for the evaluation of an expression e under an algebra $\mathcal{A}$ and a $\mathcal{A}$-valuation ρ. $\mathcal{A}, \rho$ satisfy a HOL-formula $\varphi \in \mathcal{F}_{\Sigma}(Var)$, written as $\mathcal{A}, \rho \models_{HOL} \varphi$, iff $[\![\varphi]\!]_{\mathcal{A},\rho} = tt$.

KIV allows for the convenient specification of *free algebraic datatypes* using special axioms called *generation clauses*. A generation clause for a sort s consists of special functions called *constructors*. Intuitively, a generation clause serves to express that no other representatives of the data type exist than the ones that can be built with *constructor terms* (i.e. terms built by constructor applications and variables of other sort than s). Therefore, all argument types of at least one constructor must be different from s. We call a data type *freely generated*, if two different constructor terms always represent two different elements. In the following, we will always consider freely generated data types. KIV encapsulates signatures, datatypes, variables and axioms in so-called structured *specifications*:

Definition 1. *A* specification $Sp = (\Sigma, Var, Ax, Gen)$ *consists of a signature* Σ*, variables* Var *for* Σ*, a decidable set of axioms* $Ax \subseteq \mathcal{F}_{\Sigma}(Var)$ *out of the formulae over* Σ *and* Var *as well as a set of generation clauses* Gen*. An algebra* $\mathcal{A}$ *over* Σ *is a* model *for* Sp*, written as* $\mathcal{A} \in Mod(Sp)$*, iff* $\mathcal{A} \models_{HOL} Ax$ *and* $\mathcal{A}$ *satisfies all generation clauses in* Gen*.*

Given a freely generated data type, KIV automatically generates axioms for free generation, selector functions for constructor arguments and test predicates for constructor applications, in addition to the axioms specified by the user. As mentioned before, specifications can be structured to build a hierarchy of data type definitions. Indeed, specifications can be enriched, building a modular specification graph.

Definition 2. *An* enrichment *of a specification Sp adds new symbols, axioms and generation clauses to Sp.*

For proving theorems about the specified data types, KIV uses a Gentzen-style sequent calculus whose rules follow the structure of the formula [6].

Definition 3. *A* sequent *has the form* $\Gamma \vdash \Delta$*, where the* antecedent Γ *and the* succedent Δ *are lists of formulae. An algebra* $\mathcal{A}$ *and a* $\mathcal{A}$*-valuation* ρ satisfy *a sequent, written as* $\mathcal{A}, \rho \models_{HOL} \Gamma \vdash \Delta$*, iff* $\mathcal{A}, \rho \models_{HOL} \bigwedge \Gamma \rightarrow \bigvee \Delta$.

Following the satisfaction equivalence in Definition 3, axioms of a specification in KIV are denoted as sequents as well. When constructing a proof, the calculus rules allow the proof engineer to use axioms and already proven lemmas from the specification. All calculus rules are applied backwards from the proof obligation to the rule's premises, forming a *proof tree* for the theorem. For effective proof development, KIV provides a library containing basic data types with already proven theorems, as well as a rich graphical user interface [8] supporting context-sensitive rule applications. As an additional support, KIV provides a *simplifier* for automatic and context-sensitive simplification of proof goals [6]. It applies (possibly conditional) rewrite rules modulo associativity and commutativity (AC) of operators and propositional simplification in one step, until all formulae are maximally simplified with respect to their contexts.

2.3 Syntax and Configuration

In KIV, we define the syntax of our programming language as a freely generated datatype K. Its specification contains weakly-typed constructors for all syntax constructs defined in the $\mathbb{K}$ language definition. Additionally, we map references to $\mathbb{K}$'s built-in functions to KIV library functions, and we implement a special treatment for productions with regular expressions.

The $\mathbb{K}$ framework relies on function hooks to resolve the semantics of built-in sorts by simply calling the hook operation. Therefore, we explicitly specify (a subset of) $\mathbb{K}$'s built-in sorts as data types in enrichments of KIV's basic library specifications. This allows us to offer native support for most basic types as well as collections, e.g. for integers, lists or maps. Further, we model the concept of *computations* by a data type `ksequence`. In the following, we refer to the library of specifications for built-in $\mathbb{K}$ sorts as $Lib_{\mathbb{K}}$.

$\mathbb{K}$'s internal construction scheme for sorts defined by productions with regular expressions on the right-hand side is a sort constructor taking a string argument. We rely on $\mathbb{K}$'s parser to ensure this argument matches the regular expression, e.g. that an *Id* consists only of alpha-numerical characters. Therefore, for each such *regex production*, we specify one data type in the same manner:

Definition 4. *Let p_r be a regex production for a $\mathbb{K}$ sort s^K. Then the* terminal specification Sp_s *for the $\mathbb{K}$ sort s^K enriches the* `string` *specification from $Lib_{\mathbb{K}}$ with a new freely generated data type s and a single constructor c_s :* `string` $\rightarrow s$.

Based on such *terminal specifications*, we define the basic syntax specification for the data type K. In order to embed the terminal data types in this syntax type K, we include *cast operations* from terminals to K.

```
enrich TS ∪ Lib𝕂 with
data type K =
  Stmt_:=_(. : K, . : K)
  | Stmt_*=_(. : K, . : K)
  ...
  | _(. : id)
  ...
```

(a) The basic syntax specification Sp_{Base}. Each constructor argument is denoted by a dot followed by its type.

```
enrich SpBase with
predicates isStmt : K;
...
axioms ⊢ isStmt(k0) ↔ ∃ k1, k2.
    (k0 = Stmt_:=_(k1, k2)
    ∨ k0 = Stmt_*=_(k1, k2) ∨ ...);
...
```

(b) The syntax specification Sp_{Syn}. The variables k_i are of type K.

Fig. 3. Excerpts of the basic syntax specification Sp_{Base} and the syntax specification Sp_{Syn} for our grammar from Fig. 2b

Definition 5. *Let P_S be a set of syntax productions. Further, let TS be the set of terminal specifications. Then the* basic syntax specification Sp_{Base} *enriches the union of the required specifications $TS \cup Lib_{\mathbb{K}}$ with a new freely generated data type* K *and constructors C such that:*

1. *for each syntax production $p \in P_S$ for a $\mathbb{K}$ sort s^K there is a constructor $c^p_{s^K}$:* $\mathsf{K} \times \cdots \times \mathsf{K} \rightarrow \mathsf{K} \in C$ *of the same arity as the $\mathbb{K}$ sort constructor in p,*
2. *and for each $\mathbb{K}$ sort s^K that has a corresponding KIV specification for the data type s in $Lib_{\mathbb{K}} \cup TS$, there is one* cast constructor $\_ : s \rightarrow \mathsf{K} \in C$.

An excerpt of Sp_{Base} with syntax and cast constructors derived from our grammar defined in Fig. 2b is shown in Fig. 3a. Since the data type K is freely generated, the equivalence of constructor terms of sort K is the same as equality of abstract program syntax, i.e. two KASTs are equal iff the corresponding constructor terms are equal.

As KIV does not have a notion of subsorts, the syntax specification is weakly-typed. However, to adequately describe the language semantics, we must capture the subsort relations. Thus, we define *sort predicates* for the sort K in order to guarantee well-sortedness and to take the subsort relationships of 𝕂 into account.

Definition 6. *The* syntax specification Sp_{Syn} *enriches* Sp_{Base} *with new sort predicate symbols* $isSort_{s^K} : \mathtt{K} \to \mathtt{bool}$ *for every* $\mathbb{K}$ *sort* s^K, *and corresponding axioms such that for every sort predicate* $isSort_{s^K}$, *there is an axiom which states that* $isSort_{s^K}(t)$ *evaluates to* `true` *iff* t *is an application of a constructor* c *which was derived from syntax productions for* s^K, *or any sort predicate* $isSort_{s^K_{sub}}(t)$ *for a subsort of* s^K *evaluates to* `true`.

Exemplarily, Fig. 3b shows an excerpt of Sp_{Syn} with a sort predicate and axiom for the $\mathbb{K}$ sort *Stmt*. Based on this specification, we are able to specify a *syntax translation* mapping $k2kiv_{\mathrm{syn}}(t, s)$ which translates a $\mathbb{K}$ syntax term t to a KIV term of KIV sort s. This translation is straightforward due to the unique mapping from $\mathbb{K}$ to KIV constructors: $\mathbb{K}$ constructors of built-in sorts that have associated functions in $Lib_{\mathbb{K}}$ are mapped to these KIV functions, otherwise a constructor in Sp_{Syn} is applied. The translation of variables works similarly.

The next step of the translation from $\mathbb{K}$ to KIV is to create a representation for the configuration cells. For each $\mathbb{K}$ cell, we create a single-constructor data type which takes as many arguments as the $\mathbb{K}$ cell. Each argument can either be of type `ksequence` (for computations, e.g. in the `k` cell), another built-in $\mathbb{K}$ sort that is specified in $Lib_{\mathbb{K}}$, or a KIV data type corresponding to another cell.

```
enrich SpT with
functions initialConfig : K → cellT;
...
axioms ⊢ initialConfig(pgm) = T(k(pgm.toSeq), state(∅));
...
```

Fig. 4. An excerpt of the config specification Sp_{cfg} which contains the initial configuration function of our programming language. *pgm* is a variable of type `K`.

Definition 7. *Let* $c^K : \sigma_1^K \times \cdots \times \sigma_n^K \to cfgItem_{c^K}$ *be a* $\mathbb{K}$ *configuration cell with* $\mathbb{K}$ *constructor* c^K. *We define* R *as the set of required specifications for all argument sorts* $\sigma_1^K, \cdots, \sigma_n^K$, *which contains*

- `ksequence` *and* Sp_{Syn}, *if any* σ_i^K *is a* $\mathbb{K}$ *syntax sort,*
- *the corresponding KIV cell data type if any* σ_i^K *is a* $\mathbb{K}$ *cell sort,*
- *and the corresponding KIV library data type for* σ_i^K *otherwise.*

The corresponding cell specification Sp_{c^K} *enriches* R *with a new freely generated data type* $cell_c$ *and one constructor* $c : s_1 \times \cdots \times s_n \to c$ *of same arity as* c^K *whose argument sorts correspond to* $\sigma_1^K, \cdots, \sigma_n^K$.

Thus we have now successfully specified the $\mathbb{K}$ configuration cell hierarchy in KIV. It remains to specify the initial configuration: We translate each initializer rule to our KIV cell data types and build a term of constructor applications equivalent to the initial configuration.

Definition 8. *Let Sp be the cell specification of the top-level configuration cell data type cfg. The* config specification Sp_{cfg} *for a* $\mathbb{K}$ *language definition enriches Sp with a function initialConfig* : $\texttt{K} \rightarrow cfg$ *and corresponding axiom which places a program term transformed to* `ksequence` *into the initial configuration structure represented by the corresponding constructor term.*

The config specification Sp_{cfg} for our programming language is shown in Fig. 4. The config translation $k2kiv_{\mathrm{cfg}}$ works basically the same way as $k2kiv_{\mathrm{syn}}$, but now also constructors and variables of $\mathbb{K}$ cell sorts are translated into their representatives of KIV cell data types.

2.4 From Rewrite Rules to Axioms

Now we are able to completely reproduce terms describing $\mathbb{K}$ configurations in KIV's data structures. However, in order to fully represent a language definition, we need an approach to translate the semantics in the form of rewrite rules into KIV axioms. We lift multiple rewrites within one rule to a single rewrite between top-level configuration cells, taking advantage of $\mathbb{K}$'s context transformation. A rewrite rule η **requires** ϕ always describes transitions from a configuration that matches the left-side configuration term to a configuration matching the right-side configuration term. Accordingly, the set of all rewrite rules $\mathcal{S}$ induces a transition relation $\rightarrow_{\mathcal{S},\mathcal{A}}$ between configurations.

Definition 9. *Let* $\mathcal{S}$ *be the set of rewrite rules of a* $\mathbb{K}$ *language definition. Further, let* $\mathcal{A}$ *be an algebra. The* semantic transition relation $\rightarrow_{\mathcal{S},\mathcal{A}} \subseteq \mathcal{A}_{cfg} \times \mathcal{A}_{cfg}$ *induced by* $\mathcal{S}$ *is defined as*

$$\begin{aligned}\gamma \rightarrow_{\mathcal{S},\mathcal{A}} \gamma' \iff & \textit{there exist } \rho, (\eta \textbf{ requires } \phi) \in \mathcal{S} \textit{ such that}\\ & [\![\textit{left}(\eta)]\!]_{\mathcal{A},\rho} = \gamma, [\![\textit{right}(\eta)]\!]_{\mathcal{A},\rho} = \gamma' \textit{ and } \mathcal{A}, \rho \models_{\mathrm{HOL}} \textit{k2kiv}_{\mathrm{syn}}(\phi, \texttt{bool})\end{aligned}$$

The left term *resp.* right term *of a rewrite rule* η **requires** ϕ *is defined as* $\textit{left}(\eta) = \textit{k2kiv}_{\mathrm{cfg}}(\textit{aux}_L(\eta))$ *resp.* $\textit{right}(\eta) = \textit{k2kiv}_{\mathrm{cfg}}(\textit{aux}_R(\eta))$*, where*

$$\begin{aligned}&aux_L(t \Rightarrow t') = t \quad aux_L(x) = x \quad aux_L(f(\eta_1, \dots, \eta_n)) = f(aux_L(\eta_1), \dots, aux_L(\eta_n))\\ &aux_R(t \Rightarrow t') = t' \quad aux_R(x) = x \quad aux_R(f(\eta_1, \dots, \eta_n)) = f(aux_R(\eta_1), \dots, aux_R(\eta_n))\end{aligned}$$

Given a config specification Sp_{cfg} with configuration sort *cfg*, we declare a binary predicate symbol on configurations for the semantic transition relation. We axiomatize this predicate symbol by translating rewrite rules to KIV axioms.

Definition 10. *Let cfg be the top cell type of a config specification* Sp_{cfg} *and* $\rightsquigarrow : cfg \times cfg \rightarrow \texttt{bool}$ *be a predicate symbol. The* rule translation *of a rewrite rule* $(\eta$ **requires** $\phi) \in \mathcal{S}$ *into a KIV axiom is defined as*

$$\textit{k2kiv}_{\mathrm{ax}}(\eta \textbf{ requires } \phi, \rightsquigarrow) :\equiv \Phi, \textit{k2kiv}_{\mathrm{syn}}(\phi, \texttt{bool}) \vdash \textit{left}(\eta) \rightsquigarrow \textit{right}(\eta)$$

where Φ *is the set of sort predicates for variables in the rule.*

The language specification $Sp_{\mathcal{S}} = (\Sigma, Var, Ax, Gen, \rightsquigarrow)$ *for a* $\mathbb{K}$ *language definition enriches* Sp_{cfg} *with a predicate symbol* $\rightsquigarrow : cfg \times cfg \rightarrow$ **bool**, *all rewrite rules translated to axioms by* $k2kiv_{\text{ax}}$, *and the variables used in these axioms.*

```
enrich Sp_cfg with
predicates . ⇝ . : cell_T × cell_T;
variables x,y: id; ks: ksequence; map: kmap; s: K; i,j: int;
axioms ⊢ T(k(Stmt_*=_(_(x),_(y)) ↷ ks), state((_(y) ↦ _(j))
        ⊕ (_(x) ↦ _(i)) ⊕ map))
⇝ T(k(ks), state((_(y) ↦ _(j)) ⊕ (_(x) ↦ _(i * j)) ⊕ map));

isStmt(s),i ≠ 0 ⊢ T(k(Stmt_while(_){_}(_(x),s) ↷ ks),
      state((_(x) ↦ _(i)) ⊕ map))
⇝ T(k(s ↷ Stmt_while(_){_}(_(x),s) ↷ ks),
      state((_(x) ↦ _(i)) ⊕ map))
...
```

Fig. 5. An excerpt of the language specification $Sp_{\mathcal{S}}$ for our programming language

The language specification $Sp_{\mathcal{S}}$ for our running example, containing axioms for the rewrite rules for compound assignment and while loop, is shown in Fig. 5.

Note that we under-specify the transition relation. Therefore, we can only prove that certain configurations are in relation, but not that configurations are not in relation. We will see in Sect. 3 that this is sufficient for our calculus.

Lemma 11. *Let* $Sp_{\mathcal{S}} = (\Sigma, Var, Ax, Gen, \rightsquigarrow)$ *be the language specification derived from a set of rewrite rules* $\mathcal{S}$, *with an underlying config specification* Sp_{cfg}. *Then for all* $\mathcal{A} \in Mod(Sp_{cfg})$, *it follows that* $\mathcal{A} \in Mod(Sp_{\mathcal{S}})$ *iff* $\rightsquigarrow^{\mathcal{A}} \supseteq \rightarrow_{\mathcal{S},\mathcal{A}}$.

Proof. The axioms $k2kiv_{\text{ax}}(\eta$ **requires** $\phi, \rightsquigarrow)$ *directly correspond to the "if"-direction of Definition* 9.

3 One-Path Reachability in KIV

Having defined the operational semantics, we turn to the proof system which we use to specify and prove program correctness. For this purpose, we employ *One-Path Reachability Logic* (OPR) as presented by Roşu et al. [15,17].

Traditional program logics such as Hoare Logic and Dynamic Logic constrain program states using first-order formulae over program variables. In our setting, where we have no generic notion of program variables, we instead employ patterns of configurations. In Sect. 3.1, we give a quick introduction into how such patterns are written in reachability logic, and show how we integrate them into the KIV setting. We then specify the properties of interest in Sect. 3.2, and show the proof system and its adaptation for KIV in Sect. 3.3.

3.1 Configuration Patterns

OPR makes use of (a restricted variant) of so-called *matching logic patterns* (hereafter simple *patterns*) to describe configurations. Patterns combine terms of sort *cfg*, which describe the structure of a configuration, with first-order formulae, which can be used to constrain variables occurring in such terms.

Definition 12. *The set of* matching logic patterns $\mathcal{P}_{\Sigma,cfg}(Var)$ *is defined as:*

$$\Phi ::= t = t' \mid p(t_1, \ldots, t_n) \mid \pi \mid \neg\Phi \mid \Phi_1 \vee \Phi_2 \mid \exists x \,.\, \Phi$$

where $t, t', t_1, \ldots, t_n \in \mathcal{T}_\Sigma(Var)$, $\pi \in \mathcal{T}_{\Sigma,cfg}(Var)$, $x \in Var$ *and* p *an* n*-ary predicate in* Σ. *We assume patterns to be well-typed. We call a configuration term* π *a* basic pattern, *whereas a pattern containing no basic patterns is* structureless.

Unlike formulae, patterns do not evaluate to *true* or *false*. Instead, they describe sets of configurations $\gamma \in \mathcal{A}_{cfg}$. In contrast to Roşu et al. [15], we do not assume a single configuration algebra $\mathcal{A}$. Instead, we now fix a configuration specification $Sp_{cfg} = (\Sigma, Var, Ax, Gen)$ such that Σ contains the configuration sort *cfg*. Any model $\mathcal{A} \in Mod(Sp_{cfg})$ is a *configuration model.* The detailed pattern semantics are then given by the following definition:

Definition 13 (Pattern Satisfaction [15]**).** *Let* $\mathcal{A}$ *be a* Σ*-algebra and let* ρ *be a* $\mathcal{A}$*-valuation. Satisfaction between configuration* $\gamma \in \mathcal{A}_{cfg}$ *and a matching logic pattern* Φ*, written* $(\mathcal{A}, \rho, \gamma) \models_{\mathrm{ML}} \Phi$*, is defined such that* $(\mathcal{A}, \rho, \gamma) \models_{\mathrm{ML}} \pi$ *iff* $[\![\pi]\!]_{\mathcal{A},\rho} = \gamma$ *for a basic pattern* $\Phi \equiv \pi$*, and all other constructs are defined via structural induction in the usual manner.*

In order to express such matching logic patterns in KIV, we translate them to higher-order logic expressions. We identify a pattern with the set of configurations that satisfy the pattern, represented by an expression of type $pat :\equiv cfg \to bool$.

Definition 14. *The translation from matching-logic patterns to higher-order logic expressions is defined as* $\lfloor \cdot \rfloor : \mathcal{P}_{\Sigma,cfg}(Var) \to \mathcal{E}_{\Sigma,pat}(Var), \Phi \mapsto \lambda c \,.\, \lfloor \Phi \rfloor_c$ *where* $c \in Var_{cfg}$ *is fresh, and the function* $\lfloor \cdot \rfloor_c : \mathcal{P}_{\Sigma,cfg}(Var) \to \mathcal{E}_{\Sigma,bool}(Var)$ *is inductively defined as follows:*

$$\lfloor \pi \rfloor_c :\equiv (c = \pi) \qquad \lfloor t = t' \rfloor_c :\equiv (t = t') \qquad \lfloor p(t_1, \ldots, t_n) \rfloor_c :\equiv p(t_1, \ldots, t_n)$$
$$\lfloor \neg\Phi \rfloor_c :\equiv \neg \lfloor \Phi \rfloor_c \qquad \lfloor \exists x \,.\, \Phi \rfloor_c :\equiv \exists x \,.\, \lfloor \Phi \rfloor_c \qquad \lfloor \Phi_1 \vee \Phi_2 \rfloor_c :\equiv \lfloor \Phi_1 \rfloor_c \vee \lfloor \Phi_2 \rfloor_c$$

This translation preserves the semantics of all matching logic patterns, in a sense made precise by Lemma 15. In the following, we thus make no notational distinction between a matching logic pattern Φ and its corresponding lambda expression $\lfloor \Phi \rfloor$.

Lemma 15. *Let* $\Phi \in \mathcal{P}_{\Sigma,cfg}(Var)$ *be a matching logic pattern, and let* $c \in Var_{cfg}$ *be a fresh variable not occuring in* Φ*. Then for all* Σ*-algebras* $\mathcal{A}$*,* $\mathcal{A}$*-valuations* ρ *and all* $\gamma \in \mathcal{A}_{cfg}$*, it holds that* $(\mathcal{A}, \rho, \gamma) \models_{\mathrm{ML}} \Phi$ *iff* $\mathcal{A}, \rho\{c \mapsto \gamma\} \models_{\mathrm{HOL}} \lfloor \Phi \rfloor (c)$.

Proof. By induction over the structure of the pattern Φ.

We conclude the discussion of configuration patterns with an example:

Example 16. Consider the language specification from Sect. 2, and let *fact* denote the syntax term for the factorial program in Fig. 2a. Then the basic pattern

$$T\big(k(\mathit{fact}), \mathit{state}(id(\text{“x”}) \mapsto I)\big) \quad \text{resp.} \quad \lambda c \,.\, c = T\big(k(\mathit{fact}), \mathit{state}(id(\text{“x”}) \mapsto I)\big)$$

denotes the single program configuration where the entire program *fact* remains to be executed (no step has been executed yet), the program variable `x` stores the value I (a free logical variable of the pattern), and no other variables store any value. On the other hand, the pattern

$$\exists F, m \,.\, T\big(k(.), \mathit{state}((id(\text{“f”}) \mapsto F) \oplus m)\big) \wedge F = I!$$

or, translated to the KIV setting,

$$\lambda c \,.\, \exists F, m \,.\, c = T\big(k(.), \mathit{state}((id(\text{“f”}) \mapsto F) \oplus m)\big) \wedge F = I!$$

denotes all configurations where execution has terminated (only the empty program `.` remains), and the program variable `f` stores the value $I!$ (where I is again a free variable). The values m stored by other variables are existentially quantified, they are irrelevant to the pattern.

3.2 One-Path Reachability Properties

The OPR proof system is centered around so-called *reachability properties.* We begin by defining their syntax, and then show how they connect to $\mathbb{K}$ and KIV on a semantical level. For this purpose, we fix in the following a language specification $Sp = (\Sigma, \mathit{Var}, \mathit{Ax}, \mathit{Gen}, \rightsquigarrow)$ enriching Sp_{cfg}.

Definition 17 (Reachability Properties). *A* $\rightsquigarrow$-reachability property *is of the form* $\Phi \; \langle\rightsquigarrow\rangle^{\exists} \; \Psi$*, for configuration patterns* $\Phi, \Psi \in \mathcal{E}_{\Sigma,pat}(\mathit{Var})$*.*

Intuitively, the semantics of a reachability property $\Phi \; \langle\rightsquigarrow\rangle^{\exists} \; \Psi$ is that any configuration γ matching Φ can, through a finite number of steps in the language's small-step operational semantics, reach some configuration matching Ψ. An exception is made if γ can be part of a non-terminating execution. Therefore, reachability properties correspond to partial correctness for deterministic languages. This semantics is made precise below:

Definition 18. *Let* $\mathcal{A}$ *be an algebra, let* ρ *be an* $\mathcal{A}$*-valuation, and let* $c \in \mathit{Var}_{\mathit{cfg}}$ *be a fresh variable. Then* $\mathcal{A}$ *and* ρ *satisfy a* $\rightsquigarrow$*-reachability property* $\Phi \; \langle\rightsquigarrow\rangle^{\exists} \; \Psi$*, written* $\mathcal{A}, \rho \models_{\mathrm{OPR}} \Phi \; \langle\rightsquigarrow\rangle^{\exists} \; \Psi$*, iff for all configurations* $\gamma \in \mathcal{A}_{\mathit{cfg}}$ *such that* $\mathcal{A}, \rho\{c \mapsto \gamma\} \models_{\mathrm{HOL}} \Phi(c)$*, one of the following conditions holds:*

(i) γ *can diverge, i.e., there exists an infinite* $\rightsquigarrow^{\mathcal{A}}$*-chain starting at* γ*;*
(ii) **or**, *there exists* $\gamma' \in \mathcal{A}_{cfg}$ *s.t.* $\mathcal{A}, \rho\{c \mapsto \gamma'\} \models_{\text{HOL}} \Psi(c)$ *and* $\gamma\ (\rightsquigarrow^{\mathcal{A}})^*\ \gamma'$.

In contrast to the definition above, Roşu et al. [15] define the semantics of complex reachability properties w.r.t. a language semantics expressed as a set $\mathcal{S}$ of fundamental reachability properties (also called *reachability rules*). In order to reconcile this with our setting, where the language semantics is given as a set of $\mathbb{K}$ rewrite rules over configuration terms, we connect such rewrite rules to the notions of matching logic patterns and reachability properties.

Definition 19 (Reachability Properties from Rewrite Rules). *Let* $\mathcal{S}$ *be a set of* $\mathbb{K}$ *rewrite rules. We use* $\hat{\mathcal{S}}$ *to denote the set of reachability properties*

$$\left(\lambda c\,.\, c = \mathit{left}(\eta) \wedge \mathit{k2kiv}_{\text{syn}}(\phi, \texttt{bool})\right) \langle\rightsquigarrow\rangle^{\exists} \left(\lambda c\,.\, c = \mathit{right}(\eta)\right)$$

for a $\mathbb{K}$ *rewrite rule* (η **requires** ϕ) $\in \mathcal{S}$*, where* $c \in \mathit{Var}_{cfg}$ *is fresh.*

This mapping from rewrite rules to reachability properties is quite intuitive: A rewrite rule η **requires** ϕ denotes the fact that any configuration matching the left term of η can reach in (a single step of) the small-step semantics the corresponding right term of η, if the side condition ϕ is met. In fact, this mapping is in a sense semantics-preserving, as detailed in the lemma below. In the following we will thus make no notational distinction between $\mathcal{S}$ and $\hat{\mathcal{S}}$.

Lemma 20. *Let* $\mathcal{S}$ *be a set of* $\mathbb{K}$ *rewrite rules, let* $\mathcal{A} \in \mathit{Mod}(\mathit{Sp}_{cfg})$*, and let* $\gamma, \gamma' \in \mathcal{A}_{cfg}$*. Then we have that* $\gamma \rightarrow_{\mathcal{S},\mathcal{A}} \gamma'$ *iff there exists a* ρ *and a reachability property* $(\Phi \Rightarrow^{\exists} \Psi) \in \hat{\mathcal{S}}$*, such that* $(\mathcal{A}, \rho, \gamma) \models_{\text{ML}} \Phi$ *and* $(\mathcal{A}, \rho, \gamma') \models_{\text{ML}} \Psi$*.*

In other words, the relation $\rightarrow_{\mathcal{S},\mathcal{A}}$ induced by the set of rewrite rules $\mathcal{S}$, as in Definition 9, coincides with Roşu et al.'s definition [15] of the semantic transition relation induced by a set of reachability rules, here given by $\hat{\mathcal{S}}$. Note that they allow *conditional* reachability rules, where the condition is a reachability property. As we do not consider such rules, several of the definitions simplify significantly.

Following the sequent-style of the OPR and KIV calculi, we do not consider reachability properties in isolation, but rather in the context a given set of premises assumed to hold:

Definition 21 (Reachability Entailment). *HOL-formulae* $\mathcal{L}$ *and reachability properties* $\mathcal{R}$ entail *a* $\rightsquigarrow$*-reachability property* $\Phi \langle\rightsquigarrow\rangle^{\exists} \Psi$ modulo Sp*, denoted* $\mathcal{L} \uplus \mathcal{R} \models^{\mathit{Sp}}_{\text{OPR}} \Phi \langle\rightsquigarrow\rangle^{\exists} \Psi$*, iff for all* $\mathcal{A} \in \mathit{Mod}(\mathit{Sp})$ *and all* ρ *such that* $\mathcal{A}, \rho \models_{\text{HOL}} \mathcal{L}$ *and* $\mathcal{A}, \rho \models_{\text{OPR}} \mathcal{R}$*, we have that* $\mathcal{A}, \rho \models_{\text{OPR}} \Phi \langle\rightsquigarrow\rangle^{\exists} \Psi$*.*

Example 22. As an example for this kind of statement, consider again the configuration patterns discussed in Example 16. We use them to give a partial correctness specification for the program from Fig. 2a, here again denoted as *fact*:

$$\begin{aligned}\{I \geq 0\} \uplus \emptyset \models^{\mathit{Sp}}_{\text{OPR}} & \left(\lambda c\,.\, c = T(k(\mathit{fact}), \mathit{state}(\mathit{id}(\text{“x”}) \mapsto I))\right. \\ & \langle\rightsquigarrow\rangle^{\exists}\left(\lambda c\,.\, \exists F, m\,.\, c = T(k(.), \mathit{state}((\mathit{id}(\text{“f”}) \mapsto F) \oplus m)) \wedge F = I!\right)\end{aligned}$$

All three occurences of the logical variable I – in the antecedent, in the left pattern and in the right pattern – refer to the same value. This specification states, that for non-negative initial values I of the program variable x, the factorial program reaches a configuration where execution has terminated and the program variable f stores the factorial of I (unless the program never terminates).

Our formalization differs from the formalization by Roşu et al. [15] in one important aspect: We fix a language specification *Sp*, rather than a single algebra. Thereby we consider all algebras that are models of *Sp*. Hence, instead of referring to the transition relation $\rightarrow_{\mathcal{S},\mathcal{A}}$ for algebra $\mathcal{A}$, we refer to the axiomatization of this relation, represented by the predicate symbol $\rightsquigarrow$. By Lemma 11, an interpretation $\rightsquigarrow^{A}$ of this symbol by some $\mathcal{A} \in Mod(Sp)$ is an over-approximation of the relation $\rightarrow_{\mathcal{S},\mathcal{A}}$. This approximation is tight, in the sense that for every $\mathcal{A} \in Mod(Sp)$, there exists an $\mathcal{A}' \in Mod(Sp)$ with $\rightsquigarrow^{\mathcal{A}'} = \rightarrow_{\mathcal{S},\mathcal{A}}$. Together with Lemma 20, this implies that $\emptyset \models^{Sp}_{\mathrm{OPR}} \Phi \; \langle\rightsquigarrow\rangle^{\exists} \; \Psi$, if and only if every $\mathcal{A} \in Mod(Sp)$ satisfies (in the original sense) the reachability property $\Phi \Rightarrow^{\exists} \Psi$ (here in the notation of [15]). Hence our definition coincides with the original semantics of reachability properties, allowing us to connect our setting to the results of Roşu et al.

3.3 OPR Calculus

We employ the *One-Path Reachability Calculus* [15] to prove reachability properties. This calculus derives sequents of the form $\mathcal{L} \uplus \mathcal{R} \vdash_C \Phi \; \langle\rightsquigarrow\rangle^{\exists} \; \Psi$. The additional parameter C, called *circularities*, is used to reason about repetitive behaviour such as loops or recursion. Section 4 explains the typical reasoning process for loops and invariants. Note that a semantic entailment $\mathcal{L} \uplus \mathcal{R} \models^{Sp}_{\mathrm{OPR}} \Phi \; \langle\rightsquigarrow\rangle^{\exists} \; \Psi$ connects to the sequent $\mathcal{L} \uplus \mathcal{R} \vdash_{\emptyset} \Phi \; \langle\rightsquigarrow\rangle^{\exists} \; \Psi$, i.e., a proof typically starts with an empty set of circularities. Only within the proof tree this set is populated. For details on the calculus, a correctness and a completeness statement, refer to the original paper [15]. As discussed in Sect. 3.2, we capture Roşu et al.'s semantics of reachability properties precisely, despite our slightly different formalization. Hence their correctness and completeness results equally apply in our setting.

Figure 6 shows the deduction rules for our variation of OPR. In our implementation in KIV, these rules can be combined with proof rules from KIV's existing HOL calculus. Largely, they are a straightforward adaptation of the original OPR rules to $\rightsquigarrow$-reachability properties. However, for purposes of proof convenience, we modify the rules *(Axiom)* and *(Reflexivity)* rules, and we add the rules *(One Step)*, *(Cut)* and *(Cut Constraint)*. Below we explain the modifications and argue that correctness and completeness of the calculus are not affected.

We begin with the new proof rule *(Cut Constraint)*. This rule allows moving a structure-less constraint ψ from the left-hand pattern of the succedent to the antecedent. Once moved to the antecedent, ψ – which may constrain free

Axiom:

$$\frac{}{A \cup \left\{ \Phi_1 \ \langle\leadsto\rangle^{\exists} \ \Phi_2 \right\} \vdash_C \Phi_1 \ \langle\leadsto\rangle^{\exists} \ \Phi_2}$$

One Step:

$$\frac{\mathcal{L} \vdash \forall c_1 \,.\, \Phi_1(c_1) \rightarrow \exists c_2 \,.\, c_1 \leadsto c_2 \wedge \Phi_2(c_2)}{\mathcal{L} \uplus R \vdash_C \Phi_1 \ \langle\leadsto\rangle^{\exists} \ \Phi_2}$$

Reflexivity:

$$\frac{\mathcal{L} \vdash \Phi_1 \subseteq \Phi_2}{\mathcal{L} \uplus R \vdash_{\emptyset} \Phi_1 \ \langle\leadsto\rangle^{\exists} \ \Phi_2}$$

Transitivity:

$$\frac{A \vdash_C \Phi_1 \ \langle\leadsto\rangle^{\exists} \ \Phi' \quad A \cup C \vdash_{\emptyset} \Phi' \ \langle\leadsto\rangle^{\exists} \ \Phi_2}{A \vdash_C \Phi_1 \ \langle\leadsto\rangle^{\exists} \ \Phi_2}$$

Abstraction:

$$\frac{A \vdash_C (\lambda c \,.\, \varphi\{x \mapsto y\}) \ \langle\leadsto\rangle^{\exists} \ \Phi_2}{A \vdash_C (\lambda c \,.\, \exists x \,.\, \varphi) \ \langle\leadsto\rangle^{\exists} \ \Phi_2}$$

Consequence:

$$\frac{\mathcal{L} \vdash \Phi_1 \subseteq \Phi_1' \quad \mathcal{L} \uplus \mathcal{R} \vdash_C \Phi_1' \ \langle\leadsto\rangle^{\exists} \ \Phi_2' \quad \mathcal{L} \vdash \Phi_2' \subseteq \Phi_2}{\mathcal{L} \uplus R \vdash_C \Phi_1 \ \langle\leadsto\rangle^{\exists} \ \Phi_2}$$

Circularity:

$$\frac{A \vdash_{C \cup \{\Phi_1 \langle\leadsto\rangle^{\exists} \Phi_2\}} \Phi_1 \ \langle\leadsto\rangle^{\exists} \ \Phi_2}{A \vdash_C \Phi_1 \ \langle\leadsto\rangle^{\exists} \ \Phi_2}$$

Case Analysis:

$$\frac{A \vdash_C (\lambda c \,.\, \varphi_1) \ \langle\leadsto\rangle^{\exists} \ \Phi_2 \quad A \vdash_C (\lambda c \,.\, \varphi_2) \ \langle\leadsto\rangle^{\exists} \ \Phi_2}{A \vdash_C (\lambda c \,.\, \varphi_1 \vee \varphi_2) \ \langle\leadsto\rangle^{\exists} \ \Phi_2}$$

Cut Constraint:

$$\frac{A \cup \{\psi\} \vdash_C (\lambda c \,.\, \varphi) \ \langle\leadsto\rangle^{\exists} \ \Phi_2}{A \vdash_C (\lambda c \,.\, \varphi \wedge \psi) \ \langle\leadsto\rangle^{\exists} \ \Phi_2}$$

where $c \notin freevars(\psi)$

Cut:

$$\frac{A \cup \{\psi\} \vdash_C \Phi_1 \ \langle\leadsto\rangle^{\exists} \ \Phi_2 \quad A \cup \{\neg\psi\} \vdash_C \Phi_1 \ \langle\leadsto\rangle^{\exists} \ \Phi_2}{A \vdash_C \Phi_1 \ \langle\leadsto\rangle^{\exists} \ \Phi_2}$$

Fig. 6. OPR calculus rule variants implemented in KIV. c_1, c_2 and y are assumed to be fresh variables. $\Phi_1 \subseteq \Phi_2$ is shorthand for the formula $\forall c' \,.\, \Phi_1(c') \rightarrow \Phi_2(c')$, for a fresh variable c'. A abbreviates $\mathcal{L} \uplus \mathcal{R}$ where not needed separately.

variables of the sequent – becomes eligible for usage by KIV calculus rules such as rewrites.

Lemma 23. *The rule* (Cut Constraint) *is sound.*

Proof (sketch). If under a given $\mathcal{A}, \rho$ any configuration satisfies $(\lambda c \,.\, \varphi \wedge \psi)$, then $\mathcal{A}, \rho \models_{\mathrm{HOL}} \psi$ and we apply the premise.

The rule *(Cut)* serves as a convenience rule for case distinctions. It can be derived from the existing rules by first using *(Consequence)* to transform Φ_1 to $\lambda c \,.\, (\Phi_1(c) \wedge \psi) \vee (\Phi_1(c) \wedge \neg\psi)$, then applying *(Case Distinction)*, followed by *(Cut Constraint)* in both premises. We extend *(Reflexivity)*, which originally required Φ_1 to be (syntactically) equal to Φ_2, to instead reduce to the KIV sequent $\mathcal{L} \vdash \Phi_1 \subseteq \Phi_2$. It is easy to see that the original rule can be recovered by proving the sequent $\mathcal{L} \vdash \Phi_1 \subseteq \Phi_1$. At the same time, the new version of the rule can be derived using *(Consequence)* and the original *(Reflexivity)* rule.

The main difference between our variant and the original OPR lies in the rules *(Axiom)* and *(One Step)*. Together, these rules correspond to the following rule $(Axiom_{old})$ in original OPR:

$$\frac{}{A \cup \{(\lambda c \,.\, \varphi_1) \ \langle\leadsto\rangle^{\exists} \ (\lambda c \,.\, \varphi_2)\} \vdash_C (\lambda c \,.\, \varphi_1 \wedge \psi) \ \langle\leadsto\rangle^{\exists} \ (\lambda c \,.\, \varphi_2 \wedge \psi)} \ \text{where } c \notin freevars(\psi)$$

For one, our *(Axiom)* rule omits the structure-less conjunct ψ, as this can be taken care of using the *(Cut Constraint)* rule. More importantly, we introduce the new rule *(One Step)*. The purpose of this rule is to take the place of $(Axiom_{old})$

in cases where the succedent $\Phi \langle\rightsquigarrow\rangle^{\exists} \Psi$ is a rule in $\mathcal{S}$. Unlike original OPR, we do not keep $\mathcal{S}$ as a set of reachability properties explicitly present in the antecedent, but instead encode it through axioms for the transition relation symbol $\rightsquigarrow$. It is easy to see from the definition that $\mathcal{A}, \rho \models_{\mathrm{HOL}} \forall c_1 . \Phi_1(c_1) \rightarrow \exists c_2 . c_1 \rightsquigarrow c_2 \wedge \Phi_2(c_2)$ implies $\mathcal{A}, \rho \models_{\mathrm{OPR}} \Phi \langle\rightsquigarrow\rangle^{\exists} \Psi$, for any $\mathcal{A} \in Mod(Sp_{cfg})$ and any ρ. Therefore, the *(One Step)* rule is sound; and *(Axiom)* is also sound as a special case of $(Axiom_{old})$. Thus, it only remains to show:

Lemma 24. *The rules* (Axiom) *and* (One Step) *are as complete as* $(Axiom_{old})$*, i.e., for any proof tree involving* (Axiom) *and* (One Step) *there exists a corresponding proof tree involving only* $(Axiom_{old})$ *with the same conclusion.*

4 Reducing Manual Effort

The translation of $\mathbb{K}$ semantics to KIV specifications (Sect. 2), together with the integration of the OPR calculus in KIV (Sect. 3) enable specification and correctness proofs of programs written in any language in KIV. However, the manual specification of reachability properties using the language specification is cumbersome, and manual proofs require a huge effort. Thus we show in this section how some standard techniques implemented in our tool – symbolic execution and invariant reasoning – can be applied in our setting to make proving easier.

We begin with the specification of our programs. The difficulty in specifying reachability sequents directly in KIV lies in the fact that configuration patterns can only use complete (and possibly very complicated) configuration terms. Our approach instead follows the same idea as $\mathbb{K}$: Only the relevant parts of the term need to be mentioned. Furthermore, we do not want to separate specification from program. Hence we allow the program text to be annotated with a correctness specification in the form of a reachability property, including quantifiers and logical variables. The syntax for configurations is the same as in the $\mathbb{K}$ semantics. Additionally, we allow function and predicate symbols defined in KIV. From these annotations, our tool generates proof obligations in KIV. The program itself is translated to a KIV term and stored as a constant in a KIV specification.

We extend the program syntax to allow usage of logical variables and KIV function symbols in the program itself. By reading from logical variables, programs can simulate external input and nondeterminism. This results in the program term being defined as a function rather than a constant, where the parameters correspond to the used logical variables. The usage of KIV function symbols within the program allows for incomplete programs, where certain (side effect-free) calculations are not explicitly implemented in the program. For instance, a program could refer to a KIV function symbol *gcd* for the greatest common divisor, allowing for verification modulo a correct implementation of *gcd*, e.g. at a later development stage or in an external library.

```
// lemma: initialConfig(KIV.this(I)) ∧ I ≥ 0 ⟨⇝⟩∃
//                 ∃F . (<k>.</k> <state>f ↦ F ... </state>) ∧ F = I!
x := KIV.Variable(I)
f := 1

// inv: ∃X,F . (<state>x ↦ X, f ↦ F ... </state>) ∧ X ≥ 0 ∧ F · X! = I!
while (x) {
  f *= x
  x--
}
```

Fig. 7. Annotated factorial program

Example 25. (Specification Annotation). Consider the modified factorial program in Fig. 7, annotated with a correctness specification ("lemma"). Replacement of `KIV.this` by the program function symbol *fact*, 𝕂's context transformation [16] and translation to KIV produce the following OPR sequent:

$$\emptyset \uplus \emptyset \vdash_{\emptyset} \big(\lambda c \,.\, c = \mathit{initialConfig}(\mathit{fact}(I)) \wedge I \geq 0\big)$$
$$\langle\rightsquigarrow\rangle^{\exists} \big(\lambda c \,.\, \exists F, m \,.\, c = T(k(.), \mathit{state}((\mathit{id}(\text{"f"}) \mapsto F) \oplus m)) \wedge F = I!\big)$$

The specification is essentially the same as in Example 22, except that the program explicitly stores its input I in the program variable `x` (rather than leaving it to the specification). I is implicitly universally quantified. The variable m represents values of irrelevant program variables, in particular the value of `x`, in 𝕂 syntax denoted by an ellipsis. We refer to the factorial function specified in KIV.

Having specified correctness for our program, we turn to proving it. However, a manual proof would require a lot of effort: As the underlying semantics is a *small-step* semantics – and in particular, the default expression evaluation strategy in 𝕂 generates a huge amount of very small steps – proof trees are typically huge. At the same time, complex program terms are hard to decipher for a human. Hence we developed a KIV heuristic that automatically applies OPR proof rules. It performs symbolic execution of the program, relying heavily on KIV's support for pattern matching. Given a left hand-side pattern $(\lambda c \,.\, c = t \wedge \psi)$ with $c \notin \mathit{freevars}(\psi)$, it searches for an axiom $\phi \vdash \pi_1 \rightsquigarrow \pi_2$ such that $t \equiv \pi_1\sigma$ for some substitution σ, and ψ together with the sequent's HOL-premises $\mathcal{L}$ implies $\phi\sigma$. If it finds (exactly) one such axiom, it creates the following proof tree:

$$\cfrac{\cfrac{\cfrac{\cfrac{}{\mathcal{L} \cup \{\psi\} \vdash \pi_1\sigma \rightsquigarrow \pi_2\sigma}\ \textbf{(KIV: Apply Axiom)}}{\mathcal{L} \vdash \forall c_1 \,.\, c_1 = \pi_1\sigma \wedge \psi \rightarrow \exists c_2 \,.\, c_2 = \pi_2\sigma \wedge \psi \wedge c_1 \rightsquigarrow c_2}\ \textbf{(KIV: FOL)}}{\mathcal{L} \uplus \mathcal{R} \vdash_C (\lambda c \,.\, c = \pi_1\sigma \wedge \psi)\ \langle\rightsquigarrow\rangle^{\exists}\ (\lambda c \,.\, c = \pi_2\sigma \wedge \psi)}\ \textbf{(One Step+}\beta\textbf{)} \qquad (\diamond)}{\mathcal{L} \uplus \mathcal{R} \vdash_C (\lambda c . c = \pi_1\sigma \wedge \psi)\ \langle\rightsquigarrow\rangle^{\exists}\ \Phi}\ \textbf{(Transitivity)}$$

where ($\diamond$) stands for $\mathcal{L} \uplus (\mathcal{R} \cup C) \vdash_{\emptyset} (\lambda c \,.\, c = \pi_2\sigma \wedge \psi) \langle\rightsquigarrow\rangle^{\exists} \Phi$: The heuristic has executed one step in the small-step semantics. It remains to prove ($\diamond$). Note that for non-deterministic (or concurrent) languages, more than one axiom can be found and our heuristic stops, leaving the selection of the next step to the user. More work is needed to advance automation to such languages.

The heuristic also stops symbolic execution when it encounters similar left hand-side and right hand-side patterns, and applies the *(Reflexivity)* rule instead. Furthermore, it also stops symbolic execution when a similar pattern to the current left hand-side pattern occurs in a sequent further down the proof tree. The purpose of this is to avoid infinite unrolling of loops or recursion. To deal with such repetitive constructs, we allow *invariant annotations* in the form of matching logic patterns in the program. Here configuration terms need only mention subterms that change between iterations or recursive calls. This enables the invariant to focus on those parts relevant to the loop or recursion.

To achieve this, pattern matching is employed once again. The annotations actually specify abstract invariants, which are then instantiated by the heuristic during a proof. The annotation's pattern structure is constrained to the form $\exists \vec{x} \,.\, \pi_a \wedge \psi_a$ where ψ_a is structure-less and π_a is a basic pattern. The variables $\vec{x}$ represent the aspects from which the invariant abstracts away. Free variables will be instantiated when the invariant is used. Suppose a (sub-)program p is annotated with an invariant $\exists \vec{x} \,.\, \pi_a \wedge \psi_a$. Let $cfg(p)$ denote an abstract configuration term, where $p \curvearrowright k$ (with k a fresh variable) is placed in the `<k>`-cell and all other (non-enclosing) cells are represented by fresh variables. When the heuristic encounters a left hand-side pattern of the form $\Phi_1 \equiv (\lambda c \,.\, c = \pi \wedge \psi)$, such that π is an instance of $cfg(p)$, it will try to find a substitution σ such that $\pi = \pi_a\sigma$. If found, the invariant is instantiated as $\Phi_{\text{inv}} :\equiv (\lambda c \,.\, \exists \vec{x} \,.\, c = \pi_a \wedge \psi_a)\sigma$.

Example 26 (Invariant Annotation). Consider the invariant annotation in Fig. 7. After $\mathbb{K}$'s context transformation [16] of the configuration term and translation to the KIV setting, the resulting expression is as follows:

$$\lambda c \,.\, \exists X, F \,.\, c = T(kc, state(id(\text{“x”}) \mapsto X \oplus id(\text{“f”}) \mapsto F \oplus m)) \\ \wedge X \geq 0 \wedge F \cdot X! = I!$$

In a proof of the lemma in Example 25, we encounter the pattern

$$\lambda c \,.\, c = T(k(\texttt{while...}), state(id(\text{“x”}) \mapsto I \oplus id(\text{“f”}) \mapsto 1))$$

Since the configuration term in this pattern is an instance of $cfg(\texttt{while...}) \equiv T(k(\texttt{while...}), sc)$, the heuristic applies the invariant. It finds the substitution $\sigma = \{kc \mapsto k(\texttt{while...}), X \mapsto I, F \mapsto 1, m \mapsto \emptyset\}$ and instantiates the invariant as

$$\lambda c \,.\, \exists X, F \,.\, c = T(k(\texttt{while...}), state(id(\text{“x”}) \mapsto X \oplus id(\text{“f”}) \mapsto F)) \\ \wedge X \geq 0 \wedge F \cdot X! = I!$$

This instantiation of the free variables kc and m avoids the need to explicitly include the entire loop in the invariant annotation.

To apply an invariant Φ_{inv}, the heuristic creates the following proof tree:

$$\dfrac{\mathcal{L} \vdash \Phi'_1 \subseteq \Phi_{\text{inv}} \qquad \dfrac{}{\mathcal{L} \uplus (\mathcal{R} \cup \{\Phi_{\text{inv}} \langle\rightsquigarrow\rangle^{\exists} \Phi_2\}) \vdash_{C'} \Phi_{\text{inv}} \langle\rightsquigarrow\rangle^{\exists} \Phi_2}\,(\textbf{Ax.}) \qquad \dfrac{}{\mathcal{L} \vdash \Phi_2 \subseteq \Phi_2}\,(\textbf{KIV})}{\mathcal{L} \uplus (\mathcal{R} \cup \{\Phi_{\text{inv}} \langle\rightsquigarrow\rangle^{\exists} \Phi_2\}) \vdash_{C'} \Phi'_1 \langle\rightsquigarrow\rangle^{\exists} \Phi_2}\,(\textbf{Cons.})$$

$$\vdots$$

$$\dfrac{\mathcal{L} \vdash \Phi_1 \subseteq \Phi_{\text{inv}} \qquad \dfrac{\mathcal{L} \uplus \mathcal{R} \vdash_{C \cup \{\Phi_{\text{inv}} \langle\rightsquigarrow\rangle^{\exists} \Phi_2\}} \Phi_{\text{inv}} \langle\rightsquigarrow\rangle^{\exists} \Phi_2}{\mathcal{L} \uplus \mathcal{R} \vdash_C \Phi_{\text{inv}} \langle\rightsquigarrow\rangle^{\exists} \Phi_2}\,(\textbf{Circ.}) \qquad \dfrac{}{\mathcal{L} \vdash \Phi_2 \subseteq \Phi_2}\,(\textbf{KIV})}{\mathcal{L} \uplus \mathcal{R} \vdash_C \Phi_1 \langle\rightsquigarrow\rangle^{\exists} \Phi_2}\,(\textbf{Cons.})$$

First, the *(Consequence)* rule is applied, generating two non-trivial premises: The left-hand pattern Φ_1 implies the invariant, and any configuration satisfying the invariant can reach the right-hand pattern Φ_2. Then the *(Circularity)* rule is applied to the second premise, storing a copy of the succedent in the sequent's circularities. Symbolic execution of the loop typically encounters a case distinction between continuing and exiting the loop. In the case where the loop is exited, symbolic execution continues as normal. In the case where the loop continues, symbolic execution eventually encounters the loop head again. Since this execution involves *(Transitivity)*, the reachability property $\Phi_{\text{inv}} \langle\rightsquigarrow\rangle^{\exists} \Phi_2$ is moved to the antecedent. Once the loop head is reached again, *(Consequence)* is once again applied to show the new left-hand pattern Φ'_1 implies the invariant. The second premise once again has the form $\Phi_{\text{inv}} \langle\rightsquigarrow\rangle^{\exists} \Phi_2$, which is now also present in the antecedent. Hence *(Axiom)* closes this premise.

Through the combination of symbolic execution with application of invariants our heuristic achieves a high degree of automation on simple example programs. For the program in Fig. 7, KIV requires 29 proof steps, all of which are automated. We also considered the factorial program in an only slightly more complex iterative language, called IMP. The main difference is that IMP has a simple expression language rather than only the compound multiplication and decrement statements of our language. This simple extension results in a proof with 112 steps, where only the last step (a quantifier instantiation) is manual. Similarly, another IMP program (integer multiplication through repeated addition) also requires 112 steps, out of which three are manual (a quantifier instantiation and two simple multiplication lemmas). In particular, in both cases all manual steps are first-order reasoning steps and thus out of the scope of our heuristic. Note also that quantifiers and integer multiplication quickly lead to undecidability. A completely automated approach based on SMT solving could only rely on heuristics to prove these premises.

5 Conclusion

We have presented an approach that enables interactive program verification with tool support for arbitrary programming languages. For this purpose, the approach combines the 𝕂 semantic framework, the KIV deductive proof assistant and the OPR calculus: We have shown how 𝕂 language definitions can be translated to structured algebraic specifications for KIV. We have adapted the OPR calculus and integrated it in the KIV setting: Here, we reduce OPR reasoning to HOL reasoning over the semantic transition relation between program configurations. As we capture the semantics of reachability properties precisely, the correctness and completeness results for OPR [15] carry over to our setting. An automation approach based on sophisticated heuristics performing symbolic execution, combined with invariant annotations in the program, has been greatly successful in automating proofs: For simple examples, we achieve up to 100% proof automation. Our approach has been implemented in KIV and our tool is available online (https://git.io/Jvl4x).

It has been practically demonstrated that the 𝕂 framework can be used to specify complex real-life programming languages with a wide range of different language features and programming paradigms. In our approach, the semantics is captured by a transition relation between (arbitrarily complex) program configurations: This too is a very general notion capable of modeling most reasonable language features. Our prototype tool is thus already capable of dealing with features such as concurrency, inheritance or exceptions; and an example involving concurrency is included in the link above. The limitations of our tool are mostly of an engineering flavour: In order to support complex languages such as Java or C, more work is needed to support a larger subset of 𝕂 features. Some more obscure features present conceptual challenges: For instance, to support 𝕂's feature of dynamic parsing of program text would require the specification of a parsing algorithm in KIV. However, the main obstacle for complex languages is scalability: KIV runs into problems when handling large specifications. To overcome this, both technical work (such as refactoring of certain parts of KIV) as well as conceptual improvements (such as an alternative syntax translation that generates fewer axioms) can be employed.

While further engineering work is necessary to fully support complex programming languages and to integrate our verification tool with existing language tool support, we believe that this approach represents an important step towards a future where (partially) interactive program verification is an established and highly integrated part of the day-to-day software development process, regardless of the programming language.

References

1. Bogdănaş, D., Roşu, G.: K-Java: a complete semantics of Java. In: Proceedings of the 42nd Symposium on Principles of Programming Languages (POPL 2015), pp. 445–456. ACM, January 2015
2. Chen, X., Roşu, G.: A language-independent program verification framework. In: Margaria, T., Steffen, B. (eds.) ISoLA 2018. LNCS, vol. 11245, pp. 92–102. Springer, Cham (2018). https://doi.org/10.1007/978-3-030-03421-4_7
3. Clavel, M., Durán, F., Eker, S., Lincoln, P., Martí-Oliet, N., Meseguer, J., Talcott, C.: All about Maude - a High-Performance Logical Framework: How to Specify, Program and Verify Systems in Rewriting Logic. Springer-Verlag, Berlin, Heidelberg (2007)

4. Şerbănuţă, T.F., Roşu, G.: K-Maude: a rewriting based tool for semantics of programming languages. In: Ölveczky, P.C. (ed.) WRLA 2010. LNCS, vol. 6381, pp. 104–122. Springer, Heidelberg (2010). https://doi.org/10.1007/978-3-642-16310-4_8
5. Ştefănescu, A., Park, D., Yuwen, S., Li, Y., Roşu, G.: Semantics-based program verifiers for all languages. In: Proceedings of the 31th Conference on Object-Oriented Programming, Systems, Languages, and Applications (OOPSLA 2016), pp. 74–91. ACM, November 2016
6. Ernst, G., Pfähler, J., Schellhorn, G., Haneberg, D., Reif, W.: KIV: overview and VerifyThis competition. Int. J. Softw. Tools Technol. Transfer **17**(6), 677–694 (2015)
7. Filliâtre, J.-C., Paskevich, A.: Why3—where programs meet provers. In: Felleisen, M., Gardner, P. (eds.) ESOP 2013. LNCS, vol. 7792, pp. 125–128. Springer, Heidelberg (2013). https://doi.org/10.1007/978-3-642-37036-6_8
8. Haneberg, D., et al.: The User Interface of the KIV Verification System – A System Description. Electronic Notes in Theoretical Computer Science UITP special issue (2006)
9. Hathhorn, C., Ellison, C., Roşu, G.: Defining the undefinedness of C. In: Proceedings of the 36th ACM SIGPLAN Conference on Programming Language Design and Implementation (PLDI 2015), pp. 336–345. ACM, June 2015
10. Leino, K.R.M.: This is Boogie 2, June 2008. https://www.microsoft.com/en-us/research/publication/this-is-boogie-2-2/
11. Meredith, P., Rosu, M.H.G.: An executable rewriting logic semantics of K-Scheme. In: Workshop on Scheme and Functional Programming, vol. 1, p. 10 (2007)
12. Müller, P., Schwerhoff, M., Summers, A.J.: Viper: a verification infrastructure for permission-based reasoning. In: Jobstmann, B., Leino, K.R.M. (eds.) VMCAI 2016. LNCS, vol. 9583, pp. 41–62. Springer, Heidelberg (2016). https://doi.org/10.1007/978-3-662-49122-5_2
13. Park, D., Ştefănescu, A., Roşu, G.: KJS: a complete formal semantics of JavaScript. In: Proceedings of the 36th ACM SIGPLAN Conference on Programming Language Design and Implementation (PLDI 2015), pp. 346–356. ACM, June 2015
14. Reif, W., Schellhorn, G., Stenzel, K., Balser, M.: Structured specifications and interactive proofs with KIV. In: Bibel ,W., Schmitt, P.H. (eds.) Automated Deduction – A Basis for Applications. Applied Logic Series, vol 9, pp. 13–39. Springer, Dordrecht (1998)
15. Roşu, G., Ştefănescu, A., Ciobâcă, Ş., Moore, B.M.: One-path reachability logic. In: Proceedings of the 28th Symposium on Logic in Computer Science (LICS 2013), pp. 358–367. IEEE, June 2013
16. Roşu, G., Şerbănuţă, T.F.: An overview of the K semantic framework. J. Logic Algebraic Programm. **79**(6), 397–434 (2010)
17. Rosu, G., Stefanescu, A., Ciobaca, S., Moore, B.: Reachability Logic. Technical report July 2012. https://www.ideals.illinois.edu/handle/2142/32952
18. Şerbănuţă, T., Ştefănescu, G., Roşu, G.: Defining and executing P systems with structured data in K. In: Corne, D.W., Frisco, P., Păun, G., Rozenberg, G., Salomaa, A. (eds.) WMC 2008. LNCS, vol. 5391, pp. 374–393. Springer, Heidelberg (2009). https://doi.org/10.1007/978-3-540-95885-7_26
19. Ştefănescu, A., Ciobâcă, Ş., Mereuta, R., Moore, B.M., Şerbănută, T.F., Roşu, G.: All-path reachability logic. In: Dowek, G. (ed.) RTA 2014. LNCS, vol. 8560, pp. 425–440. Springer, Cham (2014). https://doi.org/10.1007/978-3-319-08918-8_29
20. The Coq development team: The Coq proof assistant reference manual. LogiCal Project (2004). http://coq.inria.fr, version 8.0

Institution-Based Encoding and Verification of Simple UML State Machines in CASL/SPASS

Tobias Rosenberger[1,2], Saddek Bensalem[2], Alexander Knapp[3], and Markus Roggenbach[1](✉)

[1] Swansea University, Swansea, UK
{t.rosenberger.971978,m.roggenbach}@swansea.ac.uk
[2] Université Grenoble Alpes, Grenoble, France
Saddek.Bensalem@imag.fr
[3] Universität Augsburg, Augsburg, Germany
knapp@informatik.uni-augsburg.de

Abstract. We present a new approach on how to provide institution-based semantics for UML state machines. Rather than capturing UML state machines directly as an institution, we build up a new logical framework $\mathcal{M}^{\downarrow}_{\mathcal{D}}$ into which UML state machines can be embedded. A theoroidal comorphism maps $\mathcal{M}^{\downarrow}_{\mathcal{D}}$ into the CASL institution. This allows for symbolic reasoning on UML state machines. By utilising the heterogeneous toolset HETS that supports CASL, a broad range of verification tools, including the automatic theorem prover SPASS, can be combined in the analysis of a single state machine.

1 Introduction

As part of a longstanding line of research [8–10, 19], we set out on a general programme to bring together multi-view system specification with UML diagrams and heterogeneous specification and verification based on institution theory, giving the different system views both a joint semantics and richer tool support.

Institutions, a formal notion of a logic, are a principled way of creating such joint semantics. They make moderate assumptions about the data constituting a logic, give uniform notions of well-behaved translations between logics and, given a graph of such translations, automatically give rise to a joint institution.

In this paper, we will focus on UML state machines, which are an object-based variant of Harel statecharts. Within the UML, state machines are a central means to specify system behaviour. Here, we capture simple UML state machines in what we claim to be a true semantical sense. Focus of this paper are state machines running in isolation—interacting state machines and with it the notion of the event pool are left to future work.

Compared to our previous attempts to institutionalise state machines [8–10, 19], this paper takes a different approach. Rather than capturing UML state machines directly as an institution, we build up a new logical framework

M. Roggenbach (Ed.): WADT 2020, LNCS 12669, pp. 120–141, 2021.
https://doi.org/10.1007/978-3-030-73785-6_7

$\mathcal{M}^{\downarrow}_{\mathcal{D}}$ in which UML state machines can be embedded. Core of this framework is a new hybrid modal logic which allows us to logically encode the *presence* as well as the *absence* of transitions in the state machines. Data types, guards, and effects of events are specified in the algebraic specification language CASL. An algorithm translates UML state machines into $\mathcal{M}^{\downarrow}_{\mathcal{D}}$.

A theoroidal comorphism maps our logical framework $\mathcal{M}^{\downarrow}_{\mathcal{D}}$ into the CASL institution. This allows to us to utilise the heterogeneous toolset HETS [15] and its connected provers for analysing UML state machines. In this paper we demonstrate how to analyse a state machine with the automatic first-order prover SPASS [20], which is the default automated prover of HETS. Such symbolic reasoning can be of advantage as, in principle, it allows to verify properties of UML state machines with large or infinite state spaces. Such machines appear routinely in system modelling: though state machines usually have only finitely many control states, they have a large number of configurations, or even infinitely many, due to the data variables involved.

Compared to other symbolic approaches to directly encode UML state machines into a specific interactive theorem prover [1,5,11], our logical framework $\mathcal{M}^{\downarrow}_{\mathcal{D}}$ provides first an institutional semantics that is tool independent. Only in a second step, we translate $\mathcal{M}^{\downarrow}_{\mathcal{D}}$ into CASL. Via HETS, this opens access to a broad range of analysis tools, including SAT solvers, automatic first-order theorem provers, automated and interactive higher-order theorem provers, which all can be combined in the analysis of state machines.

This paper is organised as follows: First we provide some background on institutions, including the CASL institution in Sect. 2. Then we discuss simple UML state machines, how to capture their events, attributes, and transitions, and what their models are. In Sect. 4 we define a new hybrid, modal logic for specifying UML state machine transitions. Section 5 provides the translation into the CASL institution. In Sect. 6, we finally demonstrate the symbolic analysis of a simple UML state machine as enabled by the previous constructions. We conclude in Sect. 7 with an outlook to future work.

2 Background on Institutions

We briefly recall the basic definitions of institutions and theoroidal institution comorphisms as well as the algebraic specification language CASL. Subsequently we will develop an institutional frame for capturing simple UML state machines and present a theoroidal institution comorphism from this frame into CASL.

2.1 Institutions and Theoroidal Institution Comorphisms

Institutions are an abstract formalisation of the notion of logical systems combining signatures, structures, sentences, and satisfaction under the slogan "truth is invariant under change of notation". Institutions can be related in different ways by institution (forward) (co-)morphisms, where a so-called theoroidal institution comorphism covers a particular case of encoding a "poorer" logic into a "richer" one.

spec NAT =
  free type *Nat* ::= 0 | *suc*(*Nat*)
  ops $\_\_+\_\_ : Nat \times Nat \to Nat$
  pred $\_\_<\_\_ : Nat \times Nat$
  $\forall\, n, m : Nat \bullet 0 + n = n \quad \bullet\, suc(n) + m = suc(n+m)$
  $\bullet\, \neg\, n < 0 \quad \bullet\, 0 < suc(n) \quad \bullet\, suc(m) < suc(n) \Leftrightarrow m < n$
end

Fig. 1. A CASL specification of the natural numbers

Formally [4], an institution $\mathcal{I} = (\mathbb{S}^{\mathcal{I}}, Str^{\mathcal{I}}, \mathrm{Sen}^{\mathcal{I}}, \models^{\mathcal{I}})$ consists of (i) a category of *signatures* $\mathbb{S}^{\mathcal{I}}$; (ii) a contravariant *structures functor* $Str^{\mathcal{I}} : (\mathbb{S}^{\mathcal{I}})^{\mathrm{op}} \to \mathrm{Cat}$, where Cat is the category of (small) categories; (iii) a *sentence functor* $\mathrm{Sen}^{\mathcal{I}} : \mathbb{S}^{\mathcal{I}} \to \mathrm{Set}$, where Set is the category of sets; and (iv) a family of *satisfaction relations* $\models^{\mathcal{I}}_{\Sigma} \subseteq |Str^{\mathcal{I}}(\Sigma)| \times \mathrm{Sen}^{\mathcal{I}}(\Sigma)$ indexed over $\Sigma \in |\mathbb{S}^{\mathcal{I}}|$, such that the following *satisfaction condition* holds for all $\sigma : \Sigma \to \Sigma'$ in $\mathbb{S}^{\mathcal{I}}$, $\varphi \in \mathrm{Sen}^{\mathcal{I}}(\Sigma)$, and $M' \in |Str^{\mathcal{I}}(\Sigma')|$:

$$Str^{\mathcal{I}}(\sigma)(M') \models^{\mathcal{I}}_{\Sigma} \varphi \iff M' \models^{\mathcal{I}}_{\Sigma'} \mathrm{Sen}^{\mathcal{I}}(\sigma)(\varphi)\ .$$

$Str^{\mathcal{I}}(\sigma)$ is called the *reduct* functor, $\mathrm{Sen}^{\mathcal{I}}(\sigma)$ the *translation* function.

A *theory presentation* $T = (\Sigma, \Phi)$ in the institution $\mathcal{I}$ consists of a signature $\Sigma \in |\mathbb{S}^{\mathcal{I}}|$, also denoted by $Sig(T)$, and a set of sentences $\Phi \subseteq \mathrm{Sen}^{\mathcal{I}}(\Sigma)$. Its *model class* $\mathrm{Mod}^{\mathcal{I}}(T)$ is the class $\{M \in Str^{\mathcal{I}}(\Sigma) \mid M \models^{\mathcal{I}}_{\Sigma} \varphi \text{ f.a. } \varphi \in \Phi\}$ of the Σ-structures satisfying the sentences in Φ. A *theory presentation morphism* $\sigma : (\Sigma, \Phi) \to (\Sigma', \Phi')$ is given by a signature morphism $\sigma : \Sigma \to \Sigma'$ such that $M' \models^{\mathcal{I}}_{\Sigma'} \mathrm{Sen}^{\mathcal{I}}(\sigma)(\varphi)$ for all $\varphi \in \Phi$ and $M' \in \mathrm{Mod}^{\mathcal{I}}(\Sigma', \Phi')$. Theory presentations in $\mathcal{I}$ and their morphisms form the category $\mathrm{Pres}^{\mathcal{I}}$.

A *theoroidal institution comorphism* $\nu = (\nu^{\mathbb{S}}, \mu^{\mathrm{Mod}}, \nu^{\mathrm{Sen}}) : \mathcal{I} \to \mathcal{I}'$ consists of a functor $\nu^{\mathbb{S}} : \mathbb{S}^{\mathcal{I}} \to \mathrm{Pres}^{\mathcal{I}'}$ inducing the functor $\nu^{Sig} = \nu^{\mathbb{S}}; Sig : \mathbb{S}^{\mathcal{I}} \to \mathbb{S}^{\mathcal{I}'}$ on signatures, a natural transformation $\nu^{\mathrm{Mod}} : (\nu^{\mathbb{S}})^{\mathrm{op}}; \mathrm{Mod}^{\mathcal{I}'} \stackrel{.}{\to} Str^{\mathcal{I}}$ on structures, and a natural transformation $\nu^{\mathrm{Sen}} : \mathrm{Sen}^{\mathcal{I}} \stackrel{.}{\to} \nu^{Sig}; \mathrm{Sen}^{\mathcal{I}'}$ on sentences, such that for all $\Sigma \in |\mathbb{S}^{\mathcal{I}}|$, $M' \in |\mathrm{Mod}^{\mathcal{I}'}(\nu^{\mathbb{S}}(\Sigma))|$, and $\varphi \in \mathrm{Sen}^{\mathcal{I}}(\Sigma)$ the following *satisfaction condition* holds:

$$\nu^{\mathrm{Mod}}_{\Sigma}(M') \models^{\mathcal{I}}_{\Sigma} \varphi \iff M' \models^{\mathcal{I}'}_{\nu^{Sig}(\Sigma)} \nu^{\mathrm{Sen}}(\Sigma)(\varphi)\ .$$

2.2 CASL and the Institution CFOL$^=$

The algebraic specification language CASL [16] offers several specification levels: *Basic specifications* essentially list signature declarations and axioms, thus determining a category of first-order structures. *Structured specifications* serve to combine such basic specifications into larger specifications in a hierarchical and modular fashion. Of the many logics available in CASL, we will work with the institution CFOL$^=$, of which we briefly recall the main notions; a detailed account can be found e.g. in [14].

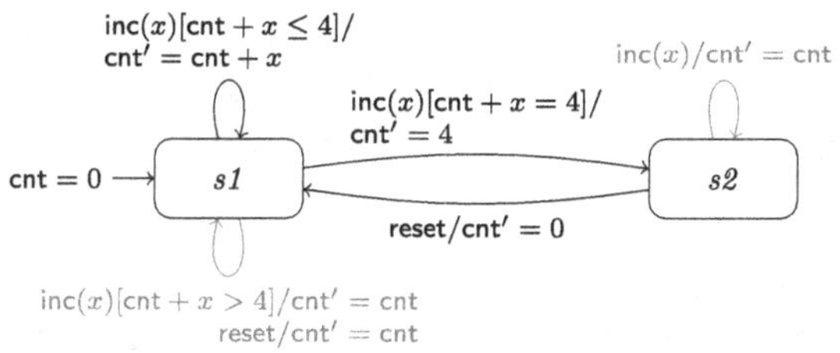

Fig. 2. Simple UML state machine *Counter*

At the level of basic specifications, cf. Fig. 1, one can declare *sorts*, *op*erations, and *pred*icates with given argument and result sorts. Formally, this defines a *many-sorted signature* $\Sigma = (S, F, P)$ with a set S of sorts, a $S^* \times S$-sorted family $F = (F_{w,s})_{w\, s \in S^+}$ of *total function symbols*, and a S^*-sorted family $P = (P_w)_{w \in S^*}$ of *predicate symbols*. Using these symbols, one may then write axioms in first-order logic. Moreover, one can specify data *types*, given in terms of alternatives consisting of data constructors and, optionally, selectors, which may be declared to be *generated* or *free*. Generatedness amounts to an implicit higher-order induction axiom and intuitively states that all elements of the data types are reachable by constructor terms ("no junk"); freeness additionally requires that all these constructor terms are distinct ("no confusion"). Basic CASL specifications denote the class of all algebras which fulfil the declared axioms, i.e., CASL has loose semantics. In structured CASL specifications, a *structured free* construct can be used to ensure freeness (i.e., initial semantics) of a specification. For functions and predicates, the effect of the structured free construct corresponds to the effect of free types on sorts. A *many-sorted* Σ*-structure* M consists of a non-empty carrier set s^M for each $s \in S$, a total function $f^M : M_w \to M_s$ for each function symbol $f \in F_{w,s}$ and a predicate p^M for each predicate symbol $p \in P_w$. A *many-sorted* Σ*-sentence* is a closed many-sorted first-order formula over Σ or a sort generation constraint.

3 Simple UML State Machines

UML state machines [17] provide means to specify the reactive behaviour of objects or component instances. These entities hold an internal data state, typically given by a set of attributes or properties, and shall react to event occurrences by firing different transitions in different control states. Such transitions may have a guard depending on event arguments and the internal state and may change, as an effect, the internal control and data state of the entity as well as raise events on their own.

Figure 2 shows the example of a bounded, resettable counter working on an attribute cnt (assumed to take values in the natural numbers) that is initialised with 0. The counter can be reset to 0 or increased by a natural number x, subject to the current control state (*s1* or *s2*) and the guards (shown in square brackets) and effects (after the slash) of the outgoing transitions. An effect describes how the data state before firing a transition (referred to by unprimed attribute names) relates to the data state after (primed names) in a single predicate; this generalises the more usual sequences of assignments such that $\mathsf{cnt}' = \mathsf{cnt} + x$ corresponds to $\mathsf{cnt} \leftarrow \mathsf{cnt} + x$ and $\mathsf{cnt}' = \mathsf{cnt}$ to a skip. The machine is specified non-deterministically: If event $\mathsf{inc}(x)$ occurs in state *s1* such that the guard $\mathsf{cnt} + x = 4$ holds, the machine can either stay in *s1* or it can proceed to *s2*. Seemingly, the machine does not react to reset in *s1* and to inc in *s2*. However, UML state machines are meant to be input-enabled such that all event occurrences to which the machine shows no explicit reacting transition are silently discarded, as indicated by the "grey" transitions. Overall, the machine *Counter* shall ensure that cnt never exceeds 4.

It is for such simple UML state machines as the counter in Fig. 2 that we want to provide proof support in SPASS via an institutional encoding in CASL. The sub-language covers the following fundamental state machine features: data, states, and (non-deterministic) guarded transitions for reacting to events. However, for the time being, we leave out not only all advanced modelling constructs, like hierarchical states or compound transitions, but also defer, most importantly, event-based communication between state machines to future work. In the following we make first precise the syntax of the machines by means of event/data signatures, data states and transitions, guards and effects. Then we introduce semantic structures for the machines and define their model class. Syntax and semantics of simple UML state machines form the basis for their institutionalisation. We thus also introduce event/data signature morphisms and the corresponding formulæ translation and structure reducts in order to be able to change the interface of simple UML state machines.

3.1 Event/Data Signatures, Data States and Transitions

We capture the events for a machine in an *event signature* E that consists of a finite set of events $|E|$ and a map $\upsilon(E)$ assigning to each $e \in |E|$ a finite set of variables, where we write $e(X)$ for $e \in |E|$ and $\upsilon(E)(e) = X$, and also $e(X) \in E$ in this case. For the data state, we use a *data signature* A consisting of a finite set of attributes. An *event/data signature* Σ consists of an event signature $E(\Sigma)$ and a data signature $A(\Sigma)$.

Example 1. The event/data signature Σ of the simple UML state machine in Fig. 2 is given by the set of events $|E(\Sigma)| = \{\mathsf{inc}, \mathsf{reset}\}$ with argument variables $\upsilon(E(\Sigma))(\mathsf{inc}) = \{x\}$ and $\upsilon(E(\Sigma))(\mathsf{reset}) = \emptyset$ such that $\mathsf{inc}(x) \in E(\Sigma)$ and $\mathsf{reset} \in E(\Sigma)$; as well as the data signature $A(\Sigma) = \{\mathsf{cnt}\}$.

For specifying transition guards and effects, we exchange UML's notorious and intricate expression and action languages both syntactically and semantically by a straightforward CASL fragment rendering guards as data state predicates and effects as data transition predicates: We assume given a fixed universe $\mathcal{D}$ of *data values* and a CASL specification *Dt* with a dedicated sort *dt* in its signature *Sig*(*Dt*) such that the universe dt^M of every model $M \in \mathrm{Mod}^{\mathrm{CASL}}(Dt)$

is isomorphic to $\mathcal{D}$, i.e., there is a bijection $\iota_{M,dt} \colon dt^M \cong \mathcal{D}$. This puts at our disposal the open formulæ $\mathscr{F}^{\text{CASL}}_{Sig(Dt),X}$ over sorted variables $X = (X_s)_{s \in S}$ and their satisfaction relation $M, \beta \models^{\text{CASL}}_{Sig(Dt),X} \varphi$ for models $M \in \text{Mod}^{\text{CASL}}(Dt)$, variable valuations $\beta \colon X \to M$, and formulæ $\varphi \in \mathscr{F}^{\text{CASL}}_{Sig(Dt),X}$.

Example 2. Consider the natural numbers $\mathbb{N}$ as data values $\mathcal{D}$. The CASL specification in Fig. 1 characterises $\mathbb{N}$ up to isomorphism as the carrier set of the dedicated sort $dt = Nat$. It specifies an abstract data type with sort *Nat*, operations $+, 0, suc$, and a predicate $<$.

The very simple choice of $\mathcal{D}$ capturing data with only a single sort can, in principal, be replaced by any institutional data modelling language that, for our purposes of a theoroidal institution comorphism (see Sect. 5), is faithfully representable in CASL; one such possibility are UML class diagrams, see [7].

Data States and Guards. A *data state* ω for a data signature A is given by a function $\omega \colon A \to \mathcal{D}$; in particular, $\Omega(A) = \mathcal{D}^A$ is the set of A-data states. The guards of a machine are *state predicates* in $\mathscr{F}^{\mathcal{D}}_{A,X} = \mathscr{F}^{\text{CASL}}_{Sig(Dt),A \cup X}$, taking A as well as an additional set X as variables of sort dt. A state predicate $\phi \in \mathscr{F}^{\mathcal{D}}_{A,X}$ is to be interpreted over an A-data state ω and valuation $\beta \colon X \to \mathcal{D}$ and we define the *satisfaction relation* $\models^{\mathcal{D}}$ by

$$\omega, \beta \models^{\mathcal{D}}_{A,X} \phi \iff M, \iota^{-1}_{M,dt} \circ (\omega \cup \beta) \models^{\text{CASL}}_{Sig(Dt),A \cup X} \phi$$

where $M \in \text{Mod}^{\text{CASL}}(Dt)$ and $\iota_{M,dt} \colon M(dt) \cong \mathcal{D}$. For a state predicate $\varphi \in \mathscr{F}^{\mathcal{D}}_{A,\emptyset}$ not involving any variables, we write $\omega \models^{\mathcal{D}}_{A} \varphi$ for $\omega \models^{\mathcal{D}}_{A,\emptyset} \varphi$.

Example 3. The guard $\mathsf{cnt} + x \leq 4$ of the machine in Fig. 2 features both the attribute cnt and the variable x. A data state fulfilling this state predicate for $x = 0$ is $\mathsf{cnt} \mapsto 3$.

Data Transitions and Effects. A *data transition* (ω, ω') for a data signature A is a pair of A-data states; in particular, $\Omega^2(A) = (\mathcal{D}^A)^2$ is the set of A-data transitions. It holds that $(\mathcal{D}^A)^2 \cong \mathcal{D}^{2A}$, where $2A = A \uplus A$ and we assume that no attribute in A ends in a prime $'$ and all attributes in the second summand are adorned with an additional prime. The effects of a machine are *transition predicates* in $\mathscr{F}^{2\mathcal{D}}_{A,X} = \mathscr{F}^{\mathcal{D}}_{2A,X}$. The satisfaction relation $\models^{2\mathcal{D}}$ for a transition predicate $\psi \in \mathscr{F}^{2\mathcal{D}}_{A,X}$, data transition $(\omega, \omega') \in \Omega^2(A)$, and valuation $\beta \colon X \to \mathcal{D}$ is defined as

$$(\omega, \omega'), \beta \models^{2\mathcal{D}}_{A,X} \psi \iff \omega + \omega', \beta \models^{\mathcal{D}}_{2A,X} \psi$$

where $\omega + \omega' \in \Omega(2A)$ with $(\omega + \omega')(a) = \omega(a)$ and $(\omega + \omega')(a') = \omega'(a)$.

Example 4. The effect $\mathsf{cnt}' = \mathsf{cnt} + x$ of the machine in Fig. 2 describes the increment of the value of attribute cnt by a variable amount x.

3.2 Syntax of Simple UML State Machines

A simple UML state machine U uses an event/data signature $\Sigma(U)$ for its events and attributes and consists of a finite set of *control states* $C(U)$, a finite set of *transition specifications* $T(U)$ of the form $(c, \phi, e(X), \psi, c')$ with $c, c' \in C(U)$, $e(X) \in E(\Sigma(U))$, a state predicate $\phi \in \mathscr{F}^{\mathcal{D}}_{A(\Sigma(U)),X}$, a transition predicate $\psi \in \mathscr{F}^{2\mathcal{D}}_{A(\Sigma(U)),X}$, an *initial control state* $c_0(U) \in C(U)$, and an *initial state predicate* $\varphi_0(U) \in \mathscr{F}^{\mathcal{D}}_{A(\Sigma(U)),\emptyset}$, such that $C(U)$ is *syntactically reachable*, i.e., for every $c \in C(U) \setminus \{c_0(U)\}$ there are $(c_0(U), \phi_1, e_1(X_1), \psi_1, c_1), \ldots, (c_{n-1}, \phi_n, e_n(X_n), \psi_n, c_n) \in T(U)$ with $n > 0$ such that $c_n = c$. Syntactic reachability guarantees initially connected state machine graphs. This simplifies graph-based algorithms (see Algorithm 1).

Example 5. The machine in Fig. 2 has as its control states $\{s1, s2\}$, as its transition specifications $\{(s1, \mathsf{cnt} + x \leq 4, \mathsf{inc}(x), \mathsf{cnt}' = \mathsf{cnt} + x, s1), (s1, \mathsf{cnt} + x = 4, \mathsf{inc}(x), \mathsf{cnt}' = 4, s2), (s2, \text{true}, \mathsf{reset}, \mathsf{cnt}' = 0, s1)\}$, as initial control state $s1$, and as initial state predicate $\mathsf{cnt} = 0$.

3.3 Event/Data Structures and Models of Simple UML State Machines

For capturing machines semantically, we use event/data structures that are given over an event/data signature Σ and consist of a transition system of configurations such that all configurations are reachable from its initial configurations. Herein, configurations show a control state, corresponding to machine states, and a data name from which a proper data state over $A(\Sigma)$ can be retrieved by a labelling function. Transitions connect configurations by events from $E(\Sigma)$ with their arguments instantiated by data from $\mathcal{D}$.

Formally, a *Σ-event/data structure* $M = (\Gamma, R, \Gamma_0, \omega)$ over an event/data signature Σ consists of a set of *configurations* $\Gamma \subseteq C \times D$ for some sets of *control states* C and *data names* D, a family of *transition relations* $R = (R_{e(\beta)} \subseteq \Gamma \times \Gamma)_{e(X) \in E(\Sigma), \beta \colon X \to \mathcal{D}}$, and a non-empty set of *initial configurations* $\Gamma_0 = \{c_0\} \times D_0 \subseteq \Gamma$ with a unique *initial control state* $c_0 \in C$ such that Γ is *reachable* via R, i.e., for all $\gamma \in \Gamma$ there are $\gamma_0 \in \Gamma_0$, $n \geq 0$, $e_1(X_1), \ldots, e_n(X_n) \in E(\Sigma)$, $\beta_1 \colon X_1 \to \mathcal{D}, \ldots, \beta_n \colon X_n \to \mathcal{D}$, and $(\gamma_i, \gamma_{i+1}) \in R_{e_{i+1}(\beta_{i+1})}$ for all $0 \leq i < n$ with $\gamma_n = \gamma$; and a *data state labelling* $\omega \colon D \to \Omega(A(\Sigma))$. We write $c(M)(\gamma) = c$ and $\omega(M)(\gamma) = \omega(d)$ for $\gamma = (c, d) \in \Gamma$, $\Gamma(M)$ for Γ, $C(M)$ for $\{c(M)(\gamma) \mid \gamma \in \Gamma(M)\}$, $R(M)$ for R, $\Gamma_0(M)$ for Γ_0, $c_0(M)$ for c_0, and $\Omega_0(M)$ for $\{\omega(M)(\gamma_0) \mid \gamma_0 \in \Gamma_0\}$.

The restriction to reachable transition systems is not strictly necessary and could be replaced by constraining all statements on event/data structures to take into account only their reachable part (see, e.g., Lemma 1).

Example 6. For an event/data structure for the machine in Fig. 2 over its signature Σ in Example 1 we may choose the control states C as $\{s1, s2\}$, and the data names D as the set $\Omega(A(\Sigma)) = \mathcal{D}^{\{\mathsf{cnt}\}}$. In particular, the data state labelling ω is just the identity. The only initial configuration is $(s1, \{\mathsf{cnt} \mapsto 0\})$. A possible transition goes from configuration $(s1, \{\mathsf{cnt} \mapsto 2\})$ to configuration $(s2, \{\mathsf{cnt} \mapsto 4\})$ with the instantiated event $\mathsf{inc}(2)$.

A $\Sigma(U)$-event/data structure M is a *model* of a simple UML state machine U if $C(U) \subseteq C(M)$ up to a bijective renaming, $c_0(M) = c_0(U)$, $\Omega_0(M) \subseteq \{\omega \in |\Omega(A(\Sigma(U)))| \mid \omega \models^{\mathcal{D}}_{A(\Sigma(U))} \varphi_0(U)\}$, and if the following holds for all $(c, d) \in \Gamma(M)$:

- for all $(c, \phi, e(X), \psi, c') \in T(U)$ and $\beta\colon X \to \mathcal{D}$ with $\omega(M)(d), \beta \models^{\mathcal{D}}_{A(\Sigma(U)),X} \phi$, there is a $((c, d), (c', d')) \in R(M)_{e(\beta)}$ with $(\omega(M)(d), \omega(M)(d')), \beta \models^{2\mathcal{D}}_{A(\Sigma(U)),X} \psi$;
- for all $((c, d), (c', d')) \in R(M)_{e(\beta)}$ there is either some $(c, \phi, e(X), \psi, c') \in T(U)$ with $\omega(M)(d), \beta \models^{\mathcal{D}}_{A(\Sigma(U)),X} \phi$ and $(\omega(M)(d), \omega(M)(d')), \beta \models^{2\mathcal{D}}_{A(\Sigma(U)),X} \psi$, or $\omega(M)(d), \beta \not\models^{\mathcal{D}}_{A(\Sigma(U)),X} \bigvee_{(c,\phi,e(X),\psi,c') \in T(U)} \phi$, $c = c'$, and $\omega(M)(d) = \omega(M)(d')$.

A model of U thus on the one hand implements each transition prescribed by U, but on the other hand must not show transitions not covered by the specified transitions. Moreover, it is *input-enabled*, i.e., every event can be consumed in every control state: If no precondition of an explicitly specified transition is satisfied, there is a self-loop which leaves the data state untouched. In fact, input-enabledness, as required by the UML specification [17], can also be rendered as a syntactic transformation making a simple UML state machine U input-enabled by adding the following set of transition specifications for idling self-loops:

$$\{(c, \neg(\bigvee_{(c,\phi,e(X),\psi,c') \in T(U)} \phi), e(X), 1_{A(\Sigma(U))}, c) \mid c \in C,\ e(X) \in E(\Sigma(U))\}\ .$$

Example 7. For the simple UML state machine in Fig. 2 the "grey" transitions correspond to an input-enabledness completion w.r.t. the "black" transitions.

The requirement of syntactic reachability for simple UML state machines is correlated with the requirement of (semantic) reachability of event/data structures, as a machine violating syntactic reachability cannot have a model. Equally, a machine with a non-satisfiable initial state predicate fails to have a model.

3.4 Event/Data Signature Morphisms, Reducts, and Translations

The external interface of a simple UML state machine is given by events, its internal interface by attributes. Both interfaces, represented as an event/data signature, are susceptible to change in the system development process which is captured by signature morphisms. Such changes have also to be reflected in the guards and effects, i.e., data state and transition predicates, by syntactical translations as well as in the interpretation domains by semantical reducts.

A *data signature morphism* from a data signature A to a data signature A' is a function $\alpha\colon A \to A'$. The *α-reduct* of an A'-data state $\omega'\colon A' \to \mathcal{D}$ along a data signature morphism $\alpha\colon A \to A'$ is given by the A-data state $\omega'|\alpha\colon A \to \mathcal{D}$

with $(\omega'|\alpha)(a) = \omega'(\alpha(a))$ for every $a \in A$; the *α-reduct* of an A'-data transition (ω', ω'') by the A-data transition $(\omega', \omega'')|\alpha = (\omega'|\alpha, \omega''|\alpha)$. The *state predicate translation* $\mathscr{F}^{\mathcal{D}}_{\alpha,X} \colon \mathscr{F}^{\mathcal{D}}_{A,X} \to \mathscr{F}^{\mathcal{D}}_{A',X}$ along a data signature morphism $\alpha \colon A \to A'$ is given by the CASL-formula translation $\mathscr{F}^{\text{CASL}}_{Sig(Dt),\alpha\cup 1_X}$ along the substitution $\alpha \cup 1_X$; the *transition predicate translation* $\mathscr{F}^{2\mathcal{D}}_{\alpha,X}$ by $\mathscr{F}^{\mathcal{D}}_{2\alpha,X}$ with $2\alpha \colon 2A \to 2A'$ defined by $2\alpha(a) = \alpha(a)$ and $2\alpha(a') = \alpha(a)'$. For each of these two reduct-translation-pairs the *satisfaction condition* holds due to the general substitution lemma for CASL:

$$\omega'|\alpha, \beta \models^{\mathcal{D}}_{A,X} \phi \iff \omega', \beta \models^{\mathcal{D}}_{A',X} \mathscr{F}^{\mathcal{D}}_{\alpha,X}(\phi)$$
$$(\omega', \omega'')|\alpha, \beta \models^{2\mathcal{D}}_{A,X} \psi \iff (\omega', \omega''), \beta \models^{2\mathcal{D}}_{A',X} \mathscr{F}^{2\mathcal{D}}_{\alpha,X}(\psi)$$

An *event signature morphism* $\eta \colon E \to E'$ is a function $\eta \colon |E| \to |E'|$ such that $\upsilon(E)(e) = \upsilon(E')(\eta(e))$ for all $e \in |E|$. An *event/data signature morphism* $\sigma \colon \Sigma \to \Sigma'$ consists of an event signature morphism $E(\sigma) \colon E(\Sigma) \to E(\Sigma')$ and a data signature morphism $A(\sigma) \colon A(\Sigma) \to A(\Sigma')$. The *$\sigma$-reduct* of a Σ'-event/data structure M' along σ is the Σ-event/data structure $M'|\sigma$ such that

- $\Gamma(M'|\sigma) \subseteq \Gamma(M')$ as well as $R(M'|\sigma) = (R(M'|\sigma)_{e(\beta)})_{e(X)\in E(\Sigma),\beta\colon X\to\mathcal{D}}$ are inductively defined by $\Gamma(M'|\sigma) \supseteq \Gamma_0(M')$ and, for all $\gamma', \gamma'' \in \Gamma(M')$, $e(X) \in E(\Sigma)$, and $\beta \colon X \to \mathcal{D}$, if $\gamma' \in \Gamma(M'|\sigma)$ and $(\gamma', \gamma'') \in R(M')_{E(\sigma)(e)(\beta)}$, then $\gamma'' \in \Gamma(M'|\sigma)$ and $(\gamma', \gamma'') \in R(M'|\sigma)_{e(\beta)}$;
- $\Gamma_0(M'|\sigma) = \Gamma_0(M')$; and
- $\omega(M'|\sigma)(\gamma') = (\omega(M')(\gamma'))|\sigma$ for all $\gamma' \in \Gamma(M'|\sigma)$.

Building a reduct of an event/data-structure does not affect the single configurations, but potentially reduces the set of configurations by restricting the available events, and the data state observable from the data name of a configuration. We denote by $\Gamma^F(M, \gamma)$ and $\Gamma^F(M)$, respectively, the set of configurations of a Σ-event/data structure M that are F-reachable from a configuration $\gamma \in \Gamma(M)$ and from an initial configuration $\gamma_0 \in \Gamma_0(M)$, respectively, with a set of events $F \subseteq E(\Sigma)$ where a $\gamma_n \in \Gamma(M)$ is *F-reachable in M from* a $\gamma_1 \in \Gamma(M)$ if there are $n \geq 1$, $e_2(X_2), \ldots, e_n(X_n) \in F$, $\beta_2 \colon X_2 \to \mathcal{D}, \ldots, \beta_n \colon X_n \to \mathcal{D}$, and $(\gamma_i, \gamma_{i+1}) \in R(M)_{e_{i+1}(\beta_{i+1})}$ for all $1 \leq i < n$.

Although it is straightforward to define a translation of simple UML state machines along an event/data signature morphism, the rather restrictive notion of their models prevents the satisfaction condition to hold. In fact, this is already true for our previous endeavours to institutionalise UML state machines [8,10]. There machines themselves were taken to be sentences over signatures comprising both events and states, and the satisfaction relation also required that a model shows exactly the transitions of such a machine sentence. For signature morphisms σ that are not surjective on states, building the reduct could result in less states and transitions, which leads to the following counterexample to the satisfaction condition [19]:

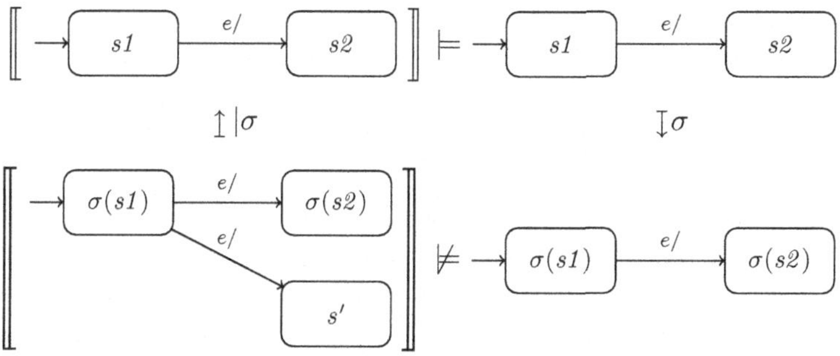

We therefore propose to make a detour through a more general hybrid modal logic. This logic is directly based on event/data structures and thus close to the domain of state machines. For forming an institution, its hybrid features allow to avoid control states as part of the signature and its event-based modalities allow to specify both mandatory and forbidden behaviour in a more fine-grained manner. Still, the logic is expressive enough to characterise the model class of a simple UML state machine syntactically.

4 A Hybrid Modal Logic for Event/Data Systems

The logic $\mathcal{M}^{\downarrow}_{\mathcal{D}}$ is a hybrid modal logic for specifying event/data-based reactive systems and reasoning about them. The $\mathcal{M}^{\downarrow}_{\mathcal{D}}$-signatures are the event/data signatures, the $\mathcal{M}^{\downarrow}_{\mathcal{D}}$-structures the event/data structures. The modal part of the logic allows to handle transitions between configurations where the modalities describe moves between configurations that adhere to a pre-condition or guard as a state predicate for an event with arguments and a transition predicate for the data change corresponding to effects. The hybrid part of the logic allows to bind control states of system configurations and to jump to configurations with such control states explicitly, but leaves out nominals as interfacing names as well as the possibility to quantify over control states. The logic builds on the hybrid dynamic logic $\mathcal{D}^{\downarrow}$ for specifying reactive systems without data [13] and its extension $\mathcal{E}^{\downarrow}$ to handle also data [6]. We restrict ourselves to modal operators consisting only of single instead of compound actions as done in dynamic logic. However, we still retain a box modality for accessing all configurations that are reachable from a given configuration. Moreover, we extend $\mathcal{E}^{\downarrow}$ by adding parameters to events.

The category of $\mathcal{M}^{\downarrow}_{\mathcal{D}}$-*signatures* $\mathbb{S}^{\mathcal{M}^{\downarrow}_{\mathcal{D}}}$ consists of the event/data signatures and signature morphisms. The Σ-event/data structures form the discrete category $Str^{\mathcal{M}^{\downarrow}_{\mathcal{D}}}(\Sigma)$ of $\mathcal{M}^{\downarrow}_{\mathcal{D}}$-*structures* over Σ. For each signature morphism $\sigma\colon \Sigma \to \Sigma'$ in $\mathbb{S}^{\mathcal{M}^{\downarrow}_{\mathcal{D}}}$ the σ-*reduct functor* $Str^{\mathcal{M}^{\downarrow}_{\mathcal{D}}}(\sigma)\colon Str^{\mathcal{M}^{\downarrow}_{\mathcal{D}}}(\Sigma') \to Str^{\mathcal{M}^{\downarrow}_{\mathcal{D}}}(\Sigma)$ is given by $Str^{\mathcal{M}^{\downarrow}_{\mathcal{D}}}(\sigma)(M') = M'|\sigma$. As the next step we introduce the formulæ and sentences of $\mathcal{M}^{\downarrow}_{\mathcal{D}}$ together with their translation along $\mathbb{S}^{\mathcal{M}^{\downarrow}_{\mathcal{D}}}$-morphisms and their satisfaction over $Str^{\mathcal{M}^{\downarrow}_{\mathcal{D}}}$. We then show that for $\mathcal{M}^{\downarrow}_{\mathcal{D}}$ the satisfaction condition holds and thus obtain $\mathcal{M}^{\downarrow}_{\mathcal{D}}$ as an institution. Subsequently, we show that

$\mathcal{M}^{\downarrow}_{\mathcal{D}}$ is simultaneously expressive enough to characterise the model class of simple UML state machines.

4.1 Formulæ and Sentences of $\mathcal{M}^{\downarrow}_{\mathcal{D}}$

$\mathcal{M}^{\downarrow}_{\mathcal{D}}$-formulæ aim at expressing control and data state properties of configurations as well as accessibility properties of configurations along transitions for particular events. The pure data state part is captured by data state sentences over $\mathcal{D}$. The control state part can be accessed and manipulated by hybrid operators for binding the control state in a state variable, $\downarrow s$; checking for a particular control state, s; and accessing all configurations with a particular control state, $@^F$, which, however, only pertains to reachable configurations relative to a set F of events. Transitions between configurations are covered by different modalities: a box modality for accessing all configurations that are reachable from a given configuration, $\Box^F$, again relative to a set F of events; a diamond modality for checking that an event with arguments is possible with a particular data state change, $\langle e(X) \,/\!\!/\, \psi \rangle$; and a modality for checking the reaction to an event with arguments according to a pre-condition and a transition predicate, $\langle\!| e(X) : \phi \,/\!\!/\, \psi |\!\rangle$.

Formally, the *Σ-event/data formulæ* $\mathscr{F}^{\mathcal{M}^{\downarrow}_{\mathcal{D}}}_{\Sigma,S}$ over an event/data signature Σ and a set of *state variables* S are inductively defined by

- φ—data state sentence $\varphi \in \mathscr{F}^{\mathcal{D}}_{A(\Sigma),\emptyset}$ holds in the current configuration;
- s—the control state of the current configuration is $s \in S$;
- $\downarrow s \,.\, \varrho$—calling the current control state s, formula $\varrho \in \mathscr{F}^{\mathcal{M}^{\downarrow}_{\mathcal{D}}}_{\Sigma,S\uplus\{s\}}$ holds;
- $(@^F s)\varrho$—in all configurations with control state $s \in S$ that are reachable with events from $F \subseteq E(\Sigma)$ formula $\varrho \in \mathscr{F}^{\mathcal{M}^{\downarrow}_{\mathcal{D}}}_{\Sigma,S}$ holds;
- $\Box^F \varrho$—in all configurations that are reachable from the current configuration with events from $F \subseteq E(\Sigma)$ formula $\varrho \in \mathscr{F}^{\mathcal{M}^{\downarrow}_{\mathcal{D}}}_{\Sigma,S}$ holds;
- $\langle e(X) \,/\!\!/\, \psi \rangle \varrho$—in the current configuration there is a valuation of X and a transition for event $e(X) \in E(\Sigma)$ with these arguments that satisfies transition formula $\psi \in \mathscr{F}^{2\mathcal{D}}_{A(\Sigma),X}$ and makes $\varrho \in \mathscr{F}^{\mathcal{M}^{\downarrow}_{\mathcal{D}}}_{\Sigma,S}$ hold afterwards;
- $\langle\!| e(X) : \phi \,/\!\!/\, \psi |\!\rangle \varrho$—in the current configuration for all valuations of X satisfying state formula $\phi \in \mathscr{F}^{\mathcal{D}}_{A(\Sigma),X}$ there is a transition for event $e(X) \in E(\Sigma)$ with these arguments that satisfies transition formula $\psi \in \mathscr{F}^{2\mathcal{D}}_{A(\Sigma),X}$ and makes $\varrho \in \mathscr{F}^{\mathcal{M}^{\downarrow}_{\mathcal{D}}}_{\Sigma,S}$ hold afterwards;
- $\neg\varrho$—in the current configuration $\varrho \in \mathscr{F}^{\mathcal{M}^{\downarrow}_{\mathcal{D}}}_{\Sigma,S}$ does not hold;
- $\varrho_1 \vee \varrho_2$—in the current configuration $\varrho_1 \in \mathscr{F}^{\mathcal{M}^{\downarrow}_{\mathcal{D}}}_{\Sigma,S}$ or $\varrho_2 \in \mathscr{F}^{\mathcal{M}^{\downarrow}_{\mathcal{D}}}_{\Sigma,S}$ hold.

We write $(@s)\varrho$ for $(@^{E(\Sigma)} s)\varrho$, $\Box\varrho$ for $\Box^{E(\Sigma)}\varrho$, $\Diamond^F \varrho$ for $\neg\Box^F\neg\varrho$, $\Diamond\varrho$ for $\Diamond^{E(\Sigma)}\varrho$, $[e(X) \,/\!\!/\, \psi]\varrho$ for $\neg\langle e(X) \,/\!\!/\, \psi \rangle\neg\varrho$, and true for $\downarrow s \,.\, s$.

Example 8. An event/data formula can make two kinds of requirements on an event/data structure: On the one hand, it can require the presence of certain mandatory transitions, on the other hand it can require the absence of certain prohibited transitions. Considering the simple UML state machine in Fig. 2, the formula

$$(@s1)\langle\!|\mathsf{inc}(x) : \mathsf{cnt} + x = 4 /\!\!/ \mathsf{cnt}' = 4|\!\rangle s2$$

requires for each valuation of $\beta\colon \{x\} \to \mathbb{N}$ such that $\mathsf{cnt} + x = 4$ holds that there is a transition from control state *s1* to control state *s2* for the instantiated event $\mathsf{inc}(\beta)$ where cnt is changed to 4. On the other hand, the formula

$$(@s2)[\mathsf{reset} /\!\!/ \neg(\mathsf{cnt}' = 0)]\mathrm{false}$$

prohibits any transitions out of *s2* that are labelled with the event reset but do not satisfy $\mathsf{cnt}' = 0$.

In the context of Fig. 2, these formulæ only have their explained intended meaning when *s1* and *s2* indeed refer to the eponymous states. However, $\mathcal{M}^{\downarrow}_{\mathcal{D}}$ does not show nominals for explicitly naming control states as part of the state machine's interface and the reference to specific states always has to build these states' context first using the modalities and the bind operator. On the other hand, as indicated in Sect. 3.4, the inclusion of nominals may interfere disadvantageously with the reduct formation.

Let $\sigma\colon \Sigma \to \Sigma'$ be an event/data signature morphism. The *event/data formulæ translation* $\mathscr{F}^{\mathcal{M}^{\downarrow}_{\mathcal{D}}}_{\sigma,S} : \mathscr{F}^{\mathcal{M}^{\downarrow}_{\mathcal{D}}}_{\Sigma,S} \to \mathscr{F}^{\mathcal{M}^{\downarrow}_{\mathcal{D}}}_{\Sigma',S}$ along σ is recursively given by

- $\mathscr{F}^{\mathcal{M}^{\downarrow}_{\mathcal{D}}}_{\sigma,S}(\varphi) = \mathscr{F}^{\mathcal{D}}_{A(\sigma),\emptyset}(\varphi)$;
- $\mathscr{F}^{\mathcal{M}^{\downarrow}_{\mathcal{D}}}_{\sigma,S}(s) = s$;
- $\mathscr{F}^{\mathcal{M}^{\downarrow}_{\mathcal{D}}}_{\sigma,S}(\downarrow s \,.\, \varrho) = \downarrow s \,.\, \mathscr{F}^{\mathcal{M}^{\downarrow}_{\mathcal{D}}}_{\sigma,S \uplus \{s\}}(\varrho)$;
- $\mathscr{F}^{\mathcal{M}^{\downarrow}_{\mathcal{D}}}_{\sigma,S}((@^F s)\varrho) = (@^{E(\sigma)(F)} s)\mathscr{F}^{\mathcal{M}^{\downarrow}_{\mathcal{D}}}_{\sigma,S}(\varrho)$;
- $\mathscr{F}^{\mathcal{M}^{\downarrow}_{\mathcal{D}}}_{\sigma,S}(\Box^F \varrho) = \Box^{E(\sigma)(F)} \mathscr{F}^{\mathcal{M}^{\downarrow}_{\mathcal{D}}}_{\sigma,S}(\varrho)$;
- $\mathscr{F}^{\mathcal{M}^{\downarrow}_{\mathcal{D}}}_{\sigma,S}(\langle e(X) /\!\!/ \psi\rangle\varrho) = \langle E(\sigma)(e)(X) /\!\!/ \mathscr{F}^{2\mathcal{D}}_{A(\sigma),X}(\psi)\rangle \mathscr{F}^{\mathcal{M}^{\downarrow}_{\mathcal{D}}}_{\sigma,S}(\varrho)$;
- $\mathscr{F}^{\mathcal{M}^{\downarrow}_{\mathcal{D}}}_{\sigma,S}(\langle\!| e(X) : \phi /\!\!/ \psi |\!\rangle\varrho) = \langle\!| E(\sigma)(e)(X) : \mathscr{F}^{\mathcal{D}}_{A(\sigma),X}(\phi) /\!\!/ \mathscr{F}^{2\mathcal{D}}_{A(\sigma),X}(\psi) |\!\rangle \mathscr{F}^{\mathcal{M}^{\downarrow}_{\mathcal{D}}}_{\sigma,S}(\varrho)$;
- $\mathscr{F}^{\mathcal{M}^{\downarrow}_{\mathcal{D}}}_{\sigma,S}(\neg\varrho) = \neg\mathscr{F}^{\mathcal{M}^{\downarrow}_{\mathcal{D}}}_{\sigma,S}(\varrho)$;
- $\mathscr{F}^{\mathcal{M}^{\downarrow}_{\mathcal{D}}}_{\sigma,S}(\varrho_1 \vee \varrho_2) = \mathscr{F}^{\mathcal{M}^{\downarrow}_{\mathcal{D}}}_{\sigma,S}(\varrho_1) \vee \mathscr{F}^{\mathcal{M}^{\downarrow}_{\mathcal{D}}}_{\sigma,S}(\varrho_2)$.

The set $\mathrm{Sen}^{\mathcal{M}^{\downarrow}_{\mathcal{D}}}(\Sigma)$ of *Σ-event/data sentences* is given by $\mathscr{F}^{\mathcal{M}^{\downarrow}_{\mathcal{D}}}_{\Sigma,\emptyset}$, the *event/data sentence translation* $\mathrm{Sen}^{\mathcal{M}^{\downarrow}_{\mathcal{D}}}(\sigma)\colon \mathrm{Sen}^{\mathcal{M}^{\downarrow}_{\mathcal{D}}}(\Sigma) \to \mathrm{Sen}^{\mathcal{M}^{\downarrow}_{\mathcal{D}}}(\Sigma')$ by $\mathscr{F}^{\mathcal{M}^{\downarrow}_{\mathcal{D}}}_{\sigma,\emptyset}$.

4.2 Satisfaction Relation for $\mathcal{M}^{\downarrow}_{\mathcal{D}}$

The $\mathcal{M}^{\downarrow}_{\mathcal{D}}$-satisfaction relation connects $\mathcal{M}^{\downarrow}_{\mathcal{D}}$-structures and $\mathcal{M}^{\downarrow}_{\mathcal{D}}$-formulæ, expressing whether in some configuration of the structure a particular formula holds with respect to an assignment of control states to state variables. Let Σ be an event/data signature, M a Σ-event/data structure, S a set of state variables, $v\colon S \to C(M)$ a state variable assignment, and $\gamma \in \Gamma(M)$. The *satisfaction relation* for event/data formulæ is inductively given by

- $M, v, \gamma \models^{\mathcal{M}^{\downarrow}_{\mathcal{D}}}_{\Sigma,S} \varphi$ iff $\omega(M)(\gamma) \models^{\mathcal{D}}_{A(\Sigma)} \varphi$;
- $M, v, \gamma \models^{\mathcal{M}^{\downarrow}_{\mathcal{D}}}_{\Sigma,S} s$ iff $v(s) = c(M)(\gamma)$;
- $M, v, \gamma \models^{\mathcal{M}^{\downarrow}_{\mathcal{D}}}_{\Sigma,S} {\downarrow} s\,.\,\varrho$ iff $M, v\{s \mapsto c(M)(\gamma)\}, \gamma \models^{\mathcal{M}^{\downarrow}_{\mathcal{D}}}_{\Sigma,S\uplus\{s\}} \varrho$;
- $M, v, \gamma \models^{\mathcal{M}^{\downarrow}_{\mathcal{D}}}_{\Sigma,S} (@^F s)\varrho$ iff $M, v, \gamma' \models^{\mathcal{M}^{\downarrow}_{\mathcal{D}}}_{\Sigma,S} \varrho$ for all $\gamma' \in \Gamma^F(M)$ with $c(M)(\gamma') = v(s)$;
- $M, v, \gamma \models^{\mathcal{M}^{\downarrow}_{\mathcal{D}}}_{\Sigma,S} \Box^F \varrho$ iff $M, v, \gamma' \models^{\mathcal{M}^{\downarrow}_{\mathcal{D}}}_{\Sigma,S} \varrho$ for all $\gamma' \in \Gamma^F(M, \gamma)$;
- $M, v, \gamma \models^{\mathcal{M}^{\downarrow}_{\mathcal{D}}}_{\Sigma,S} \langle e(X) \mathbin{/\!\!/} \psi \rangle \varrho$ iff there is a $\beta\colon X \to \mathcal{D}$ and a $\gamma' \in \Gamma(M)$ such that $(\gamma, \gamma') \in R(M)_{e(\beta)}$, $(\omega(M)(\gamma), \omega(M)(\gamma')), \beta \models^{2\mathcal{D}}_{A(\Sigma),X} \psi$, and $M, v, \gamma' \models^{\mathcal{M}^{\downarrow}_{\mathcal{D}}}_{\Sigma,S} \varrho$;
- $M, v, \gamma \models^{\mathcal{M}^{\downarrow}_{\mathcal{D}}}_{\Sigma,S} \langle\!\langle e(X) : \phi \mathbin{/\!\!/} \psi \rangle\!\rangle \varrho$ iff for all $\beta\colon X \to \mathcal{D}$ with $\omega(M)(\gamma), \beta \models^{\mathcal{D}}_{A(\Sigma),X} \phi$ there is some $\gamma' \in \Gamma(M)$ such that $(\gamma, \gamma') \in R(M)_{e(\beta)}$, $(\omega(M)(\gamma), \omega(M)(\gamma')), \beta \models^{2\mathcal{D}}_{A(\Sigma),X} \psi$, and $M, v, \gamma' \models^{\mathcal{M}^{\downarrow}_{\mathcal{D}}}_{\Sigma,S} \varrho$;
- $M, v, \gamma \models^{\mathcal{M}^{\downarrow}_{\mathcal{D}}}_{\Sigma,S} \neg\varrho$ iff $M, v, \gamma \not\models^{\mathcal{M}^{\downarrow}_{\mathcal{D}}}_{\Sigma,S} \varrho$;
- $M, v, \gamma \models^{\mathcal{M}^{\downarrow}_{\mathcal{D}}}_{\Sigma,S} \varrho_1 \vee \varrho_2$ iff $M, v, \gamma \models^{\mathcal{M}^{\downarrow}_{\mathcal{D}}}_{\Sigma,S} \varrho_1$ or $M, v, \gamma \models^{\mathcal{M}^{\downarrow}_{\mathcal{D}}}_{\Sigma,S} \varrho_2$.

This satisfaction relation is well-behaved with respect to reducts of $\mathcal{M}^{\downarrow}_{\mathcal{D}}$-structures. On the one hand, this is due to the use of abstract data names rather than data states in the structures, and on the other hand to the satisfaction condition of $\mathcal{D}$ and $2\mathcal{D}$.

Lemma 1. *Let $\sigma\colon \Sigma \to \Sigma'$ be a event/data signature morphism and M' a Σ'-event/data structure. For all $\varrho \in \mathscr{F}^{\mathcal{M}^{\downarrow}_{\mathcal{D}}}_{\Sigma,S}$, all $\gamma' \in \Gamma(M'|\sigma) \subseteq \Gamma(M')$, and all $v\colon S \to C(M'|\sigma) \subseteq C(M')$ it holds that*

$$M'|\sigma, v, \gamma' \models^{\mathcal{M}^{\downarrow}_{\mathcal{D}}}_{\Sigma,S} \varrho \iff M', v, \gamma' \models^{\mathcal{M}^{\downarrow}_{\mathcal{D}}}_{\Sigma',S} \mathscr{F}^{\mathcal{M}^{\downarrow}_{\mathcal{D}}}_{\sigma,S}(\varrho)\ .$$

For a $\Sigma \in |\mathbb{S}^{\mathcal{M}^{\downarrow}_{\mathcal{D}}}|$, an $M \in |Str^{\mathcal{M}^{\downarrow}_{\mathcal{D}}}(\Sigma)|$, and a $\rho \in \mathrm{Sen}^{\mathcal{M}^{\downarrow}_{\mathcal{D}}}(\Sigma)$ the *satisfaction relation* $M \models^{\mathcal{M}^{\downarrow}_{\mathcal{D}}}_{\Sigma} \rho$ holds if, and only if, $M, \emptyset, \gamma_0 \models^{\mathcal{M}^{\downarrow}_{\mathcal{D}}}_{\Sigma,\emptyset} \rho$ for all $\gamma_0 \in \Gamma_0(M)$.

Theorem 1. $(\mathbb{S}^{\mathcal{M}^{\downarrow}_{\mathcal{D}}}, Str^{\mathcal{M}^{\downarrow}_{\mathcal{D}}}, \mathrm{Sen}^{\mathcal{M}^{\downarrow}_{\mathcal{D}}}, \models^{\mathcal{M}^{\downarrow}_{\mathcal{D}}})$ *is an institution.*

Algorithm 1. Constructing an $\mathcal{M}^{\downarrow}_{\mathcal{D}}$-sentence from a set of transition specifications

Require: $T \equiv$ a set of transition specifications
$Im_T(c) = \{(\phi, e(X), \psi, c') \mid (c, \phi, e(X), \psi, c') \in T\}$
$Im_T(c, e(X)) = \{(\phi, \psi, c') \mid (c, \varphi, e(X), \psi, c') \in T\}$

function $\mathrm{sen}(c, I, V, B)$ ▷ c: state, I: image to visit, V: states to visit, B: bound states
  if $I \neq \emptyset$ **then**
    $(\phi, e(X), \psi, c') \leftarrow$ **choose** I
    if $c' \in B$ **then**
      return $(@c)\langle\!|e(X) : \phi /\!\!/ \psi|\!\rangle(c' \wedge \mathrm{sen}(c, I \setminus \{(\phi, e(X), \psi, c')\}, V, B))$
    else
      return $(@c)\langle\!|e(X) : \phi /\!\!/ \psi|\!\rangle(\downarrow c' \,.\, \mathrm{sen}(c, I \setminus \{(\phi, e(X), \psi, c')\}, V, B \cup \{c'\}))$
  $V \leftarrow V \setminus \{c\}$
  if $V \neq \emptyset$ **then**
    $c' \leftarrow$ **choose** $B \cap V$
    return $\mathrm{sen}(c', Im_T(c'), V, B)$
  return $(\bigwedge_{c \in B} \mathrm{fin}(c)) \wedge \bigwedge_{c_1 \in B, c_2 \in B \setminus \{c_1\}} \neg(@c_1)c_2$

function $\mathrm{fin}(c)$
  return $(@c)\bigwedge_{e(X) \in E(\Sigma(U))} \bigwedge_{P \subseteq Im_T(c, e(X))}$
$[e(X) /\!\!/ (\bigwedge_{(\phi,\psi,c') \in P}(\phi \wedge \psi)) \wedge$
$\neg(\bigvee_{(\phi,\psi,c') \in Im_T(c,e(X)) \setminus P}(\phi \wedge \psi))](\bigvee_{(\phi,\psi,c') \in P} c')$

4.3 Representing Simple UML State Machines in $\mathcal{M}^{\downarrow}_{\mathcal{D}}$

The hybrid modal logic $\mathcal{M}^{\downarrow}_{\mathcal{D}}$ is expressive enough to characterise the model class of a simple UML state machine U by a single sentence ϱ_U, i.e., an event/data structure M is a model of U if, and only if, $M \models^{\mathcal{M}^{\downarrow}_{\mathcal{D}}}_{\Sigma(U)} \varrho_U$. Such a characterisation is achieved by means of Algorithm 1 that is a slight variation of the characterisation algorithm for so-called operational specifications within $\mathcal{E}^{\downarrow}$ [6] by including also events with data arguments. The algorithm constructs a sentence expressing that semantic transitions according to explicit syntactic transition specifications are indeed possible and that no other semantic transitions not adhering to any of the syntactic transition specifications exist. For a set of transition specifications T, a call $\mathrm{sen}(c, I, V, B)$ performs a recursive breadth-first traversal starting from c, where I holds the unprocessed quadruples $(\phi, e(X), \psi, c')$ of transitions in T outgoing from c, V the remaining states to visit, and B the set of already bound states. The function first requires the existence of each outgoing transition of I in the resulting formula, binding any newly reached state. Having visited all states in V, it requires that no other transitions from the states in B exist using calls to fin, and adds the requirement that all states in B are pairwise different. Formula $\mathrm{fin}(c)$ expresses that at c, for all events $e(X)$ and for all subsets P of the transitions in T outgoing from c, whenever an $e(X)$-transition can be done with the combined effect of P but not adhering to any of the effects of the currently not selected transitions, the $e(X)$-transition must have one of the states as its target that are target states of P.

Example 9. Applying Algorithm 1 to the set of explicitly mentioned, "black" transition specifications T of the simple UML state machine *Counter* in Fig. 2, i.e., calling $\mathrm{sen}(s1, Im_T(s1), \{s1, s2\}, \{s1\})$ yields $\varrho_{s1,s1}$ with

$$\begin{aligned}
\varrho_{s1,s1} &= (@s1)\langle\!|\mathsf{inc}(x) : \mathsf{cnt} + x \leq 4 /\!\!/ \mathsf{cnt}' = \mathsf{cnt} + x|\!\rangle(s1 \wedge \varrho_{s1,s2}) \\
\varrho_{s1,s2} &= (@s1)\langle\!|\mathsf{inc}(x) : \mathsf{cnt} + x = 4 /\!\!/ \mathsf{cnt}' = \mathsf{cnt} + x|\!\rangle{\downarrow}s2 \,.\, (\varrho_{s2,s1}) \\
\varrho_{s2,s1} &= (@s2)\langle\!|\mathsf{reset} : \mathrm{true} /\!\!/ \mathsf{cnt}' = 0|\!\rangle(s1 \wedge \varrho_{\mathrm{fin}}) \\
\varrho_{\mathrm{fin}} &= \varrho_{\mathrm{fin}(s1)} \wedge \varrho_{\mathrm{fin}(s2)} \wedge \neg(@s1)s2 \\
\varrho_{\mathrm{fin}(s1)} &= (@s1)\big([\mathsf{inc}(x) /\!\!/ \neg((\mathsf{cnt} + x \leq 4 \wedge \mathsf{cnt}' = \mathsf{cnt} + x) \vee \\
&\qquad\qquad (\mathsf{cnt} + x = 4 \wedge \mathsf{cnt}' = 4))]\mathrm{false} \wedge \\
&\qquad [\mathsf{inc}(x) /\!\!/ (\mathsf{cnt} + x \leq 4 \wedge \mathsf{cnt}' = \mathsf{cnt} + x) \wedge \\
&\qquad\qquad \neg(\mathsf{cnt} + x = 4 \wedge \mathsf{cnt}' = 4)]s1 \wedge \\
&\qquad [\mathsf{inc}(x) /\!\!/ (\mathsf{cnt} + x = 4 \wedge \mathsf{cnt}' = 4) \wedge \\
&\qquad\qquad \neg(\mathsf{cnt} + x \leq 4 \wedge \mathsf{cnt}' = \mathsf{cnt} + x)]s2 \wedge \\
&\qquad [\mathsf{inc}(x) /\!\!/ (\mathsf{cnt} + x \leq 4 \wedge \mathsf{cnt}' = \mathsf{cnt} + x) \wedge \\
&\qquad\qquad (\mathsf{cnt} + x = 4 \wedge \mathsf{cnt}' = 4)](s1 \vee s2) \wedge \\
&\qquad [\mathsf{reset} /\!\!/ \mathrm{true}]\mathrm{false}\big) \\
\varrho_{\mathrm{fin}(s2)} &= (@s2)\big([\mathsf{inc}(x) /\!\!/ \mathrm{true}]\mathrm{false} \wedge \\
&\qquad [\mathsf{reset} /\!\!/ \neg(\mathsf{cnt}' = 0)]\mathrm{false} \wedge \\
&\qquad [\mathsf{reset} /\!\!/ \mathsf{cnt}' = 0]s1\big)
\end{aligned}$$

In fact, there is no outgoing "black" transition for reset from $s1$, thus $P = \emptyset$ is the only choice for this event in $\mathrm{fin}(s1)$ and the clause $[\mathsf{reset} /\!\!/ \mathrm{true}]\mathrm{false}$ is included. For $\mathsf{inc}(x)$ there are two outgoing transitions resulting four different clauses checking whether none, the one or the other, or both transitions are executable.

In order to apply the algorithm to simple UML state machines, the idling self-loops for achieving input-enabledness first have to be made explicit. For a syntactically input-enabled simple UML state machine U a characterising sentence then reads

$$\varrho_U = {\downarrow}c_0 \,.\, \varphi_0 \wedge \mathrm{sen}(c_0, Im_{T(U)}(c_0), C(U), \{c_0\}) \ ,$$

where $c_0 = c_0(U)$ and $\varphi_0 = \varphi_0(U)$. Due to syntactic reachability, the bound states B of Algorithm 1 become $C(U)$ when sen is called for $B = \{c_0(U)\}$ and V reaches $\emptyset$.

5 A Theoroidal Comorphism from $\mathcal{M}^{\downarrow}_{\mathcal{D}}$ to CASL

We define a theoroidal comorphism from $\mathcal{M}^{\downarrow}_{\mathcal{D}}$ to CASL. The construction mainly follows the standard translation of modal logics to first-order logic [2] which has been considered for hybrid logics also on an institutional level [3,12].

from *Basic/StructuredDatatypes* **get** SET % import finite sets
spec $\text{TRANS}_\Sigma = Dt$
then free type $\text{Evt} ::= \tau_e(E(\Sigma))$
$\% \ \tau_e(\{e(X)\}) = e(dt^{|X|}), \tau_e(\{e(X)\} \cup E) = e(dt^{|X|}) \mid \tau_e(E)$
free type $\text{EvtNm} ::= \tau_n(E(\Sigma))$ % $\tau_n(\{e(X)\}) = e, \tau_n(\{e(X)\} \cup E) = e \mid \tau_n(E)$
op $\text{nm} : \text{Evt} \to \text{EvtNm}$
axiom $\forall x_1, \ldots, x_n : dt \cdot \text{nm}(e(x_1, \ldots, x_n)) = e$ % for each $e(x_1, \ldots, x_n) \in E(\Sigma)$
then SET[sort EvtNm]
then sort Ctrl
free type $\text{Conf} ::= \text{conf}(\text{c} : \text{Ctrl}; \tau_a(A(\Sigma)))$
$\% \ \tau_a(\{a\}) = a : dt, \tau_a(\{a\} \cup A) = a : dt; \tau_a(A)$
preds init : Conf;
trans : Conf × Evt × Conf
• $\exists g : \text{Conf} \cdot \text{init}(g)$ % there is some initial configuration
• $\forall g, g' : \text{Conf} \cdot \text{init}(g) \wedge \text{init}(g') \Rightarrow \text{c}(g) = \text{c}(g')$ % single initial control state
free { **pred** reachable : *Set*[EvtNm] × Conf × Conf
$\forall g, g', g'' : \text{Conf}, E : Set[\text{EvtNm}], e : \text{Evt}$
• $\text{reachable}(E, g, g)$
• $\text{reachable}(E, g, g') \wedge \text{nm}(e) \in E \wedge \text{trans}(g', e, g'') \Rightarrow \text{reachable}(E, g, g'')$ }
then preds $\text{reachable}(E : Set[\text{EvtName}], g : \text{Conf}) \Leftrightarrow$
$\exists g_0 : \text{Conf} \cdot \text{init}(g_0) \wedge \text{reachable}(E, g_0, g);$
$\text{reachable}(g : \text{Conf}) \Leftrightarrow \text{reachable}(E(\Sigma), g)$
end

Fig. 3. Frame for translating $\mathcal{M}^{\downarrow}_{\mathcal{D}}$ into CASL

The basis is a representation of $\mathcal{M}^{\downarrow}_{\mathcal{D}}$-signatures and the frame given by $\mathcal{M}^{\downarrow}_{\mathcal{D}}$-structures as a CASL-specification as shown in Fig. 3. The signature translation

$$\nu^{\mathbb{S}} : \mathbb{S}^{\mathcal{M}^{\downarrow}_{\mathcal{D}}} \to \text{Pres}^{\text{CASL}}$$

maps a $\mathcal{M}^{\downarrow}_{\mathcal{D}}$-signature Σ to the CASL-theory presentation given by TRANS_Σ and a $\mathcal{M}^{\downarrow}_{\mathcal{D}}$-signature morphism to the corresponding theory presentation morphism. TRANS_Σ first of all covers the events and event names according to $E(\Sigma)$ (types Evt and EvtNm with several alternatives separated by "|") and the configurations (type Conf with a single constructor "conf") with their control states (sort Ctrl) and data states given by assignments to the attributes from $A(\Sigma)$ (separated by ";"). The remainder of TRANS_Σ sets the frame for describing reachable transition systems with a set of initial configurations (predicate init), a transition relation (predicate trans) and reachability predicates. The specification of the predicate reachable uses CASL's "structured free" construct to ensure reachability to be inductively defined. The model translation

$$\nu^{\text{Mod}}_\Sigma : \text{Mod}^{\text{CASL}}(\nu^{\mathbb{S}}(\Sigma)) \to Str^{\mathcal{M}^{\downarrow}_{\mathcal{D}}}(\Sigma)$$

then can rely on this encoding. In particular, for a model $M' \in \text{Mod}^{\text{CASL}}(\nu^{\mathbb{S}}(\Sigma))$, there are, using the bijection $\iota_{M',dt} : dt^{M'} \cong \mathcal{D}$, an injective map

$\iota_{M',\mathrm{Conf}} \colon \mathrm{Conf}^{M'} \rightarrowtail \mathrm{Ctrl}^{M'} \times \Omega(A(\Sigma))$ and a bijective map $\iota_{M',\mathrm{Evt}} \colon \mathrm{Evt}^{M'} \cong \{e(\beta) \mid e(X) \in E(\Sigma),\ \beta \colon X \to \mathcal{D}\}$. The $\mathcal{M}^{\downarrow}_{\mathcal{D}}$-structure resulting from a CASL-model of TRANS_{Σ} can thus be defined by

- $\Gamma(\nu^{\mathrm{Mod}}_{\Sigma}(M')) = \iota^{-1}_{M',\mathrm{Conf}}(\{g' \in M'_{\mathrm{Conf}} \mid \mathrm{reachable}^{M'}(g')\})$
- $R(\nu^{\mathrm{Mod}}_{\Sigma}(M'))_{e(\beta)} = \{(\gamma, \gamma') \in \Gamma(\nu^{\mathrm{Mod}}_{\Sigma}(M')) \times \Gamma(\nu^{\mathrm{Mod}}_{\Sigma}(M')) \mid$ $\mathrm{trans}^{M'}(\iota_{M',\mathrm{Conf}}(\gamma), \iota^{-1}_{M',\mathrm{Evt}}(e(\beta)), \iota_{M',\mathrm{Conf}}(\gamma'))\})$
- $\Gamma_0(\nu^{\mathrm{Mod}}_{\Sigma}(M')) = \{\gamma \in \Gamma(\nu^{\mathrm{Mod}}_{\Sigma}(M')) \mid \mathrm{init}^{M'}(\iota_{M',\mathrm{Conf}}(\gamma))\})$
- $\omega(\nu^{\mathrm{Mod}}_{\Sigma}(M')) = \{(c, \omega) \in \Gamma(\nu^{\mathrm{Mod}}_{\Sigma}(M')) \mapsto \omega\}$

For $\mathcal{M}^{\downarrow}_{\mathcal{D}}$-sentences, we first define a formula translation

$$\nu^{\mathscr{F}}_{\Sigma,S,g} \colon \mathscr{F}^{\mathcal{M}^{\downarrow}_{\mathcal{D}}}_{\Sigma,S} \to \mathscr{F}^{\mathrm{CASL}}_{\nu^{Sig}(\Sigma),S\cup\{g\}}$$

which, mimicking the standard translation, takes a variable $g : \mathrm{Conf}$ as a parameter that records the "current configuration" and also uses a set S of state names for the control states. The translation embeds the data state and 2-data state formulæ using the substitution $A(\Sigma)(g) = \{a \mapsto a(g) \mid a \in A(\Sigma)\}$ for replacing the attributes $a \in A(\Sigma)$ by the accessors $a(g)$. The translation of $\mathcal{M}^{\downarrow}_{\mathcal{D}}$-formulæ then reads

- $\nu^{\mathscr{F}}_{\Sigma,S,g}(\varphi) = \mathscr{F}^{\mathrm{CASL}}_{\nu^{Sig}(\Sigma),A(\Sigma)(g)}(\varphi)$
- $\nu^{\mathscr{F}}_{\Sigma,S,g}(s) = (s = \mathrm{c}(g))$
- $\nu^{\mathscr{F}}_{\Sigma,S,g}({\downarrow} s \,.\, \varrho) = \exists s : \mathrm{Ctrl} \,.\, s = \mathrm{c}(g) \wedge \nu^{\mathscr{F}}_{\Sigma,S\uplus\{s\},g}(\varrho)$
- $\nu^{\mathscr{F}}_{\Sigma,S,g}((@^F s)\varrho) = \forall g' : \mathrm{Conf} \,.\, (\mathrm{c}(g') = s \wedge \mathrm{reachable}(F, g')) \Rightarrow \nu^{\mathscr{F}}_{\Sigma,S,g'}(\varrho)$
- $\nu^{\mathscr{F}}_{\Sigma,S,g}(\Box^F \varrho) = \forall g' : \mathrm{Conf} \,.\, \mathrm{reachable}(F, g, g') \Rightarrow \nu^{\mathscr{F}}_{\Sigma,S,g'}(\varrho)$
- $\nu^{\mathscr{F}}_{\Sigma,S,g}(\langle e(X) /\!\!/ \psi \rangle \varrho) = \exists X : dt \,.\, \exists g' : \mathrm{Conf} \,.\, \mathrm{trans}(g, e(X), g') \wedge$ $\mathscr{F}^{\mathrm{CASL}}_{\nu^{Sig}(\Sigma),A(\Sigma)(g)\cup A(\Sigma)(g')\cup 1_X}(\psi) \wedge \nu^{\mathscr{F}}_{\Sigma,S,g'}(\varrho)$
- $\nu^{\mathscr{F}}_{\Sigma,S,g}(\langle\!| e(X) : \phi /\!\!/ \psi |\!\rangle \varrho) = \forall X : dt \,.\, \mathscr{F}^{\mathrm{CASL}}_{\nu^{Sig}(\Sigma),A(\Sigma)(g)\cup 1_X}(\phi) \Rightarrow$ $\exists g' : \mathrm{Conf} \,.\, \mathrm{trans}(g, e(X), g') \wedge$ $\mathscr{F}^{\mathrm{CASL}}_{\nu^{Sig}(\Sigma),A(\Sigma)(g)\cup A(\Sigma)(g')\cup 1_X}(\psi) \wedge \nu^{\mathscr{F}}_{\Sigma,S,g'}(\varrho)$
- $\nu^{\mathscr{F}}_{\Sigma,S,g}(\neg\varrho) = \neg\nu^{\mathscr{F}}_{\Sigma,S,g}(\varrho)$
- $\nu^{\mathscr{F}}_{\Sigma,S,g}(\varrho_1 \vee \varrho_2) = \nu^{\mathscr{F}}_{\Sigma,S,g}(\varrho_1) \vee \nu^{\mathscr{F}}_{\Sigma,S,g}(\varrho_2)$

Example 10. The translation of $(@s1)\langle\!| \mathsf{inc}(x) : \mathsf{cnt} + x \leq 4 /\!\!/ \mathsf{cnt}' = \mathsf{cnt} + x |\!\rangle s1$ over the state set $\{s1\}$ and the configuration variable g is

$$\begin{aligned}
&\nu^{\mathscr{F}}_{\Sigma,\{s1\},g}((@s1)\langle\!| \mathsf{inc}(x) : \mathsf{cnt} + x \leq 4 /\!\!/ \mathsf{cnt}' = \mathsf{cnt} + x |\!\rangle s1) \\
=\ &\forall g' : \mathrm{Conf} \,.\, (\mathrm{c}(g') = s1 \wedge \mathrm{reachable}(g')) \Rightarrow \\
&\quad \nu^{\mathscr{F}}_{\Sigma,\{s1\},g'}(\langle\!| \mathsf{inc}(x) : \mathsf{cnt} + x \leq 4 /\!\!/ \mathsf{cnt}' = \mathsf{cnt} + x |\!\rangle s1) \\
=\ &\forall g' : \mathrm{Conf} \,.\, (\mathrm{c}(g') = s1 \wedge \mathrm{reachable}(g')) \Rightarrow \\
&\quad \forall x : dt \,.\, \mathrm{cnt}(g') + x \leq 4 \Rightarrow \\
&\qquad \exists g'' : \mathrm{Conf} \,.\, \mathrm{trans}(g', \mathrm{inc}(x), g'') \wedge \\
&\qquad\qquad \mathrm{cnt}(g'') = \mathrm{cnt}(g') + x \wedge \nu^{\mathscr{F}}_{\Sigma,\{s1\},g''}(s1)
\end{aligned}$$

$$\begin{aligned} = \ & \forall g' : \mathrm{Conf} \,.\, (\mathrm{c}(g') = \mathit{s1} \wedge \mathrm{reachable}(g')) \Rightarrow \\ & \quad \forall x : \mathit{dt} \,.\, \mathrm{cnt}(g') + x \leq 4 \Rightarrow \\ & \quad\quad \exists g'' : \mathrm{Conf} \,.\, \mathrm{trans}(g', \mathrm{inc}(x), g'') \wedge \\ & \quad\quad\quad\quad \mathrm{cnt}(g'') = \mathrm{cnt}(g') + x \wedge \mathit{s1} = \mathrm{c}(g'') \end{aligned}$$

Building on the translation of formulæ, the sentence translation

$$\nu^{\mathrm{Sen}}_{\Sigma} \colon \mathrm{Sen}^{\mathcal{M}^{\downarrow}_{\mathcal{D}}}(\Sigma) \to \mathrm{Sen}^{\mathrm{CASL}}(\nu^{\mathit{Sig}}(\Sigma))$$

only has to require additionally that evaluation starts in an initial state:

- $\nu^{\mathrm{Sen}}_{\Sigma}(\rho) = \forall g : \mathrm{Conf} \,.\, \mathrm{init}(g) \Rightarrow \nu^{\mathscr{F}}_{\Sigma,\emptyset,g}(\rho)$

The translation of CASL-models of TRANS_{Σ} into $\mathcal{M}^{\downarrow}_{\mathcal{D}}$-structures and the translation of $\mathcal{M}^{\downarrow}_{\mathcal{D}}$-formulæ into CASL-formulæ over TRANS_{Σ} fulfil the requirements of the "open" satisfaction condition of theoroidal comorphisms:

Lemma 2. *For a* $\varrho \in \mathscr{F}^{\mathcal{M}^{\downarrow}_{\mathcal{D}}}_{\Sigma,S}$, *an* $M' \in \mathrm{Mod}^{\mathrm{CASL}}(\nu^{\mathbb{S}}(\Sigma))$, *a* $v \colon S \to C(\nu^{\mathrm{Mod}}_{\Sigma}(M'))$, *and a* $\gamma \in \Gamma(\nu^{\mathrm{Mod}}_{\Sigma}(M'))$ *it holds with* $\beta'_{M',g}(v,\gamma) = \iota^{-1}_{M',\mathrm{Ctrl}} \circ v \cup \{g \mapsto \iota_{M',\mathrm{Conf}}(\gamma)\}$ *that*

$$\nu^{\mathrm{Mod}}_{\Sigma}(M'), v, \gamma \models^{\mathcal{M}^{\downarrow}_{\mathcal{D}}}_{\Sigma,S} \varrho \iff M', \beta'_{M',g}(v,\gamma) \models^{\mathrm{CASL}}_{\nu^{\mathit{Sig}}(\Sigma),S\cup\{g\}} \nu^{\mathscr{F}}_{\Sigma,S,g}(\varrho) \,.$$

Theorem 2. $(\nu^{\mathbb{S}}, \nu^{\mathrm{Mod}}, \nu^{\mathrm{Sen}})$ *is a theoroidal comorphism from* $\mathcal{M}^{\downarrow}_{\mathcal{D}}$ *to* CASL.

6 Proving Properties of UML State Machines with HETS and SPASS

We implemented the translation of simple UML state machines into CASL specifications within the heterogeneous toolset HETS [15]. Based on this translation we explain how to prove properties symbolically in the automated theorem prover SPASS [20] for our running example of a counter.

6.1 Implementation in HETS

For a HETS chain from simple UML state machine to CASL and SPASS, we first defined the input language UMLSTATE and extended HETS with a parser for this language. The syntax of UMLSTATE closely follows the ideas of PlantUML [18], such that, in particular, its textual specifications can potentially be rendered graphically as UML state machines. Listing 1 gives a representation of our running example *Counter*, cf. Sect. 3, in UMLSTATE. Note that UMLSTATE uses more conventional UML syntax for effects on transitions, e.g., "$\mathsf{cnt} := \mathsf{cnt} + x$". Next, we extended HETS with a syntax representation of our logic $\mathcal{M}^{\downarrow}_{\mathcal{D}}$, cf. Sect. 4, and implemented Algorithm 1 in HETS to automatically translate UMLSTATE specifications into $\mathcal{M}^{\downarrow}_{\mathcal{D}}$ specifications, where we arrive at

```
logic UMLState
spec Counter =
  var cnt;
  event inc(x);
  event reset;
  states s1, s2;
  init s1 : cnt = 0;
  trans s1 --> s1 : inc(x) [cnt + x < 4] / { cnt := cnt + x };
  trans s1 --> s2 : inc(x) [cnt + x = 4] / { cnt := cnt + x };
  trans s2 --> s1 : reset [cnt = 4] / { cnt := 0 };
end
```

Listing 1. Representation of the simple UML state machine *Counter* in UMLState

the institutional level. In this step, effects on transitions are turned into logical formulæ, like "$\mathsf{cnt}' = \mathsf{cnt} + x$". Finally, we extended HeTS with an implementation of the comorphism from $\mathcal{M}^{\downarrow}_{\mathcal{D}}$ into Casl, cf. Sect. 5. The implementation has been bundled in a fork of HeTS (https://github.com/spechub/hets) and provides a translation chain from UMLState via Casl to the input languages of various proof tools, such as the automated theorem prover Spass.

6.2 Proving in Spass

Figure 4 shows the Casl specification representing the state machine from Fig. 2, extended by a proof obligation %(Safe)% and proof infrastructure for it. We want to prove the safety property that cnt never exceeds 4 using the automated theorem prover Spass.

The Casl specification Counter imports a specification Trans which instantiates the generic frame translating $\mathcal{M}^{\downarrow}_{\mathcal{D}}$ into Casl, cf. Fig. 3. However, the first-order theorem prover Spass does not support Casl's structured free that we use for expressing reachability. For invariance properties this deficiency can be circumvented by loosely specifying *reachable* (i.e., omitting the keyword `free`), introducing a predicate *invar*, and adding a first-order induction axiom. This means that we have to establish the safety property for a larger model class than we would have with freeness. When carrying out symbolic reasoning for invariant referring to a single configuration, the presented induction axiom suffices. Other properties would require more involved induction axioms, e.g., referring to several configurations.

Then the specification provides the machine axioms as stated (partially) in Example 9. The axioms following the *%implies* directive are treated as proof obligations. We first state the safety property that we wish to establish: in all reachable configurations, the counter value is less or equal 4 – %(Safe)%. The remainder steers the proving process in Spass by providing suitable case distinctions. For invariants referring to a single configuration, these could also be generated automatically based on the transition structure of the state machine.

spec COUNTER = TRANS
then pred $invar(g : Conf) \Leftrightarrow (c(g) = s1 \wedge cnt(g) \leq 4) \vee (c(g) = s2 \wedge cnt(g) \leq 4)$
%% induction scheme for "reachable" predicate, instantiated for "invar":
$\cdot\ ((\forall\, g : Conf \cdot init(g) \Rightarrow invar(g))$
$\wedge \forall\, g, g' : Conf; e : Evt$
$\cdot\ (reachable(g) \Rightarrow invar(g)) \wedge reachable(g) \wedge trans(g, e, g') \Rightarrow invar(g'))$
$\Rightarrow \forall\, g : Conf \cdot reachable(g) \Rightarrow invar(g)$
then ... *machine axioms* ...
then %implies
%% the safety assertion for our counter:
$\forall\, g : Conf \cdot reachable(g) \Rightarrow cnt(g) \leq 4$ %(Safe)%
%% steering SPASS with case distinction lemmas, could be generated algorithmically:
$\forall\, g, g' : Conf; e : Evt; k : Nat$
$\cdot\ init(g) \Rightarrow invar(g)$ %(InvarInit)%
$\cdot\ (reachable(g) \Rightarrow invar(g)) \wedge reachable(g) \wedge trans(g, e, g') \wedge e = reset$
$\Rightarrow invar(g')$ %(InvarReset)%
$\cdot\ (reachable(g) \Rightarrow invar(g)) \wedge reachable(g) \wedge trans(g, e, g') \wedge e = inc(k)$
$\Rightarrow invar(g')$ %(InvarInc)%
$\cdot\ (reachable(g) \Rightarrow invar(g)) \wedge reachable(g) \wedge trans(g, e, g')$
$\Rightarrow invar(g')$ %(InvarStep)%
$\cdot\ invar(g) \Rightarrow cnt(g) \leq 4$ %(InvarImpliesSafe)%

Fig. 4. CASL specification of our running example

As proof of concept, we automatically verified this safety property in SPASS. In this experiment, we performed some optimising, semantics-preserving logical transformations on the result of applying the comorphism, to make the specification more digestible to the theorem prover. These transformations include the removal of double negations, splitting a conjunction into separate axioms, and turning existentially quantified control states into constants by Skolemisation.

7 Conclusions and Future Work

We have described a new, institution-based logical framework $\mathcal{M}^{\downarrow}_{\mathcal{D}}$ that captures simple UML state machines. This is in contrast to previous approaches that modelled UML parts directly as an institution and ran into difficulties in establishing the satisfaction condition [19]. By (1) defining an institution-based translation from $\mathcal{M}^{\downarrow}_{\mathcal{D}}$ into the CASL institution and (2) implementing and thus automatising our translation within HETS, we made it possible to analyse UML state machines with the broad range of provers accessible via HETS.

The resulting tool chain allows us to apply an automatic prover (as demonstrated here using the theorem prover SPASS), or several automatic provers, where they work and switch to interactive tools like Isabelle where necessary (not needed in the analysis of our example *Counter*). Not only does this switch require no manual reformulation into the interactive tool's input language, rather, it can be done even within one development: We could possibly show some lemmas via automatic first-order provers, some lemmas via domain-specific tools, then use those to prove a difficult lemma in an interactive prover, then apply all those lemmas to automatically prove the final theorem. HETS allows us to use the best language and the best tool for each job, and takes care of linking the results together under the hood.

It is future work to extend $\mathcal{M}^{\downarrow}_{\mathcal{D}}$ to cover more elements of UML state machines, such as hierarchical states and communication networks. The main challenge here will be to enrich $\mathcal{M}^{\downarrow}_{\mathcal{D}}$ in such a way that it offers suitable logical representations for the additional structural elements (hierarchical states or communication networks) rather than to flatten these: We anticipate symbolic reasoning on UML state machines to be "easier" if their structural elements are still "visible" in their CASL representations.

In the long term, we work towards heterogeneous verification of different UML diagrams. One possible setting would be to utilise interactions as a specification mechanism, where communicating state machines model implementations.

References

1. Balser, M., Bäumler, S., Knapp, A., Reif, W., Thums, A.: Interactive verification of UML state machines. In: Davies, J., Schulte, W., Barnett, M. (eds.) ICFEM 2004. LNCS, vol. 3308, pp. 434–448. Springer, Heidelberg (2004). https://doi.org/10.1007/978-3-540-30482-1_36
2. Blackburn, P., de Rijke, M., Venema, Y.: Modal Logic, Cambridge Tracts in Theoretical Computer Science, vol. 53. Cambridge University Press (2001)
3. Diaconescu, R., Madeira, A.: Encoding hybridized institutions into first-order logic. Math. Struct. Comp. Sci. **26**(5), 745–788 (2016)
4. Goguen, J.A., Burstall, R.M.: Institutions: abstract model theory for specification and programming. J. ACM **39**, 95–146 (1992)
5. Grönniger, H.: Systemmodell-basierte Definition objektbasierter Modellierungssprachen mit semantischen Variationspunkten. Ph.D. thesis, RWTH Aachen (2010)
6. Hennicker, R., Madeira, A., Knapp, A.: A Hybrid Dynamic Logic for Event/Data-Based Systems. In: Hähnle, R., van der Aalst, W. (eds.) FASE 2019. LNCS, vol. 11424, pp. 79–97. Springer, Cham (2019). https://doi.org/10.1007/978-3-030-16722-6_5
7. James, P., Knapp, A., Mossakowski, T., Roggenbach, M.: Designing domain specific languages – a craftsman's approach for the railway domain using CASL. In: Martí-Oliet, N., Palomino, M. (eds.) WADT 2012. LNCS, vol. 7841, pp. 178–194. Springer, Heidelberg (2013). https://doi.org/10.1007/978-3-642-37635-1_11
8. Knapp, A., Mossakowski, T.: UML interactions meet state machines – an institutional approach. In: Bonchi, F., König, B. (eds.) Proceedings of 7th International Conference Algebra and Coalgebra in Computer Science (CALCO 2017). LIPIcs, vol. 72, pp. 15:1–15:15 (2017)
9. Knapp, A., Mossakowski, T., Roggenbach, M.: Towards an Institutional Framework for Heterogeneous Formal Development in UML. In: De Nicola, R., Hennicker, R. (eds.) Software, Services, and Systems. LNCS, vol. 8950, pp. 215–230. Springer, Cham (2015). https://doi.org/10.1007/978-3-319-15545-6_15

10. Knapp, A., Mossakowski, T., Roggenbach, M., Glauer, M.: An institution for simple UML state machines. In: Egyed, A., Schaefer, I. (eds.) FASE 2015. LNCS, vol. 9033, pp. 3–18. Springer, Heidelberg (2015). https://doi.org/10.1007/978-3-662-46675-9_1
11. Kyas, M., et al.: Formalizing UML Models and OCL Constraints in PVS. In: Lüttgen, G., Mendler, M. (eds.) Proc. Ws. Semantic Foundations of Engineering Design Languages (SFEDL 2004). Electr. Notes Theo. Comp. Sci., vol. 115 (2005)
12. Madeira, A.: Foundations and Techniques for Software Reconfigurability. Ph.D. thesis, Universidade do Minho (2013)
13. Madeira, A., Barbosa, L.S., Hennicker, R., Martins, M.A.: Dynamic logic with binders and its application to the development of reactive systems. In: Sampaio, A., Wang, F. (eds.) ICTAC 2016. LNCS, vol. 9965, pp. 422–440. Springer, Cham (2016). https://doi.org/10.1007/978-3-319-46750-4_24
14. Mossakowski, T.: Relating CASL with other specification languages: the institution level. Theo. Comp. Sci. **286**(2), 367–475 (2002)
15. Mossakowski, T., Maeder, C., Lüttich, K.: The heterogeneous tool set, HETS. In: Grumberg, O., Huth, M. (eds.) TACAS 2007. LNCS, vol. 4424, pp. 519–522. Springer, Heidelberg (2007). https://doi.org/10.1007/978-3-540-71209-1_40
16. Mosses, P.D.: CASL Reference Manual – The Complete Documentation of the Common Algebraic Specification Language, Lect. Notes Comp. Sci., vol. 2960. Springer (2004)
17. Object Management Group: Unified Modeling Language. Standard formal/17-12-05, OMG (2017). http://www.omg.org/spec/UML/2.5.1
18. Roques, A.: PlantUML. https://plantuml.com/. Accessed 2020-02-11
19. Rosenberger, T.: Relating UML State Machines and Interactions in an Institutional Framework. Master's thesis, Elite Graduate Program Software Engineering (Universität Augsburg, Ludwig-Maximilians-Universität München, Technische Universität München) (2017)
20. Weidenbach, C., Dimova, D., Fietzke, A., Kumar, R., Suda, M., Wischnewski, P.: SPASS version 3.5. In: Schmidt, R.A. (ed.) CADE 2009. LNCS (LNAI), vol. 5663, pp. 140–145. Springer, Heidelberg (2009). https://doi.org/10.1007/978-3-642-02959-2_10

Structure-Preserving Diagram Operators

Navid Roux(✉) and Florian Rabe

Computer Science, FAU Erlangen-Nürnberg, Erlangen, Germany
{navid.roux,florian.rabe}@fau.de

Abstract. Theory operators are meta-level operators in logic that map theories to theories. Often these are functorial in that they can be extended to theory morphisms and possibly enjoy further valuable properties such as preserving inclusions. Thus, it is possible to apply them to entire diagrams at once, often in a way that the output diagram mimics any morphisms or modular structure of the input diagram. Our results are worked out using the MMT language for structured theories instantiated with the logical framework LF for basic theories, but they can be easily transferred to other languages. We investigate how MMT/LF diagram operators can be defined conveniently and give multiple examples.

1 Introduction and Related Work

Motivation. Diagrams of theories and theory morphisms have long been used successfully to build large networks of theories both in algebraic specification languages [9,24,25] and in deduction systems [12,18,23,27]. In particular, they enable the use of meta-level operators on theories such as union and translation to build large structured theories in a modular way.

Recently, inspired by ideas in [3,10], the second author generalized this idea to diagram operators [26], where an operator is applied not to a single theory but to an entire diagram. In this paper, we focus on the special case of diagram operators that are induced by applying operators on basic theories to every theory and morphism in a diagram at once. For example, we can form the diagram `Magmas` of the magma-hierarchy (defining theories for semigroup, commutative magma, etc.) and apply an operator to obtain in one step the corresponding diagram of homomorphisms (defining theories for semigroup homomorphisms, etc.).

Our main challenge here is to combine two conflicting goals. On the one hand, it must be **easy to define and implement** new diagram operators. This is critical for scalability as many diagram operators will be contributed by users, who may not be perfectly familiar with the overall framework and therefore need an interface as easy as possible. Moreover, it is critical for correctness: diagram operators tend to be very difficult to correctly specify and implement. On the other hand, diagram operators shine when applied to large diagrams, and **large diagrams are inevitably built with complex language features**. This applies both to the base logic, e.g., adding nodes to diagrams that require more expressive logics than originally envisioned, and to the structuring features for building larger theories.

M. Roggenbach (Ed.): WADT 2020, LNCS 12669, pp. 142–163, 2021.
https://doi.org/10.1007/978-3-030-73785-6_8

Contribution. We identify a class of diagram operators, for which these conflicting goals can be achieved. The general design uses two steps. Firstly, our diagram operators are **defined and implemented for flat theories** only. In particular, the language of structured theories remains transparent to users adding diagram operators. Secondly, every such definition is automatically **lifted to an operator on structured theories**. This lifting should preserve the structure and commute with flattening. Our work focuses on defining and implementing such diagram operators efficiently and reliably while providing only minimal metatheoretical analysis.

We present several concrete examples. Firstly, many constructions from universal algebra fall in this class, e.g., the operator that maps a first-order theory T to the theory $\mathtt{Hom}(T)$ of homomorphisms between two T-models. Secondly, we give an operator we call *polymorphify*, which maps a typed first-order theory T to a polymorphic theory $\mathtt{Poly}(T)$, in which types become unary type operators. Applied to `Magmas`, this yields various theories of collection datatypes: polymorphic monoids (i.e., lists), polymorphic commutative monoids (i.e., multisets), and polymorphic bounded semilattices (i.e., sets)—all derived from the single concise expression `Poly(Magmas)`. All of these operators are functorial and preserve structure, e.g., `Poly(Magmas)` contains theory morphisms and inclusions wherever `Magmas` does.

Our operators are defined within the framework for MMT diagram operators developed in [26]. We specialize our presentation to the LF logical framework [16] as defined inside MMT. This choice is made for the sake of simplicity and concreteness, and our results can be easily transferred to other formal systems. More precisely, our results are applicable to any formal system whose syntax is described by a category of theories in which theories consist of lists of named declarations. In fact, MMT was introduced specifically as an abstract definition capturing exactly those formal systems [21]. Moreover, as LF is a logical framework designed specifically for representing the syntax and proof theory of formal systems, even the restriction to MMT/LF subsumes diagram operators for many important logics and type theories (see [7] for examples). Our implementation is already applicable to any framework defined in MMT with LF as used here being just one example (see [20] for others).

Regarding structuring features, we limit attention to the two simplest and arguably most important features: definitions and inclusions. This choice is made for brevity, and our results generalize to the more complex structuring features supported by MMT such as renaming and translation.

Related Work. In parallel to the present work, [2] also expands on the development of diagram operators. That work has a similar focus and even includes some of the same examples as ours. It focuses on programmatically generating many theories derived from the algebraic hierarchy, whereas we focus on structure preservation.

[17] introduces syntactic theory functors in the setting where theories are pairs of a signature and a set of axioms. Because signatures are kept abstract, the setting cannot be directly compared to ours, but their treatment of axioms

corresponds to ours, and several of their concrete examples fit our framework. They also consider what we will call include-preservation but do not consider morphisms.

Following [26], while our diagrams are formalized in MMT, our diagram operators are implemented as self-contained objects in the programming language underlying MMT. Recently, several systems for dependent type theory have introduced meta-programming capabilities [5,11]. That would allow defining diagrams and diagram operators in the same language and is an interesting avenue of future work. However, these systems tend to use different structuring principles and in particular do not support theory morphisms. Therefore, in practice our results cannot be directly ported to those systems even though they apply to them in theory.

Programmatic definitions of universal algebra have been done in multiple settings, e.g., in [1] in Coq. Our work emphasizes the general framework in which these operators are defined and allows applications to structured theories. To the best of our knowledge, the polymorphify operator, while folklore in principle, is formalized here for the first time.

Overview. We sketch the diagram operator framework of [26] and the theory structuring features of MMT in Sect. 2. Then we develop our main results in Sect. 3 and present example applications in Sect. 4.1 and 4.2. We conclude in Sect. 5.

2 Preliminaries

The logical framework LF [16] is a dependent type theory designed for defining a wide variety of formal systems including many variants of first- and higher-order logic and set and type theory [6]. We work with LF as realized in MMT [21], which induces a language of structured theories for any such formal system defined in LF. MMT uses structured theories and theory morphisms akin to algebraic specification languages like OBJ [15] and CASL [9].

The **grammar** for MMT/LF is given in Fig. 1. There and in the sequel, we use S, T for theory identifiers, v, w for morphism identifiers, and c and x for constant and variable identifiers, respectively. In the following, we first discuss flat theories and morphisms (the non-underlined parts of Fig. 1) and state their semantics. Then we discuss our structuring features (underlined), and finally the parts of the grammar that deal with diagram expressions D.

The **flat theories** are inspired by LF-style languages and are anonymous lists of typed/kinded declarations $c\colon A$. Correspondingly, a **flat morphism** σ between two flat theories Σ and Σ' is an anonymous list of assignments $c := a$ such that, if $c\colon A$ is declared in Σ, then a must be a Σ'-expression of type $\overline{\sigma}(A)$, where $\overline{\sigma}$ is the homomorphic extension of σ. The flat theories and morphisms form a category $\mathbb{LF}^\flat$. Further details of the type system are not essential for our purposes, and we refer to [21].

For example, the theory `TFOL` for typed first-order logic can be defined as below. There, `prop` and `tp` are the LF-types holding the `TFOL`-propositions and

Diag	::=	$(Thy \mid Morph \mid \textbf{install } D)^*$	diagrams
Thy	::=	$T = \{Decl^*\}$	theory definition
Decl	::=	$c\colon A\,\underline{[= A]} \mid \underline{\textbf{include } T}$	declarations in a theory
Morph	::=	$v\colon S \to T = \{Ass^*\}$	morphism definition
Ass	::=	$c := A \mid \underline{\textbf{include } v}$	assignments in a morphism
A	::=	$\textbf{type} \mid c \mid x \mid A\ A \mid$ $\lambda x{:}A.\,A \mid \Pi x{:}A.\,A \mid A{\to}A$	terms
D	::=	$\mathrm{Diagram}(T^*, v^*) \mid O(D)$	diagram expressions

Fig. 1. MMT/LF grammar

TFOL-types, respectively. For any TFOL-type $A\colon \mathtt{tp}$, the LF-type $\mathtt{tm}\,A$ holds the TFOL-terms of TFOL-type A. We only give a few connectives as examples. Following the judgments-as-types paradigm, the validity of a proposition $F\colon \mathtt{prop}$ is captured by the non-emptiness of the type $\vdash F$, which holds the proofs of F.

$$\mathtt{TFOL} = \left\{\begin{array}{ll} \mathtt{prop} & : \mathtt{type} \\ \mathtt{tp} & : \mathtt{type} \\ \mathtt{tm} & : \mathtt{tp} \to \mathtt{type} \\ \neg & : \mathtt{prop} \to \mathtt{prop} \\ \Rightarrow & : \mathtt{prop} \to \mathtt{prop} \to \mathtt{prop} \\ \doteq & : \Pi A\colon \mathtt{tp}.\ \mathtt{tm}\ A \to \mathtt{tm}\ A \to \mathtt{prop} \\ \forall & : \Pi A\colon \mathtt{tp}.\ (\mathtt{tm}\ A \to \mathtt{prop}) \to \mathtt{prop} \\ \vdash & : \mathtt{prop} \to \mathtt{type} \end{array}\right\}$$

The underlined parts in the grammar in Fig. 1 are the structuring principles that LF inherits from MMT and that give rise to **structured theories and morphisms**. For simplicity, we restrict attention to the two most important structuring principles: defined constants and includes. In theories, a **definition** $c\colon A = a$ is valid if a has type A. In morphisms, defined constants are subject to the implicit assignment $c := \overline{v}(a)$. **Include** declarations allow combining theories into theories and morphisms into morphisms. MMT provides further structuring features, in particular for translating theories and renaming constants during an include. We expect our results to carry over to those features, but we omit them here due to space constraints.

TFOL-theories can now be represented as LF-theories that include TFOL, and similarly TFOL-theory morphisms as LF-morphisms that include the identity morphism of TFOL. More precisely, the image of this representation contains theories that include TFOL and then only add declarations of certain shapes, namely $t\colon \mathtt{tp}$ for a type symbol, $f\colon \mathtt{tm}\ t_1 \to \ldots \to \mathtt{tm}\ t_n \to \mathtt{tm}\ t$ for a function symbol, $p\colon \mathtt{tm}\ t_1 \to \ldots \to \mathtt{tm}\ t_n \to \mathtt{prop}$ for a predicate symbol, and $a\colon \vdash F$ for an axiom. More generally, we can choose to allow polymorphic declarations which are represented, e.g., as $\mathtt{list}\colon \mathtt{tp} \to \mathtt{tp}$ and $\mathtt{cons}\colon \Pi A\colon \mathtt{tp}.\ \mathtt{tm}\ A \to \mathtt{tm}\ \mathtt{list}\,A \to \mathtt{tm}\ \mathtt{list}\,A$.

The semantics of MMT structuring features is given by the flattening operation $-^\flat$ that transforms structured theories and morphisms into flat ones as sketched in Fig. 2. There, A^δ is the expression arising from A by recursively replacing any reference to a defined constant with its definiens.

We say a theory S is **included** into a theory T if $S^\flat \subseteq T^\flat$. This is the case, in particular, if **include** S occurs in the body of T. Thus, inclusion is a preorder relation on theories.

$$
\begin{aligned}
S^\flat &= \Sigma^\flat \quad \text{if } S = \{\Sigma\} \\
\cdot^\flat &= \varnothing \\
(c\colon A, \Sigma)^\flat &= \{c\colon A^\delta\} \cup \Sigma^\flat \\
(c\colon A = a, \Sigma)^\flat &= \Sigma^\flat \\
(\textbf{include } T, \Sigma)^\flat &= T^\flat \cup \Sigma^\flat
\end{aligned}
\qquad
\begin{aligned}
v^\flat &= \sigma^\flat \quad \text{if } v\colon S \to T = \{\sigma\} \\
\cdot^\flat &= \varnothing \\
(c := A, \sigma)^\flat &= \begin{cases} \{c := A^\delta\} \cup \sigma^\flat & c\colon A' \text{ in } S \\ \sigma^\flat & c\colon A' = a' \text{ in } S \end{cases} \\
(\textbf{include } w, \sigma)^\flat &= w^\flat \cup \sigma^\flat.
\end{aligned}
$$

Fig. 2. Flattening

Diagram expressions D were introduced in [26]: they are used in a third toplevel declaration **install** D, whose semantics is to declare all theories and morphisms in D at once. For our purposes, it is sufficient to consider only two simple cases for D: Diagram(T^*, v^*) builds an anonymous diagram by aggregating some previously defined theories and morphisms. And $O(D)$ applies a diagram operator O to the diagram D. Here, O is simply an identifier that MMT binds to a user-provided computation rule implemented in the underlying programming language.

Remark 1. The exact nature of diagram expressions and the install declaration in MMT is still somewhat of an open question. Here, we follow [26] and add them to the formal syntax of the language. Alternatively, we could relegate all diagram expressions to the meta-level. For example, a preprocessor could be used to compute $O(D)$ and generate the theory and morphism declarations in it.

One indication against the latter is that we have already identified some operators that take more arguments than just a diagram. For example, pushout takes a morphism m and returns the diagram operator $O = P_m$. Such operators can benefit from a tight integration with the type checker.

Further work with larger case studies is necessary to identify the most convenient syntax and work flow for utilizing diagram operators. However, large case studies are best done with structured diagrams, which is why we have prioritized the present work. In any case, the work presented here is independent of how that question is answered, and the current implementation can be easily adapted to other work flows.

For simplicity, we will restrict attention to `TFOL` in our examples below. But our results apply to any formal system defined in LF. In fact, MMT allows implementing many other logical frameworks [20], and our results apply to most of them as well. In order to pin down the **limitations** of our work more precisely, we introduce the following definition: A formal system is called **straight** if

- its theories consist of lists of declarations $c\colon A$,
- the well-formedness of theories is checked declaration-wise, i.e., $\Sigma, c\colon A$ is a well-formed theory if c is a fresh name and A satisfies some well-formedness condition $\mathrm{WF}_\Sigma(A)$ relative to Σ, and
- $\mathrm{WF}_\Sigma(A)$ depends only on those declarations in Σ that can be reached by following the occurs-in relation between declarations.

Thus, in a straight language, $\mathrm{WF}_\Sigma(A)$ can be reduced to $\mathrm{WF}_{\Sigma_0}(A)$ where Σ_0 consists of the set of declarations in Σ whose names transitively occur in A. We call Σ_0 the **dependencies** of c. In a straight language, it is easy and harmless to **identify theories up to reordering of declarations**, and we will do so in the sequel.

Straightness is a very natural condition and is satisfied by LF and thus any formal system defined in it. However, there are practically relevant counterexamples. Most of those use proof obligations as part of defining $\mathrm{WF}_\Sigma(A)$ and discharging them may have to make use of all declarations in Σ. Typical examples are languages with partial functions, subtyping, or soft typing. (Many of these can be defined in LF as well, but only by enforcing straightness at the cost of simplicity.) Moreover, any kind of backward references such as in mutually recursive declarations violates straightness. We expect that our results can be generalized to such languages, but we have not investigated that question yet.

3 Structure-Preserving Diagram Operators

3.1 Motivation: The Pushout Operator

As a motivating example, we consider the pushout operator P_m for a fixed morphism $m\colon S \to T$ in the category $\mathbb{LF}^\flat$. P_m maps extensions X of S to the pair of $P_m(X)$ and m^X such that the square below on the left is a pushout. Moreover, as indicated below on the right, it extends to a functor by mapping morphisms f to the universal morphism out of $P_m(X)$.

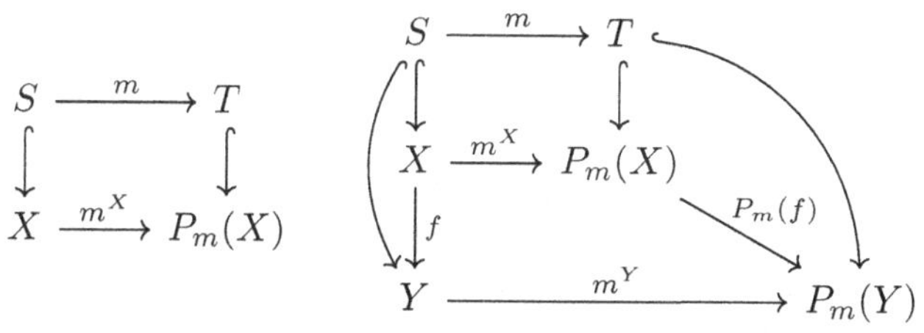

These are defined as

$$P_m(S) = T \qquad P_m(S, \Sigma, c\colon A) = P_m(S, \Sigma), c\colon \overline{m^{S,\Sigma}}(A)$$
$$P_m(id_S) = id_T \qquad P_m(id_S, \sigma, c := a) = P_m(id_S, \sigma), c := \overline{m^Y}(a)$$
$$m^S = m \qquad m^{S,\Sigma,c:A} = m^{S,\Sigma}, c := c$$

We can observe a number of abstract structural properties that are helpful for implementing this operator at large scales and that we often see in other operators. Firstly, it maps extensions of S to extensions of T. And it can be extended to a functor mapping morphisms $f\colon X \to Y$ that agree with id_S (i.e., commutative triangles of S over $X \xrightarrow{f} Y$) to morphisms between extensions of T that agree with id_T. The following definition captures this property:

Definition 1 (Functorial). *A* ***functorial*** *theory operator is a functor from a subcategory of* $\mathbb{LF}^{\flat}$ *to* $\mathbb{LF}^{\flat}$. *Thus,* O *is a partial map of objects and morphisms such that: if* O *is defined for an object* X, *it is also defined for* id_X; *if it is defined for morphisms* f, g, *it is also defined for their domains, codomains, and (if composable) their composition.*

We say that O *is* ***from*** S ***to*** T *if it (i) is only defined for theories extending* S *and then returns theories extending* T, *and (ii) if defined for theories* X, Y, *is only defined for morphisms* $f\colon X \to Y$ *that agree with* id_S *and then returns morphisms that agree with* id_T.

Thus, P_m is functorial from S to T for $m\colon S \to T$.

This situation is very common. For example, it is typical for transporting developments relative to a base language S to a different base language T. Concretely, to represent a language L (e.g., a type theory or logic) in LF, we usually employ an LF-theory S to represent the syntax and possibly proof calculus of L. L-theories are then represented as LF-theories extending S, and L-morphisms between L-theories as LF-morphisms that agree with id_S. Now given two such representations S and T for two languages, many language translations can be represented as functorial operators from S to T.

Remark 2 (Partiality). In Definition 1, we do *not* require that O is defined for all extensions of S. There are two reasons for this. Firstly, the representation of L-theories as LF-theories extending S is usually not surjective. Theory operators specific to L can usually only be defined on the image of that representation. Secondly, defining operators may run into name clashes: it may be straightforward to define a functor up to renaming of declarations (a special case of isomorphism) but awkward or impossible to do so on the nose. For example, we discussed this problem in depth for the pushout functor in [8]. In those cases, the best trade-off may sometimes be to leave the operator undefined for some inputs.

Remark 3 (Functoriality). In Definition 1, we do require that O is functorial where defined. In our experience, there are few interesting operators where functoriality fails. Essentially, it means that operators (i) are defined for morphisms, not just for theories, and (ii) preserve identity and composition of morphisms. An operator failing the first requirement usually cannot be extended to theories with definitions – a critical requirement in practice. And an operator failing the second requirement would be highly unusual. It is, however, common to find transformations in the literature where only the definition on theories is worked out and the extension to a functorial operator requires additional work.

A second property of the pushout operator that often occurs in general is that it is defined declaration-wise: the declarations in the input are processed in a row, each resulting in a declaration that occurs in the output theory. Moreover, the output only depends on the input declaration (and its dependencies) and not on any other preceding or succeeding declaration. An abstract way to capture the essence of this property is the following:

Definition 2 (Include-Preservation). *An operator O is **include-preserving** if whenever O is defined for flat LF-theories X, Y, we have that $X \subseteq Y$ implies $O(X) \subseteq O(Y)$ and accordingly for morphisms.*

This property is frequently fulfilled for theory operators because they are typically defined by induction on the list of declarations in a theory, as is the case with the pushout operator.

As a third property, include-preservation in particular allows us to extend the pushout to diagrams of structured theories: if we map every theory T in a diagram to T', we can map every declaration **include** T to **include** T' and thus preserve the structure. Similarly, the pushout can be extended to theories with definitions. If the input theory contains the declaration $c\colon A = a$, we can put the definition $c\colon \overline{m^{S,\Sigma}}(A) = \overline{m^{S,\Sigma}}(a)$ into the output theory. Then in any subsequent occurrence of c in the input, we do not need to expand the definition before applying m^X. Instead, we can map any occurrence of the defined constant c in X to the correspondingly defined constant c in $P_m(X)$.

Definition 3 (Structure-Preservation). *A partial map O on LF-diagrams is a **structure-preserving** diagram operator if the following holds: if $O(D)$ is defined for a diagram D, then for every theory/morphism named n in D there is a corresponding theory/morphism named $O(n)$ in $O(D)$, and we have $O(n)^\flat = O(n^\flat)$.*

If we extend P_m to diagrams using includes and definitions as sketched above, we obtain a structure-preserving diagram operator.

Structure-preservation is satisfied by many interesting diagram operators. However, it is often awkward to define them—it is much more convenient to define an operator only for flat theories/morphisms, where category theory provides an elegant and expressive meta-theory. Indeed, many formal definitions in the literature do only that.

3.2 Linear Operators

Even though the preceding properties make intuitively sense to demand upon operators, they are also abstract in nature and do not help much users in easily specifying and implementing operators. We tackle this problem in the sections to come by developing a more accessible class of operators which are given more concretely and yet fulfill the abstract properties.

In particular, we start by identifying general patterns of operators on flat theories that allow lifting them to structure-preserving diagram operators. The following definition identifies a large class of such cases:

Definition 4 (Linear Operator). *Given two theories S and T, a* ***linear*** *diagram operator O from S to T is a partial endofunctor on flat theories mapping extensions of S to extensions of T such that*

- *O is defined for extensions of S declaration-wise:*

$$O(S) = T \qquad O(S, \Sigma, c\colon A) = O(S, \Sigma), \Delta_\Sigma(c\colon A)$$

  for some $\Delta_-(-)$,
- *O is defined similarly for morphisms $S, \Sigma \to S, \Sigma'$ that are of the form id_S, σ:*

$$O(id_S) = id_T \qquad O(id_S, \sigma, c := a) = O(id_S, \sigma), \delta_\sigma(c := a)$$

  for some $\delta_-(-)$,
- *the definedness and result of $\Delta_\Sigma(c\colon A)$ are determined by $\Delta_{\Sigma_0}(c\colon A)$ where Σ_0 are the dependencies of c, and*
- *the definedness and result of $\delta_\sigma(c := a)$ are determined by $\delta_{\sigma_0}(c := a)$ where σ_0 is the fragment of σ acting on the dependencies of c.*

It is straightforward to see that P_m is linear for every m. Moreover, we have the following basic property:

Theorem 1. *Every linear operator is functorial from S to T and preserves includes.*

Proof. Straightforward.

In contrast, functorial operators that preserve includes are not necessarily linear. For example, by setting $O(\Sigma) = \{c_1\_c_2\colon \texttt{type} \mid c_1, c_2 \in \Sigma\}$ we can define an operator that produces a single declaration for every ordered pair of declarations in Σ. This operator still preserves includes but fails to fulfill the above third requirement on linear operators.

The functions Δ and δ serve to output a *list* of declarations for every input declaration. They are uniquely determined by O, and vice versa, (fixing S and T) O is uniquely determined by Δ and δ. Therefore, to implement linear operators, we can fix $O(S)$ and implement the functions Δ and δ. Moreover, the argument Σ in $\Delta_\Sigma(c\colon A)$ is only needed to look up the types of constants occurring in Σ. Thus, implementing a linear operator essentially means to map declarations $c\colon A$ individually. That makes them much simpler to implement than arbitrary operators on theories.

Concerning the declarations output by Δ and δ, the pushout operator also satisfies the following stricter property:

Definition 5 (Strongly Linear Operator). *A linear operator is called* ***strongly linear*** *if $\Delta_\Sigma(c\colon A)$ always contains exactly one declaration, which is also named c.*

Strongly linear operators are even simpler to implement because they are already determined by a pair (E, ε) of expression translation functions by means of $\Delta_\Sigma(c\colon A) = c\colon E_\Sigma(A)$ and $\delta_\sigma(c := a) = c := \varepsilon_\sigma(a)$. Namely, developers of operators only need to worry about the inductive expression translation functions, and the framework can take over all bureaucracy for names and declarations. Moreover, it is even simpler to check that two arbitrary functions (E, ε) induce a strongly linear operator. We omit the details, but essentially we only have to check that the typing judgement $a\colon A$ implies $\varepsilon(a)\colon E(A)$.

For the pushout operator we even have $E_\Sigma = \varepsilon_\sigma$, but that is not common enough to deserve its own definition. However, it is often the case that E_Σ and ε_σ are very similar, e.g., they might be the same except that E inserts a Π-binder where ε inserts a λ one.

3.3 Structure-Preserving Lifting of Linear Operators

Our goal now is to extend linear operators O from S to T—which by definition act on flat theories and morphisms only—to operators on diagrams D of structured theories. We make some simplifying assumptions to state our rigorous definitions.

Firstly, we assume that every theory in D starts by including S and every morphism by including id_S. Correspondingly, theories and morphisms in $O(D)$ will include T and id_T, respectively. However, we will not mention these includes in the syntax and instead assume that they are fixed globally for the entire diagram. This mimics how diagrams are actually implemented in MMT. For example, S could be `TFOL` and D a diagram of `TFOL`-theories. It would then be very awkward to manually include `TFOL` in every theory in D. Instead, MMT provides a mechanism for declaring D to be a `TFOL`-diagram, in which case `TFOL` is available in all theories and fixed by all morphisms in D.

Secondly, we assume that D is self-contained, i.e., every theory mentioned in D, be it in an include declaration or as the (co)domain of a morphism, is also defined in D.

Thirdly, we assume that there are no name clashes between theories defined in D and the theory T: other than the names already declared in S, no theory in D should declare names also used in T. In particular, this means that no theory in D may include T or any named theory that is transitively included into T (unless S itself includes that theory). This requirement can be dropped in practice because MMT anyway distinguishes two constants of the same name, one declared in a theory in D and one declared in T. But it is necessary here to (i) avoid explaining MMT's name disambiguation mechanism, and (ii) alert to this subtlety any reader who plans to implement the lifting in other systems.

Our output will be the diagram $O(D)$ that contains the results of applying O to every theory and morphism in D. Our goal is that $O(D)$ mirrors as much of the structure of D as possible.

We need to generate fresh names for the new theories and morphisms in $O(D)$. These new names should not be arbitrary but obtained from the names in D in a systematic way that is predictable for the user. That is necessary to enable users to actually make use of the new theories and morphisms after having applied O to obtain them. For example, when applying the operator P_m to a theory defined as $X = \{\Sigma\}$, we could obtain the theory definition $\texttt{pushout}.m.X = \{P_m(\Sigma)\}$. Therefore, we define:

Definition 6. *A **liftable operator** O is an operator together with a function that maps names to names. We denote this function also by $O(-)$. The composition of liftable operators is defined by composing both the operators and their name maps.*

Thus, we can map the theory definition $X = \{\Sigma\}$ to the theory definition $O(X) = \{O(\Sigma)\}$. To avoid confusion, keep in mind that X, Y, v, w are always names that O maps to other names, and that Σ and σ are lists of declarations/assignments for which O is defined inductively.

Then we can finally define the lifting:

Definition 7 (Lifting). *Given a linear liftable operator O, we define its lifting $O(-)$ to diagrams as follows:*

- *For every theory $X = \{\Sigma\}$ in D, $O(D)$ contains the theory $O(X) = \{O(\Sigma)\}$ where*

$$O(\cdot) = \cdot \qquad O(\Sigma,\ c\colon A) = O(\Sigma),\ \Delta_\Sigma(c\colon A)$$
$$O(\Sigma,\ c\colon A = a) = O(\Sigma),\ \mathrm{AsDef}(\delta_{id_\Sigma}(c := a))$$
$$O(\Sigma,\ \textbf{include}\, Y) = O(\Sigma),\ \textbf{include}\, O(Y)$$

  and AsDef$(-)$ *as defined below.*
- *For every morphism $v\colon X \to Y = \{\sigma\}$ in D, $O(D)$ contains the morphism $O(v)\colon O(X) \to O(Y) = \{O(\sigma)\}$ where*

$$O(\cdot) = \cdot \qquad O(\sigma,\ c := a) = O(\sigma),\ \delta_\sigma(c := a)$$
$$O(\sigma,\ \textbf{include}\, w) = O(\sigma),\ \textbf{include}\, O(w).$$

Here, the subscripts of Δ and δ technically must be flattened first. But we omit that from the notation.

Definition 7 looks complex but is mostly straightforward. It uses Δ and δ for the flat cases and maps includes to includes. The only subtlety is the case for defined constants. Here, we exploit the general property of MMT that a constant definition $\Sigma,\ c\colon A = a$ is well-formed iff $id_\Sigma,\ c := a$ is a well-formed morphism from $\Sigma,\ c\colon A$ to Σ. This is easy to see—in both directions the key property is the typing judgment $\vdash_\Sigma a\colon A$. This equivalence lets us turn a definition into a morphism assignment, apply O, and then turn the resulting assignments back into definitions. Using the morphism above, O yields the morphism $O(id_\Sigma),\ \delta_{id_\Sigma}(c := a)$ from $O(\Sigma),\ \Delta_\Sigma(c\colon A)$ to $O(\Sigma)$. We define the function AsDef$(-)$ to turn this morphism back into a sequence of definitions: it replaces every assignment $c' := a'$ for a constant $c'\colon A'$ in $\Delta_\Sigma(c\colon A)$ with the definition $c'\colon A' = a'$.

AsDef(−) is only needed in our definition on paper. When implementing the lifting in MMT, it is not even needed because declarations in a theory and assignments in a morphism are internally represented in the same way.

Remark 4 (Strongly Linear Lifting). By definition, every strongly linear operator O with expression translation functions (E, ε) is linear, and hence its lifting (via an arbitrary name map) is a special case of the above.

The case of defined constants is particularly interesting: Applying the definition, we see that it maps defined constants by

$$O(\Sigma,\ c\colon A = a) = O(\Sigma),\ c\colon E_\Sigma(A) = \varepsilon_{id_\Sigma}(a)$$

Thus, E and ε can be seen as using one translation function for types and one for typed terms.

3.4 Structure-Preservation of the Lifting

It remains to show that the lifted operators behave as expected. This is captured formally in our main theorem:

Theorem 2 (Structure Preservation). *Consider a well-formed diagram D and an operator O as in Definition 7. Then, $O(D)$ is a well-formed diagram, and*

- *for every theory named X defined in D, we have $O(X^\flat) = O(X)^\flat$*
- *for every morphism named v defined in D, we have $O(v^\flat) = O(v)^\flat$.*

In particular, O is structure-preserving.

Proof. The proof of well-formedness of $O(D)$ proceeds by induction on the well-formedness derivation for D in the MMT/LF calculus. Only the case for defined constants is non-obvious. The argument for that case is already sketched in the remarks explaining the use of AsDef(−) after Definition 7.

Because linear operators preserve includes, it is easy to see that the preservation statements hold for diagrams that do not contain definitions.

To account for definitions, we observe that a constant c' in $O(X)$ is defined iff the lifting generates it when translating a defined constant c in X. Moreover, linearity guarantees that the lifting handles undefined constants in the same way regardless of whether defined constants in the same theory are eliminated or not. Thus, $O(X^\flat)$ and $O(X)^\flat$ contain the same declarations.

3.5 Composing Operators

While we do not focus on the meta-theoretical analysis of our operators, it is critical to study the composition of operators. This is because our language allows repeated application as in $O'(O(D))$. All properties defined above are preserved under composition in the following sense:

Theorem 3 (Composition of Theory Operators). *Consider two operators O, O' on $\mathbb{LF}^b$ such that O' is defined on the image of O. Then:*

- *If O is functorial (from R to S) and O' is functorial (from S to T), then $O' \circ O$ is functorial (from R to T).*
- *If O and O' preserve includes, so does $O' \circ O$.*

Proof. All proofs are straightforward.

Theorem 4 (Composition of Diagram Operators). *Consider two liftable operators O, O' on LF-diagrams such that O' is defined on the image of O. Then:*

- *If O and O' are structure-preserving, then so is $O' \circ O$.*
- *If O and O' are (strongly) linear, then so is $O' \circ O$. Moreover, its lifting is the composition of the liftings of O' and O.*

Proof. All proofs are straightforward.

4 Applications

Linear operators occur in all areas of formal languages. Before we describe some operators in detail below, we give a list of examples that we are aware of:

- Universal algebra provides many constructions that correspond to linear operators from TFOL to itself. Examples include the operators that map any TFOL-theory X to the theory of homomorphisms between two X-models, the sub-models of an X-model, and congruence relations of an X-model, respectively. [2] reports on a systematic survey identifying dozens more, which are applied uniformly to a diagram of over 200 algebraic theories.
- As described in [6], many translations are already special cases of the pushout P_m for an appropriate m. Examples include the relativization translations from modal or description logics to unsorted first-order logic and the interpretation of type theory in set theory.
  But many more complex translations are functorial operators from S to T that cannot be represented as pushouts, and that was one of the original motivations of the present work. Typical examples are translations that use encodings to eliminate features such as:
  - The negative translation from classical to intuitionistic logic is strongly linear but cannot be given by a pushout: being strongly linear, the output theory declares a propositional variable p whenever the input theory does; but all references to p are translated to $\neg\neg p$ (whereas the pushout would translate them to p).
  - The type-erasure translation from typed to untyped first-order logic is linear but not strongly linear: it maps every typed declaration to an untyped declaration *and* an axiom capturing the typing properties.

- Logical frameworks often allow multiple different encodings for the same formal system, in which case there are often systematic syntactic transformations that mediate between them. For example, many type theoretical features (function types, product types, etc.) can be formalized both using intrinsic (terms carry their type) and using extrinsic (terms are assigned types by the environment) encodings of typing. Because both have their merit, they are usually both done in practice. Using a linear operator, we cannot only generate one from the other, but we can also generate the transformations between them.
- Many structural operations needed to manage large libraries can be seen as linear operators. Examples include the conversion between different packaging conventions in the sense of [13] and promotion in Z in the sense of [4]. Often these are written ad hoc for a subset of the theories of the library, sometimes multiple times for the same theory. They are especially valuable to automate in order to reduce workload and ensure the uniform application of boilerplate constructions across the library.

4.1 Universal Algebra

The algebraic hierarchy in which theories are developed is a prime example of a diagram of structured theories due to the high degree of reuse in that domain. Therefore, the combination of the two is an ideal match. We develop two operators as examples: one that maps a TFOL-theory X (whose models are the X-models) to the TFOL-theory of X-homomorphisms (whose models are the homomorphisms between X-models). And another that maps a TFOL-theory X to the TFOL-theory of X-submodels (whose models are the pairs of a X-model and a submodel of it). Other constructions such as product and quotient models can be handled accordingly.

In both cases, we use the following structured diagram of magma-based theories as an example:

$$
\begin{array}{ccccc}
 & & & \texttt{Comm} & \\
 & & \nearrow & & \\
\texttt{Set} & \hookrightarrow & \texttt{Magma} & & \\
 & & \searrow & & \\
 & & & \texttt{SemiGr} \hookrightarrow & \texttt{Monoid}
\end{array}
$$

We start with $\texttt{Set} = \{U\colon \texttt{tp}\}$ and build the hierarchy in a straightforward way:

$$
\texttt{Magma} = \left\{ \begin{array}{l} \textbf{include}\ \texttt{Set} \\ \circ\colon \texttt{tm}\ U \to \texttt{tm}\ U \to \texttt{tm}\ U \end{array} \right\}
\qquad
\texttt{Comm} = \left\{ \begin{array}{l} \textbf{include}\ \texttt{Magma} \\ \texttt{ax\_comm}\colon \vdash \ldots \end{array} \right\}
$$

$$
\texttt{SemiGr} = \left\{ \begin{array}{l} \textbf{include}\ \texttt{Magma} \\ \texttt{ax\_assoc}\colon \vdash \ldots \end{array} \right\}
\qquad
\texttt{Monoid} = \left\{ \begin{array}{ll} \textbf{include}\ \texttt{SemiGr} & \\ \texttt{e} & \colon \texttt{tm}\ U \\ \texttt{ax\_neut} & \colon \vdash \ldots \end{array} \right\}
$$

For later application of our operators, let us by Magmas abbreviate the MMT diagram expression Diagram(Set, Magma, Comm, SemiGr, Monoid).

Homomorphisms. We define the operator $\mathtt{Hom}$ such that it is linear by construction and only define Δ and δ. We map every type, function, or predicate symbol declaration $c\colon A$ via Δ to three declarations. Two of them serve as renamed copies to build up the domain and codomain of the homomorphism, and the third declaration accounts for the actual homomorphism. Axioms are mapped to two declarations only, one each for domain and codomain:

- In a type symbol declaration, we have $A = \mathtt{tp}$, and $\Delta_\Sigma(t\colon A)$ contains

$$t^d\colon \mathtt{tp},\ t^c\colon \mathtt{tp},\ t^h\colon \mathtt{tm}\ t^d \to \mathtt{tm}\ t^c$$

  Here, the superscripts indicate different systematic renamings of the constant t.
- In a function symbol declaration, A is of the form $\mathtt{tm}\ t_1 \to \ldots \to \mathtt{tm}\ t_n \to \mathtt{tm}\ t$, and $\Delta_\Sigma(f\colon A)$ contains

$$\begin{aligned}&f^d\colon A^d, \quad f^c\colon A^c,\\ &f^h\colon \vdash \forall x_1\colon \mathtt{tm}\ t_1^d, \ldots, x_n\colon \mathtt{tm}\ t_n^d.\ t^h(f^d(x_1,\ldots,x_n)) \doteq f^c(t_1^h(x_1),\ldots,t_n^h(x_n))\end{aligned}$$

  Here and below, the superscripts as in A^d indicate the translation of the expression A by renaming all constants occurring in it.
- In a predicate symbol declaration, A is of the form $\mathtt{tm}\ t_1 \to \ldots \to \mathtt{tm}\ t_n \to \mathtt{prop}$, and $\Delta_\Sigma(p\colon A)$ contains

$$\begin{aligned}&p^d\colon A^d, \quad p^c\colon A^c,\\ &p^h\colon \vdash \forall x_1\colon \mathtt{tm}\ t_1^d, \ldots, x_n\colon \mathtt{tm}\ t_n^d.\ p^d(x_1,\ldots,x_n) \Rightarrow p^c(t_1^h(x_1),\ldots,t_n^h(x_n))\end{aligned}$$

- In an axiom declaration, A is of the form $\vdash F$, and $\Delta_\Sigma(a\colon A)$ contains $a^d\colon A^d$, $a^c\colon A^c$.

Moreover, for any TFOL-theory $X = \{\Sigma\}$, we define the theory morphism $X^d\colon X \to \mathtt{Hom}(X) = \{\sigma^d\}$ where σ^d contains **include** Y^d for every **include** Y in Σ and $s := s^d$ for every constant s in Σ. Analogously, we define the morphism $X^c\colon X \to \mathtt{Hom}(X) = \{\sigma^c\}$. Thus, $\mathtt{Hom}$ is more than a functor: it maps a single theory X to the diagram

$$X \underset{X^c}{\overset{X^d}{\rightrightarrows}} \mathtt{Hom}(X).$$

It is this diagram-valued behavior that inspired MMT diagram operators in the first place.

The definition of δ is the same in principle but there is a subtle issue: Hom is not actually functorial on all morphisms between TFOL-theories. We refer to [22] for a detailed analysis of the problem. Because our framework uses partial functors anyway, we can remedy this with the following definition: A formula is called *monotone* if it only uses the connectives $\wedge$, $\vee$, $\doteq$, and $\exists$ (but not $\neg$, $\Rightarrow$, or $\forall$). The intuition behind monotone formulas is that they are preserved along homomorphisms. Then we restrict the applicability of Hom as follows: If a TFOL-theory contains a defined predicate symbol, the definiens must be monotone.

And in a morphism between TFOL-theories, all predicate symbols must be assigned a monotone expression. This partiality is a bit awkward but desirable in practice: users trying to apply Hom to a theory or morphism violating the restriction are usually unaware of this issue and thus have inconsistent expectations of the behavior of Hom.

After making this restriction, we can define δ as follows:

- For a type symbol assignment, $\delta_\sigma(t := E) = t^d := E^d,\ t^c := E^c,\ t^h := E^h$. Here, the superscripts on E again denote the translations that replace every constant accordingly. Note that in TFOL, up to β-normalization in LF, E can only be a type *symbol*, never a complex expression.
- For a function symbol $f\colon A$ as above, $\delta_\sigma(f := E) = f^d := E^d,\ f^c := E^c,\ f^h := P$. Here, P is a proof that

$$\forall x_1\colon \mathtt{tm}\ \widehat{t_1^d}, \dots, x_n\colon \mathtt{tm}\ \widehat{t_n^d}.\\ \widehat{t^h}\left(E^d(x_1, \dots, x_n)\right) \doteq E^c\left(\widehat{t_1^h}(x_1), \dots, \widehat{t_n^h}(x_n)\right),$$

  where the circumflex $\widehat{\ }$ abbreviates the application of $\overline{\mathtt{Hom}(\sigma)}$; a property provable in TFOL for every well-typed expression E.
- For a predicate symbol $p\colon A$ as above, $\delta_\sigma(p := E) = p^d := E^d,\ p^c := E^c,\ p^h := P$. Here, P is a proof that

$$\forall x_1\colon \mathtt{tm}\ \widehat{t_1^d}, \dots, x_n\colon \mathtt{tm}\ \widehat{t_n^d}.\ E^d\left(x_1, \dots, x_n\right) \Rightarrow E^c\left(\widehat{t_1^h}(x_1), \dots, \widehat{t_n^h}(x_n)\right),$$

  a property provable in TFOL for every monotone well-typed expression E.
- For an axiom symbol assignment, $\delta_\sigma(a := E) = a^d := E^d,\ a^c := E^c$.

Theorem 5. Hom(−) *is linear from* TFOL *(restricted to monotone theories and morphisms) to* TFOL.

Proof. It is well-known that Hom as defined above is indeed a functor, see e.g., [22]. Then linearity is obvious.

Consequently, we can immediately apply Hom to our diagram of structured theories: The MMT declaration **install** Hom(Magmas) adds the encircled diagram shown in Fig. 3 to the previous diagram Magmas also shown there. As an example, we show the generated theories for Set and Magma:

$$\mathtt{Hom(Set)} = \left\{\begin{array}{ll} U^d & : \mathtt{tp} \\ U^c & : \mathtt{tp} \\ U^h & : \mathtt{tm}\ U^d \to \mathtt{tm}\ U^c \end{array}\right\}$$

$$\mathtt{Hom(Magma)} = \left\{\begin{array}{ll} \multicolumn{2}{l}{\textbf{include}\ \mathtt{Hom(Set)}} \\ \circ^d & : \mathtt{tm}\ U^d \to \mathtt{tm}\ U^d \to \mathtt{tm}\ U^d \\ \circ^c & : \mathtt{tm}\ U^c \to \mathtt{tm}\ U^c \to \mathtt{tm}\ U^c \\ \circ^h & : \vdash \forall x_1\colon \mathtt{tm}\ U^d, x_2\colon \mathtt{tm}\ U^d. \\ & \qquad U^h(x_1 \circ^d x_2) \doteq U^h(x_1) \circ^c U^h(x_2) \end{array}\right\}$$

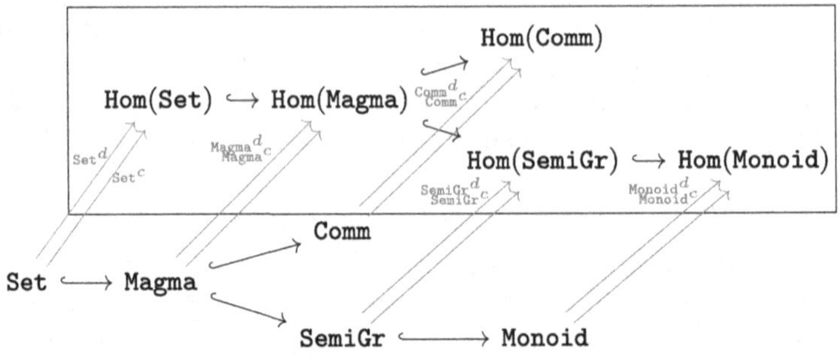

Fig. 3. Diagrams Magmas and (boxed) Hom(Magmas)

Submodels. We proceed in essentially the same way to define a theory that pairs a model with one of its submodels. Again, we translate and rename all declarations of the input, but this time only once using the superscript ^{p} for the parent of the submodel. We use the superscript ^{s} for the declarations building the submodel. We define Δ by:

- Every type symbol declaration $t\colon \mathtt{tp}$ is mapped to two declarations: $t^p\colon \mathtt{tp}$ for the parent model and $t^s\colon \mathtt{tm}\ t^p \to \mathtt{prop}$ for the predicate singling out the values of the submodel.
- Every function symbol declaration $f\colon A$ (of the form as above) is mapped to two declarations, $f^p\colon A^p$ for the parent model and

$$f^s\colon \vdash \forall x_1\colon \mathtt{tm}\ t_1^p, \ldots, x_n\colon \mathtt{tm}\ t_n^p.\ t_1^s(x_1) \wedge \ldots \wedge t_n^s(x_n) \Rightarrow t^s(f^p(x_1, \ldots, x_n))$$

  for the closure property of the submodel.
- Predicate symbols are not relevant for submodels, and we simply translate $c\colon A$ to $c^p\colon A^p$.
- Axioms $a\colon \vdash F$ are translated to $a^p\colon \vdash F^p$ for the parent model and $a^s\colon \vdash F'$ for the submodel. Here, F' arises from F^p by relativizing every quantifier on a type t^p using the predicate t^s.

In the same way as for Hom, we obtain a morphism $X^p\colon X \to \mathtt{Sub}(T)$ that assigns $c := c^p$. Hypothetically, if we worked in a stronger logic that allowed taking subtypes, we could define a morphism $X^s\colon X \to \mathtt{Sub}(X)$ that maps, e.g., a type t to the subtype of t^p given by t^s.

Finally, we define δ by:

- Every type symbol assignment $t := E$ is mapped to $t^p := E^p$, $t^s := E^s$.
- Every function symbol assignment $f := E$ is mapped to $f^p := E^p$, $f^s := P$ where P is a proof that the result of E is in the submodel whenever all its arguments are.
- Predicate symbol assignments $c := E$ are mapped to $c^p := E^p$.
- Axiom assignments $a := E$ are translated to $a^p := E^p$, $a^s := E'$ where E' arises from E^p by adapting all occurrences of quantifier rules to the relativized variants.

Theorem 6. *The operator* Sub(−) *is linear from* TFOL *to* TFOL.

Proof. The proof proceeds as for Hom.

These examples give a first glimpse of the power of composing diagram operators. We can, for example, use **install** Hom(Sub(Magmas)) to obtain the theories of homomorphisms between submodels. By further combining that with a diagram operator for coequalizers, we can then obtain the theory of homomorphisms between submodels of the *same* parent model.

Future Work: Provable Axioms. The submodel example indicates an important avenue of future work: many of the axioms a^s we copy to Sub(X) are in fact provable. For example, all axioms using only $\forall$ and $\doteq$ (i.e., the axioms primarily used in universal algebra) are automatically true in each submodel. Here, Sub could do much better and translate such axioms to theorems by synthesizing an appropriate proof and adding it as the definiens of a^s. More generally, we could run a theorem prover on every axiom we generate (independent of its shape) and generate a definiens whenever a proof can be found.

This issue can be more subtle as a similar example with Hom shows: sometimes the generated axioms become provable in the context of stronger theories. For example, every magma homomorphism between groups is automatically a group homomorphism. Thus, the preservation axioms e^h for the neutral element and i^h (where i is the unary function symbol for the inverse element) are provable in the theory Hom(Group), at which place it would therefore be desirable for Hom to add definitions. However, this makes it trickier for the operator to be structure-preserving: the theory Hom(Monoid) must still contain e^h without a definition, and the definition should only be added when Hom(Monoid) is included into Hom(Group).

4.2 Polymorphic Generalization

We give a linear operator Poly(−) from TFOL to polymorphic first-order logic PFOL. PFOL uses the same LF-theory as TFOL. But the well-formed symbol declarations in a PFOL-theory are more general: they are like the ones in TFOL-theories except that they may be polymorphic in type variables. Concretely, PFOL allows type *operator* declarations $t\colon \mathtt{tp} \to \ldots \to \mathtt{tp} \to \mathtt{tp}$ and *polymorphic* function symbol declarations $f\colon \Pi\, u_1\colon \mathtt{tp}.\ \ldots\ \Pi\, u_m\colon \mathtt{tp}.\ \ \mathtt{tm}\ t_1 \to \ldots \to \mathtt{tm}\ t_m \to \mathtt{tm}\ t$, where all t_i and t may now contain the type variables u_i. Accordingly, PFOL allows polymorphic predicate symbols and polymorphic axioms.

Poly is strongly linear by construction, i.e., we only need to give expression translation functions E_Σ for types in declarations $c\colon A$ and ε_σ for expressions in assignments $c := a$. These are defined as

- $E_\Sigma(A) = \Pi u\colon \mathtt{tp}.\ A^{\Sigma,u}$
- $\varepsilon_\sigma(a) = \lambda u\colon \mathtt{tp}.\ a^{\Sigma,u}$ where Σ is the codomain of σ

where the function $-^{\Sigma,u}$ replaces every occurrence of a constant c declared in Σ with $c\,u$. Here, u is any variable name that does not occur bound anywhere in the argument.

Applying the definition, we see that $\texttt{Poly}(X)$ maps declarations in X as follows:

- Every type $t\colon \texttt{tp}$ yields a unary type operator $t\colon \Pi u\colon \texttt{tp}.\ \texttt{tp}$ (i.e., $t\colon \texttt{tp} \to \texttt{tp}$).
- Every function symbol $f\colon \texttt{tm}\ t_1 \to \ldots \to \texttt{tm}\ t_n \to \texttt{tm}\ t$ yields a polymorphic function symbol $f\colon \Pi u\colon \texttt{tp}.\ \texttt{tm}\ t_1 u \to \ldots \to \texttt{tm}\ t_n u \to \texttt{tm}\ t u$. Thus f abstracts over an arbitrary type u and replaces every X-type symbol t with the type $t\,u$, which arises by applying the $\texttt{Poly}(X)$-unary type operator t to u.
- Every predicate symbol is mapped in essentially the same way as function symbols.
- Every axiom $c\colon \vdash F$ yields an axiom $c\colon \Pi u\colon \texttt{tp}.\ \vdash F^{\Sigma,u}$ where the operation $-^{\Sigma,u}$ now affects all type, function, and predicate symbols occurring in F.

Theorem 7. $\texttt{Poly}(-)$ *is a strongly linear operator.*

Proof. We only need to show that Poly indeed yields well-typed theories and morphisms. For theories, that is obvious. For morphisms, the critical step of the inductive proof considers a TFOL-morphism $id_{\texttt{TFOL}}, \sigma, c := a$ from $\texttt{TFOL}, \Sigma, c\colon A$ to $\texttt{TFOL}, \Sigma'$. Applying the definition of Poly, we see that the well-typedness of the resulting morphism hinges on $\varepsilon_\sigma(a)\colon \overline{\texttt{Poly}(id_{\texttt{TFOL}}, \sigma)}(E_\Sigma(A))$ to hold over $\overline{\texttt{Poly}(\texttt{TFOL}, \Sigma')}$. That follows from the definitions of E and ε and the fact that $a\colon \overline{id_{\texttt{TFOL}}, \sigma}(A)$ over Σ'.

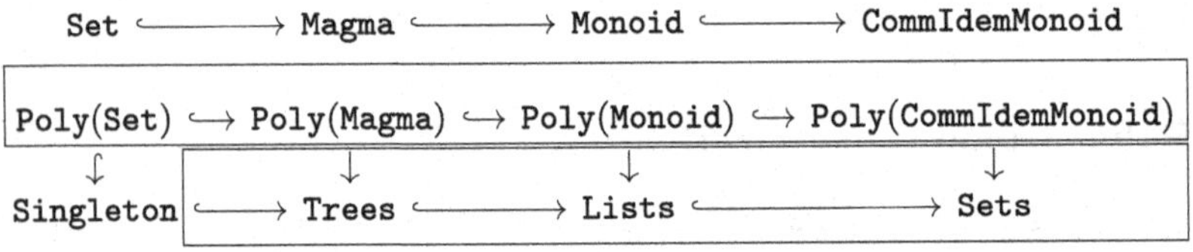

Fig. 4. Diagrams Magmas, Singleton and (boxed) results of applying Poly

Consider Fig. 4 for an example application: the first row draws and extends on a fragment of Magmas, while the second row shows the corresponding theories and morphisms emerging from **install** Poly(Magmas). For instance, $\texttt{Poly}(\texttt{Monoid})^\flat$ is given by

$$U\colon \texttt{tp} \to \texttt{tp},\ \circ : \Pi u\colon \texttt{tp}.\ \texttt{tm}\ U u \to \texttt{tm}\ U u \to \texttt{tm}\ U u,\ e\colon \Pi u\colon \texttt{tp}.\ \texttt{tm}\ U u,\ \ldots$$

where we omit the axioms. That already looks very close to the theory of lists with $U\,u$ for the type of lists over u and $\circ$ and e for concatenation and empty list. Similarly, magmas, commutative monoids, and commutative-idempotent monoids yield theories close to the collection data types for trees, multisets, and sets over a type u.

In all of these cases, the only thing missing to complete the specification of the collection data type is an operator for creating singleton trees, lists, and sets. We can uniformly inject it into all theories in the diagram by defining the theory

$$\texttt{Singleton} = \{\textbf{include}\,\texttt{Poly(Set)},\ \texttt{singleton}\colon \Pi u\colon \texttt{tp}.\ \texttt{tm}\ u \rightarrow \texttt{tm}\ U u\}$$

and then applying $P_{\texttt{Singleton}}$ to Poly(Magmas) where $P_{\texttt{Singleton}}$ takes the pushout along the inclusion Poly(Set) $\hookrightarrow$ Singleton. The result is shown in the third row in Fig. 4.

5 Conclusion and Future Work

We introduced a class of structure-preserving functorial diagram operators, and showed how to define them easily and lift them to large diagrams. They allow building small diagram expressions that evaluate to large diagrams whose structure remains intuitive and predictable to users.

They can be seen as different degrees of compositionality-breaking: pushout-based translations are induced by the homomorphic extension of a morphism and thus entirely compositional; strongly linear operators use arbitrary expression translation functions and extend them compositionally to declarations and theories; linear operators use arbitrary declaration translation functions and extend them compositionally to theories; finally, the most general class translates theories without any constraint. Thus, our work can be seen as identifying good trade-offs between the rather restrictive pushout-based and the unpredictable arbitrary operators.

A drawback of our approach is the lack of a static type system at the diagram expression level: all our diagram operators are partial, and the only way to check that $O(D)$ is defined is to successfully evaluate it. That is frustrating, but our experiments in this direction have indicated that any type system that could predict definedness would be too complicated to be practical. Moreover, in practice, the immediate evaluation of diagram expressions is needed anyway for two reasons: Firstly, many operators can only be type-checked if their arguments are fully evaluated, thus obviating the main advantage of static type-checking. Secondly, because diagram expressions introduce theories that are to be used as interfaces later, their evaluation is usually triggered soon after type-checking.

We presented two applications centered around the algebraic hierarchy. We chose these examples because their simplicity and partial overlap allowed for a compact presentation. But linear operators occur widely in many formal systems. In particular, compared to the pushout-based definitions of logic translations used in the LATIN atlas [6], linear operators significantly increase the expressivity while retaining some desirable structural properties.

Future work will focus on defining and implementing more operators such as the ones from universal algebra or the gaps in the LATIN atlas. This can now be done extremely efficiently. We will also present the generalization of our results to all structuring features of MMT, in particular renaming and translation, in a longer report. Additionally, it is interesting to extend our work to the framework of institutions [14]. This would replace MMT with an abstract definition of declaration-based theories such as an institution with symbols [19]. Then structure-preservation could be restated in terms of models and satisfaction, e.g., by relating include-preservation to forgetful model reduction.

References

1. Capretta, V.: Universal algebra in type theory. In: Bertot, Y., Dowek, G., Théry, L., Hirschowitz, A., Paulin, C. (eds.) TPHOLs 1999. LNCS, vol. 1690, pp. 131–148. Springer, Heidelberg (1999). https://doi.org/10.1007/3-540-48256-3_10
2. Carette, J., Farmer, W.M., Sharoda, Y.: Leveraging the information contained in theory presentations. In: Benzmüller, C., Miller, B. (eds.) CICM 2020. LNCS (LNAI), vol. 12236, pp. 55–70. Springer, Cham (2020). https://doi.org/10.1007/978-3-030-53518-6_4
3. Carette, J., O'Connor, R.: Theory presentation combinators. In: Jeuring, J., Campbell, J.A., Carette, J., Dos Reis, G., Sojka, P., Wenzel, M., Sorge, V. (eds.) CICM 2012. LNCS (LNAI), vol. 7362, pp. 202–215. Springer, Heidelberg (2012). https://doi.org/10.1007/978-3-642-31374-5_14
4. Castro, P., Aguirre, N., Pombo, C.L., Maibaum, T.: Categorical foundations for structured specification in Z. Formal Asp. Comput. **27**(5–6), 831–865 (2015)
5. Christiansen, D., Brady, E.: Elaborator reflection: extending idris in idris. In: Garrigue, J., Keller, G., Sumii, E. (eds.) International Conference on Functional Programming, pp. 284–297. ACM (2016)
6. Codescu, M., Horozal, F., Kohlhase, M., Mossakowski, T., Rabe, F.: Project abstract: logic atlas and integrator (LATIN). In: Davenport, J.H., Farmer, W.M., Urban, J., Rabe, F. (eds.) CICM 2011. LNCS (LNAI), vol. 6824, pp. 289–291. Springer, Heidelberg (2011). https://doi.org/10.1007/978-3-642-22673-1_24
7. Codescu, M., Horozal, F., Kohlhase, M., Mossakowski, T., Rabe, F., Sojakova, K.: Towards logical frameworks in the heterogeneous tool set hets. In: Mossakowski, T., Kreowski, H.-J. (eds.) WADT 2010. LNCS, vol. 7137, pp. 139–159. Springer, Heidelberg (2012). https://doi.org/10.1007/978-3-642-28412-0_10
8. Mossakowski, T., Rabe, F., Codescu, M.: Canonical selection of colimits. In: James, P., Roggenbach, M. (eds.) WADT 2016. LNCS, vol. 10644, pp. 170–188. Springer, Cham (2017). https://doi.org/10.1007/978-3-319-72044-9_12
9. CoFI (The Common Framework Initiative): CASL Reference Manual, LNCS, vol. 2960. Springer (2004). https://doi.org/10.1007/b96103
10. DOL editors: The distributed ontology, modeling, and specification language (DOL). Technical report, Object Management Group (2018). https://www.omg.org/spec/DOL/About-DOL/
11. Ebner, G., Ullrich, S., Roesch, J., Avigad, J., de Moura, L.: A metaprogramming framework for formal verification. In: Proceedings of the ACM on Programming Languages **1**(ICFP), 34:1–34:29 (2017)
12. Farmer, W., Guttman, J., Thayer, F.: IMPS: an interactive mathematical proof system. J. Autom. Reason. **11**(2), 213–248 (1993)

13. Garillot, F., Gonthier, G., Mahboubi, A., Rideau, L.: Packaging mathematical structures. In: Berghofer, S., Nipkow, T., Urban, C., Wenzel, M. (eds.) TPHOLs 2009. LNCS, vol. 5674, pp. 327–342. Springer, Heidelberg (2009). https://doi.org/10.1007/978-3-642-03359-9_23
14. Goguen, J., Burstall, R.: Institutions: abstract model theory for specification and programming. J. Assoc. Comput. Mach. **39**(1), 95–146 (1992)
15. Goguen, J., Winkler, T., Meseguer, J., Futatsugi, K., Jouannaud, J.: Introducing OBJ. In: Goguen, J., Coleman, D., Gallimore, R. (eds.) Applications of Algebraic Specification using OBJ, Cambridge (1993)
16. Harper, R., Honsell, F., Plotkin, G.: A framework for defining logics. J. Assoc. Comput. Mach. **40**(1), 143–184 (1993)
17. Haveraaen, M., Roggenbach, M.: Specifying with syntactic theory functors. J. Log. Algebraic Methods Program **113** (2020)
18. Kammüller, F., Wenzel, M., Paulson, L.C.: Locales A sectioning concept for Isabelle. In: Bertot, Y., Dowek, G., Théry, L., Hirschowitz, A., Paulin, C. (eds.) TPHOLs 1999. LNCS, vol. 1690, pp. 149–165. Springer, Heidelberg (1999). https://doi.org/10.1007/3-540-48256-3_11
19. Mossakowski, T.: Specifications in an arbitrary institution with symbols. In: Bert, D., Choppy, C., Mosses, P.D. (eds.) WADT 1999. LNCS, vol. 1827, pp. 252–270. Springer, Heidelberg (2000). https://doi.org/10.1007/978-3-540-44616-3_15
20. Müller, D., Rabe, F.: Rapid prototyping formal systems in MMT: case studies. In: Miller, D., Scagnetto, I. (eds.) Logical Frameworks and Meta-languages: Theory and Practice, pp. 40–54 (2019)
21. Rabe, F.: How to Identify, Translate, and Combine Logics? J. Log. Comput. **27**(6), 1753–1798 (2017)
22. Rabe, F.: Morphism Axioms. Theoret. Comput. Sci. **691**, 55–80 (2017)
23. Rabe, F., Kohlhase, M.: A scalable module system. Inf. Comput. **230**(1), 1–54 (2013)
24. Sannella, D., Tarlecki, A.: Specifications in an arbitrary institution. Inf. Control **76**, 165–210 (1988)
25. Sannella, D., Wirsing, M.: A Kernel language for algebraic specification and implementation extended abstract. In: Karpinski, M. (ed.) FCT 1983. LNCS, vol. 158, pp. 413–427. Springer, Heidelberg (1983). https://doi.org/10.1007/3-540-12689-9_122
26. Rabe, F., Sharoda, Y.: Diagram combinators in MMT. In: Kaliszyk, C., Brady, E., Kohlhase, A., Sacerdoti Coen, C. (eds.) CICM 2019. LNCS (LNAI), vol. 11617, pp. 211–226. Springer, Cham (2019). https://doi.org/10.1007/978-3-030-23250-4_15
27. Srinivas, Y.V., Jüllig, R.: Specware: formal support for composing software. In: Möller, B. (ed.) MPC 1995. LNCS, vol. 947, pp. 399–422. Springer, Heidelberg (1995). https://doi.org/10.1007/3-540-60117-1_22

Author Index

Printed in the United States
by Baker & Taylor Publisher Services